Environmental Valuation
A Worldwide Compendium of Case Studies

Edited by
Jennifer Rietbergen-McCracken and Hussein Abaza

UNEP

Earthscan

D0322455

First published in the UK in 2000 by Earthscan Publications Limited
for and on behalf of the United Nations Environment Programme

Copyright © United Nations Environment Programme, 2000

A catalogue record for this book is available from the British Library

ISBN: 1 85383 695 8

Typesetting and page design by PCS Mapping & DTP, Newcastle upon Tyne
Printed and bound by Biddles Ltd, Guildford and King's Lynn
Cover design by Susanne Harris

For a full list of publications please contact:

Earthscan Publications Limited
120 Pentonville Road
London N1 9JN
Tel: +44 (0)20 7278 0433
Fax: +44 (0)20 7278 1142
Email: earthinfo@earthscan.co.uk
http://www.earthscan.co.uk

Earthscan is an editorially independent subsidiary of Kogan Page Limited and publishes
in association with WWF-UK and the International Institute for Environment and
Development

This book is printed on elemental chlorine-free paper from sustainably managed forests

CONTENTS

Eastern and Central Europe Region Case Studies

Latin America Region Case Studies

LIST OF TABLES

PREFACE

How has environmental valuation been applied in developing countries and countries in transition (CITs)? What range of methods have been used and for what kinds of purposes? What types of problems have been encountered? This compendium seeks to address these questions, by reviewing a select sample of environmental valuation studies from Africa, Asia, Eastern and Central Europe, and Latin America and the Caribbean. The cases have been chosen to cover the main valuation methods available and the major environmental issues to which these methods have been applied. The topics investigated by the case studies range from the value of wildlife viewing, to the value of conserving rainforests, mangroves, or coral reefs, to the value of supplying rural water supplies or controlling urban air pollution.

The reviews, undertaken by researchers from developing countries and CITs, reveal some common difficulties that have affected the valuation studies, including methodological limitations and contextual factors, which have impacted the quality and applicability of the valuation results. In critiquing these studies – many of which represent first-time attempts to use particular methods or value particular resources – the compendium highlights some of the key lessons learned and offers suggestions as to how valuation studies can be strengthened in the future. The focus throughout the book is on how environmental valuations can be adapted to suit the particular conditions in developing countries and CITs, and the overall conclusion can be summarized as 'Make the method fit the study's audience and objectives, and the valuation will be a valuable one'.

ACKNOWLEDGEMENTS

This long-term project involved a great many people who deserve to be thanked, although space does not allow them all to be mentioned here.

The editors would like to thank the regional coordinators for their participation in this project and their willingness to assist in finalizing the chapters for publication – in particular, Anthony Leiman (Africa); Sergei Tikhonov and Renat Perelet (Eastern and Central Europe); Marian delos Angeles (Asia); and Edgar Fürst and Gerardo Jiménez (Latin America and Caribbean). In UNEP, Deborah Vorhies and Ivonne Higuero were responsible for the overall coordination of this project and Naomi Poulton undertook the initial editing work.

The editors would also like to thank Frank Vorhies (Head of Economic Services Unit, IUCN, Gland) and Ali Dehlavi (Economics, Trade and Environment Unit, UNEP) for their kind assistance, and Simon Rietbergen for his support and advice, and wish to publicly absolve them of any responsibility for any remaining errors.

INTRODUCTION

Jennifer Rietbergen-McCracken

BACKGROUND

This compendium is the product of several years' collaborative work by researchers in a wide range of developing countries and countries in transition (CITs), facilitated and coordinated by the Economics, Trade and Environment Unit of the United Nations Environment Programme (UNEP). In 1993 UNEP commissioned the Centre for Social and Economic Research of the Global Environment (CSERGE) to prepare a collection of valuation methodologies and studies in developing countries. The following year, UNEP convened a consultative expert group meeting on the valuation of environmental and natural resources, to review the existing methodologies and applications, and then held follow-up workshops with institutions from Africa, Asia, Eastern and Central Europe, and Latin America.

From these discussions and reviews of the use of valuation methods, it was concluded that the extensive literature on the subject included few examples of their application in developing countries and CITs. It was therefore decided to produce a compendium of case studies to show the possibilities and practicalities associated with using valuation methods in these countries. Research institutions were chosen from each of the four regions – Africa, Asia, Eastern and Central Europe, and Latin America – to help coordinate the selection and production of the case studies. Several rounds of discussion meetings and workshops brought together the regional coordinators to develop a consistent approach and ensure that the cases covered a range of different applications.[1] A paper by Kuik et al (1990) provided the initial framework for the analyses, which was then adapted in the course of the work. Most of the chapters were drafted between 1995 and 1996 and reviewed during 1996 and 1997. A companion compendium on the use of *economic instruments* in developing countries and CITs is also available (Rietbergen-McCracken and Abaza, 2000).

OBJECTIVE AND AUDIENCE

This compendium is intended to serve three main purposes:

- to present evidence of the feasibility of using valuation methods in developing countries and CITs;
- to provide practical guidance on the particular issues that need to be addressed in using valuation methods in these countries; and
- to give researchers in developing countries and CITs the opportunity, by writing their chapters, to present their own critiques of the applications described.

Up until recently, there was considerable skepticism, particularly among international development organizations and developing country governments (as end users of the valuation results) about the possibilities of using valuation methods outside the relatively research resource-rich and data-rich environments of developed countries. It was generally felt that developing countries and CITs presented too many difficulties (including a scarcity of statistical information; the presence of price distortions or undeveloped markets; and in some cases largely illiterate communities) to allow valuation methods to produce meaningful results. However, over the last five to ten years, a growing body of evidence has emerged to refute these claims and this compendium will hopefully contribute to the realization that applying valuation methods in developing countries and CITs has much to offer, not only to international development institutions, but also to policy makers in the countries concerned.

Another trend that has been seen up until recently, and one that applies to the field of environmental economics as a whole, has been the dominance of western academics in the literature. Researchers from developing countries and CITs have had relatively few opportunities to present their views and perspectives to an international audience.[2] By involving research institutions from within the four regions, UNEP has purposely tried to correct this imbalance, while at the same time encouraging networking between the different institutions.

The main audience for this book comprises economists in developing countries and CITs, who are looking for practical descriptions of and guidance on how valuation methods can be applied in their countries. The cases will also provide useful material for researchers and university lecturers in the fields of environmental economics and environmental policy. As something of a 'how to' case book, the compendium is intended to provide training material. The cases therefore go beyond descriptions of the valuation methods used, to include critical analyses, suggestions on alternative methodologies and other possible applications, and references to other studies and the theoretical literature.

Policy makers in developing countries and international and national development agency staff may also have an interest in the empirical evidence presented by the cases, as they consider the potential applications of such methods in their own spheres of influence. Finally, readers without formal training in economics should not feel unwelcome. The book has also been written with them in mind, and this introductory chapter and the extensive glossary should help them make their way through (or round) the economics involved.

SCOPE

In selecting the cases to be included in this collection, the coordinators tried to ensure that all major valuation methods were covered and a range of applications represented.[3] The following valuation methods are included (the numbers in parentheses refer to the number of cases in which they are described):

- Loss of Income and/or Production (7)
- Contingent Valuation Method (6)
- Travel Cost Method (4)
- Replacement/Reproduction Cost Method (4)
- Benefit Transfers (4)
- Mitigation Cost Avoided (2)
- Opportunity Cost Approach (2)
- Discounted Income Method (1)
- Damage Cost Avoided (1)
- Hedonic Property Pricing (1)

Table I.1 lists the valuation methods described in the cases and the particular environmental issues addressed. In most instances, the cases review previous valuation studies taken from the literature.

Quite a few of these studies represent first-time attempts at valuing a particular resource, or using a particular combination of valuation methods, in the regions concerned. Other cases, for example those from Eastern and Central Europe, present original work by the authors, or propose the use of particular valuation methods to address the shortcomings of more traditional approaches to valuation. Most of the studies provide results of direct relevance to policy makers, for example in decisions on price setting, development planning, or pollution control.

Table I.1 *Valuation Methods Included in this Compendium*

Country	Environmental issue	Valuation methods or components
Africa		
Kenya	Value of time spent collecting water	Revealed preference approach (application of discrete choice theory); Random utility theory approach
Kenya	Value of wildlife viewing	Travel Cost Method; Contingent Valuation Method
Ghana	Determinants of land values in Accra	Hedonic Pricing Method
Cameroon	Costs of rainforest conservation	Costs of forgone benefits from commercial logging and hunting; Benefits from tourism, fisheries protection, flood control, and soil fertility maintenance
Asia		
Philippines	Profitability of forest plantations	Replacement cost method; Change in productivity method; Loss of earnings method; Shadow project method
Taiwan	Air pollution and health	Contingent Valuation Method
Sri Lanka	Environmental impacts of highway construction	Loss of productivity of fisheries and agriculture; Loss of non-agricultural land and buildings; Costs of noise, air, and water pollution
Eastern and Central Europe		
Poland	Air pollution-related damage to forests	Loss of productivity; Losses from premature felling; Reconstruction costs; Loss of non-productive uses
Estonia	Environmental problems of oil shale extraction	Costs of land reclamation; Costs of compensation payments; Reproduction costs of (polluted) water resources
Russian Federation	Forest parks in the Moscow region	Reproduction cost method; Discounted income method; Travel Cost Method
Latin America and Caribbean		
Chile	Air pollution control in Santiago	Human capital approach; Mitigation cost approach
Netherlands Antilles	Reef conservation	Loss of income method; Contingent Valuation Method; Costs of protection
Haiti	Water services	Contingent valuation method
Mexico	Forest valuation	Damage costs avoided; Mitigation costs avoided; Loss of production avoided; Contingent Valuation Method; Travel Cost Method
Nicaragua	Valuation of mangroves	Loss of income method; Change in productivity method; Contingent Valuation Method; Travel expenditure method

APPLYING VALUATION METHODS IN DEVELOPING COUNTRIES AND COUNTRIES IN TRANSITION

While the cases describe a wide range of different applications, they revealed some common issues. The following is a summary of the most common issues that emerged, including those related to the valuation *methodologies*, and those related to the socio-economic and political *context* of the valuations (there is, of course, considerable overlap between these two sets of issues).[4]

METHODOLOGICAL ISSUES

A tabular summary of the strengths and weaknesses of some of the main methods is provided in Table I.2. For more information on the pros and cons of the various valuation methods, interested readers are referred to the growing body of literature on this subject, including Georgiou et al (1997), Pearce and Moran (1994) and Pearce and Turner (1990). Each of the main valuation methods is described briefly in the glossary in this compendium.

A few of the lessons learned regarding the use of specific valuation methodologies are presented in Table I.3. By and large, the kinds of *common* methodological issues that appeared *across* the different studies relate to either the *inputs* (ie the availability and quality of information) or the *outputs* (ie the quality of the estimates produced) of the valuation methods used.

Data Availability

The majority of the valuation studies explicitly mention limitations imposed by the lack of available data, for example, time-series data on resource use of productivity, or socio-economic statistics on visitors to natural resource amenities. This lack of information can result in one or more of the following: (i) the valuation relying on rough approximations rather than accurate data; (ii) the valuation being based on a set of simplified assumptions; and (iii) uncertainty as to whether the sample surveyed (eg of visitors to national parks) is representative of the population (of visitors) as a whole. Another possible consequence of the unavailability of data – in this case, specifically data on the benefits provided by particular resources – is the need to use 'off-the-shelf' values from other locations or countries, where these kinds of data are more available. This issue of 'benefit transfer' is discussed below.[5] The scarcity of statistical and market data also tends to favour the use of those valuation methods that employ primary data collection rather than secondary data sources. This, according to Georgiou et al (1997), may explain the evident success of contingent valuation, discrete choice, and travel cost techniques (all of which are based on surveys) in developing countries.

Table I.2 *Strengths and Weaknesses of Some Valuation Methods and Approaches*

Valuation Method/ Approach	Strengths	Weaknesses/Limitations
Market prices	Market/shadow prices are usually the best estimate of WTP; Market prices reflect stakeholders' decision-making reality (they are the prices faced when making decisions).	Market and policy failure mean that shadow prices need calculating to find WTP; Prices underestimate true value since they don't include consumer surplus; Prices vary by season, so averages mislead; Care is needed over the assumption that output will not affect price (elasticity of supply).
Replacement Cost and Preventive Expenditure	Relatively easy to calculate (sometimes based on observed behaviour) and useful as second-best estimate.	Difficult to establish if people really would be prepared to incur costs of secure benefits in 'without project' situation; Difficult to establish if net benefits of prevention or replacement would be same as the 'with project' intervention.
Proxy/ Substitute Products	Relatively easy to collect data.	Proxies are rarely perfect substitutes; Same limitations as market prices.
Change in Productivity	If data exist, easily understood by decision makers.	Quantitative input-output data needed on physical relationships; Difficulty of isolating cause and effect.
Opportunity Cost	Useful for subsistence production with high labour requirements, and one land use precluding another.	Only useful for gross value, since the product is effectively valued by its cost, and labour opportunity cost can be difficult and costly to value properly.
Travel Cost Method	Useful for recreational facilities and eco-tourism; More accurate when travel distances are short.	Assumptions required to develop demand curve (eg whether travel is uni- or multi-purpose); Estimated parameters and benefits highly sensitive to opportunity cost of time estimates; Data intensive and complex/costly.
Hedonic Pricing	Has potential in high-income or semi-urban areas.	Relies on highly developed property markets; Difficult to isolate the explanatory variable.
Contingent Valuation Methods	Reliable if strict procedures followed and pre-testing done; Only method available for non-use values; Includes consumer surplus; Gives net value, so no need to deduct costs.	People find it difficult to separate environmental from wider values (embedding problem); Biases; Credibility problems; Low income as a constraint on WTP or WTA; Ethical issues, especially in low-income countries.

Source: Adapted from Davies and Richards (1998)

Cost Considerations versus Credibility

While a number of the studies were commissioned and supported by international organizations (for instance, three of the cases from Latin America and the Caribbean were based on World Bank-supported valuation work), many others did not benefit from outside financial assistance, and had to operate on quite tight budgets. This directly affected the way in which the methodologies were applied. Cost considerations tended to decrease the time which could be spent on the studies (particularly the field work); reduce the sample sizes; and preclude the use of more sophisticated techniques. All of these impacts in turn influenced the quality of the results and their potential credibility with policy makers. In noting this problem, van Zyl, Store and Leiman (1996) recommend that valuation studies start with a careful analysis of the feasibility of adequately applying the proposed techniques, to help achieve the best results possible. In some cases, they say, it may be wiser to increase sample sizes, instead of producing estimates that are not reliable anyway and represent a waste of resources.

Accuracy and Reliability of Results

Data scarcity also affects the level of accuracy of the valuation estimates. This however is not necessarily a problem, depending on the purpose of the study. Obviously, if the valuation is intended to provide an estimate that will be used, for example, to set user fees for parks or determine acceptable levels of resource use, then accuracy is important. However, several cases describe studies that were designed to provide order-of-magnitude estimates, for more general policy purposes. This was the case in the study by Fallon Scura and van't Hof (1993) (reviewed by Fürst et al in Chapter 11), which valued the costs and benefits of reef conservation on a small Caribbean island. The study was intended to address questions such as 'Are protection and tourism compatible?' and 'Are there physical limits on the multiple uses of protected marine ecosystems?'. Given the relatively undiversified economy of the island, and the general kinds of questions to be addressed, the rough-and-ready nature of the study (necessitated by time and data constraints) was considered justified. By using a simplified version of contingent valuation and a 'gross revenues and expenditures' approach, the study was able to identify a threshold level of scuba dives per site per year, and to suggest an upward adjustment of the modest entrance fee for the marine park. These very useful findings probably would not have required a more exact valuation approach.

Another 'order-of-magnitude' study, by Pearce et al (1993) (reviewed by Fürst et al in Chapter 13), attempted to calculate the Total Economic Value of forests in Mexico. The level of aggregation this required and the very mixed quality of the little data that was available meant that the final estimate was inaccurate and unreliable, and therefore considered of little

Table I.3 *Some Lessons Learned re Valuation Methodologies*[6]

Contingent Valuation Method

- when CVM studies are used for policy purposes, it is useful to have some form of validity test;
- CVM studies must address bias problems explicitly;
- although cost considerations are always important in valuation studies, samples must be of a significant size for the generation of reliable estimates, particularly if the results are to be used for policy purposes;
- pre-test and pilot surveys can help to enhance the reliability and validity of the study;
- caution must be exercised when using WTA question formats, to ensure they are phrased appropriately;
- WTA formats may produce unreliable results, which represent an opportunity cost – more comprehensive and reliable results may be produced if complementary elicitation methods are used together.

Source: van Zyl, Store and Leiman, Chapter 2, this compendium

---

Travel Cost Method

- when valuing amenities that are used by both foreigners and residents, two separate demand functions should be estimated;
- both zonal and individual observations should be used, to determine which gives more reliable estimates;
- researchers should be careful in the definition of travel costs, travel time, and on-site time costs;
- comprehensive statistical analysis should be undertaken for the selection of the best functional form.

Source: van Zyl, Store and Leiman, Chapter 2, this compendium

---

Hedonic Pricing Method

- variables used in the analysis should reflect the sociological and cultural circumstances of the residents;
- a broad spectrum of variables should be included to improve accuracy and comprehensiveness;
- the choice of functional form used in regression analysis should be explicitly validated;
- special treatment must be given to unusual circumstances (including political changes) that affect the property market.

Source: van Zyl, Store and Leiman, Chapter 3, this compendium

---

use except for general awareness-raising purposes. Indeed, Fürst et al raise the question 'Is an inaccurate monetary value more useful than the alternative of no value at all?' and suggest that such a generalized approach to valuation may provide few applied policy guidelines that may not otherwise be deduced from environmental economics theory.

In Chapter 5, delos Angeles et al review an evaluation study of forest plantations in the Philippines (by Niskanen, 1995), and outline the steps taken to increase the reliability of the estimates, given the major inaccuracies in the methodology. Firstly, the study report clearly describes the methodology used and all the assumptions made. Secondly, the study uses conservative figures in key economic data such as yield and prices, so as not to overemphasize the impacts of plantation forestry. Thirdly, the study conducted a sensitivity analysis for all the types of cost-benefit analysis performed.

Several studies attempted to increase the reliability of the valuation estimates by using two different methods and comparing the convergence of the results obtained. However, as cited in a number of cases, Mitchell and Carson (1989) have pointed out that a convergent validation only contributes to the credibility of the results and does not prove the accuracy of either of the methods used.

Discounting

One of the most contentious issues in valuation methodology, discounting refers to the common practice of lowering the value of a resource (and its use) over time – in other words, 'preferring' present use over future use. Discounting using market interest rates, many environmentalists (and some environmental economists) argue, has a built-in bias against future generations and makes unsustainable exploitation seem preferable, in economic terms, to sustainable use. Thus, they say, market discount rates need to be adjusted downwards to social rates, to incorporate the interests of future generations. Others (such as Pearce et al, 1989) argue that this would be difficult to achieve, both in methodological and administrative terms, and that, in any case, the lower rate would tend to favour development projects, thus increasing the demand for natural resources. Pearce et al therefore recommend that, instead of lowering the discount rate, efforts should be concentrated on, *inter alia*, improving the actual valuation techniques, to better value future costs and benefits.

Several cases raise concerns about the practice of discounting. Kjabbi, in Chapter 8 on the valuation of oil shale in Estonia, avoids discounting altogether, as she feels it is inappropriate in the economic context of former Soviet Union countries. While others may contest her argument, she says it is impossible to substantiate the application of any discount rate, because of problems associated with inflation and the economic stagnation common in these countries. Further, she argues that the increasing scarcity of natural resources means that the future values of these disappearing resources will *increase*.

Other chapters take issue, not with the fact that the original studies used discounting, but with the choice of the actual discount rate applied. In a few instances, the rate seems to have been plucked from the air, and no justification given for the selection. In two cases, discount rates were chosen according to the rates used by the World Bank in its financing of development projects (see the study by Windevoxhel (1992), reviewed by Fürst et al in Chapter 14, and the study by Niskanen, reviewed by delos Angeles et al in Chapter 5). As several reviewers point out, the discount rate chosen is often the main determinant of the valuation results and the associated recommendations. For example, the valuation of costs of rainforest conservation in Cameroon (by Ruitenbeek, 1991, reviewed by van Zyl et al in Chapter 4) sought to determine the amount of international transfer needed to compensate Cameroon for the costs involved. Using a discount rate of 8 per cent, the study found that a transfer of 3605 million CFAF would be necessary.[7] However, if the discount rate were lowered to 6 per cent, the result would be quite different. Indeed, no transfer would be necessary and the conservation of the rainforest would actually yield a Net Present Value of 319 million CFAF.

To increase credibility, valuation studies that use discount rates should therefore include a sensitivity analysis for the discount rate, and the report should make explicit the assumptions and limitations of the rate chosen. However, discounting is likely to remain a contentious issue for some time, as Georgiou et al (1997) admit: 'The discount rate problem remains and none of the recent developments in the literature will assist the analyst in resolving the problem in any clear-cut fashion.'

Benefit Transfers

The use of benefit transfers – that is, the transfer of benefit estimates or benefit functions from another location or country to the site being valued – is sometimes seen as a 'necessary evil', though others (including Georgiou et al, 1997) see it in a more positive light, as a potentially useful and low-cost alternative to conducting full-blown valuation studies in developing countries.[8] What is clear is that the use of benefit transfers needs to be accompanied by a validation analysis to test the applicability of the outside values to the situation at hand.

CONTEXTUAL ISSUES

A few general comments can be made about the way in which the prevailing socio-economic situation can influence the valuation methodology, and the potential applicability of the valuation results by policy makers.

Market Failure[9]

The countries in which the valuation studies were conducted represented, especially at that time, an enormous range of socio-economic and political conditions. They ranged from Nicaragua (emerging from a civil war) to Taiwan and Chile (both rapidly growing economic 'tigers') to Poland, Estonia and Russia (undergoing transition and suffering economic recession). Despite the huge influence which market failure (as well as government failure) has on valuation results, relatively few of the studies addressed this issue directly. Ignoring such market distortions in the valuation work can make the results meaningless.

Some cases in the compendium do make mention of the existence of market distortions, due to situations of high inflation, high interest rates, or centrally-administered prices, pointing out the effect this may have on the results. For example, the study by Windevoxhel (1992) (reviewed by Fürst et al in Chapter 14), recognized labour market distortions, due to long-term and seasonal unemployment, and corrected the market wage rates accordingly. One study, by Asabere (1981) (reviewed by van Zyl et al in Chapter 3), went further and attempted to measure the significance of the effect of market distortions. The hedonic pricing technique used in this study of the urban land market in Accra, Ghana, included variables for several factors thought to have potential distorting effects. Indeed, the regression results revealed *legislative* market distortions, from government zoning practices and rent controls, and *socio-political* distortions, from traditional land tenure systems and ethnic clustering. The analysis also examined the land market over several time periods, to capture the potential impact of the artificial price suppression that was experienced for several years under the rule of a military dictatorship.

Reflecting on the distortions in the Haitian economy during the early 1980s, Fürst et al, in Chapter 12, suggest that direct surveys of resource user WTP may be more reliable than methods that rely on the observation of very distorted market prices. A similar comment is made by Georgiou et al (1997), who cite market distortions as the reason why valuation methods such as the hedonic property and hedonic wage pricing techniques are the least common types of valuation in developing countries. However, they qualify this remark by pointing out that there *is* scope for applying these techniques in developing countries, especially for land values, where markets often work well. The relative advantages of survey-based techniques under market distortions are even stronger when statistical and market data are not readily available, as mentioned earlier. These advantages are partly offset by a number of limitations of these approaches, notably the higher risk of non-random error, including various biases.[10]

Distributional Issues

In countries with highly skewed income distributions, valuation studies should ideally take distributional issues into account in two ways. Firstly, the existing distribution patterns should be considered, and if necessary incorporated, in the valuation process, to make the results more meaningful. Secondly, the studies' recommendations would need to include forecasts of how the policies proposed could have different impacts on different income groups.

There are surprisingly few examples of either of these considerations in the studies reviewed in this book. Two studies did calculate the social shadow price of labour, in one case (Niskanen, 1995) to reflect society's marginal WTP for non-educated labourers, in the other case (Windevoxhel, 1992) to take into account the high level of unemployment, as mentioned above. In addition, the Contingent Valuation Method (CVM) and Travel Cost Method (TCM) study on the value of wildlife viewing in Kenya, by Navrud and Mungatana (1994) (reviewed by van Zyl et al in Chapter 2), differentiated between residents' and non-residents' WTP and the elasticities of their demand for recreation, thereby incorporating, at least implicitly, some distributional consideration.

However, most cases either ignore distributional issues completely, or mention them without incorporating them into the analysis, as is the case with the study on air pollution in Santiago, Chile, by Eskeland (1994) (reviewed by Fürst et al in Chapter 10). The report of this study drew attention to the fact that air pollution may disproportionately affect the poor, yet the valuation used a single minimum wage to value the loss of productive labour to the economy, due to the health-impacts of pollution.

The only study that makes explicit mention of the possible impact of its policy recommendations on particular groups in society is the valuation of time spent collecting water in a Kenyan town, by Whittington et al (1990). This study found that households' preferences for the three main water sources available (ie, buying water from kiosks, or vendors, or getting water from open wells) were significantly influenced by the total income of the households and the number of adult women in the households – both distributional issues. And, in considering the possible implications of replacing vending and/or kiosk systems with piped water systems, the review by van Zyl et al in Chapter 1 highlights the distributional trade-off that would result, from the removal of the employment opportunities that the former two systems provide the local community.

Applicability of Results

While the vast majority of the studies provided results that could be used by policy makers, relatively few actually provided detailed proposals on how the results could be applied in practice. This kind of information is key, if policy makers are to become convinced about the credibility and applicability of valuation results. As Fürst et al (1996) point out, it was only recently that valuation methods gained a wider acceptance outside of the western academic community. The challenge now is to show their relevance to governments in developing countries and CITs, and this will require a good deal of 'hard evidence' in the form of cases where valuation results provided immediately useful information for policy makers.

A good example from this compendium is the study by Navrud and Mungatana (1994) (reviewed by van Zyl et al in Chapter 2) of the value of viewing wildlife in a national park in Kenya. The fact that the Kenya Wildlife Service used the pricing estimates obtained from this study to increase the entrance fees for non-residents by 310 per cent illustrates the applicability of the Travel Cost and Contingent Valuation methods used. Another study that paid attention to the applicability of the results was that by Fallon Scura and van't Hof (1993) (reviewed by Fürst et al in Chapter 11). In valuing the costs and benefits of reef conservation on the Caribbean island of Bonaire, the researchers made very practical suggestions on how best to avoid damage from the high visitation rates. The authors of the study report were aware that the cooperation of an important group of stakeholders – the diving holiday operators – was vital to the successful implementation of the recommended policies. They therefore recommended, alongside the imposition of a limit on the number of visits and/or higher park user fees, the introduction of incentives to increase the local economy multipliers, to increase the benefits to the tourism-dependent sectors on the island.

Van Zyl, Store and Leiman (1996) suggest that, for valuation studies that are to be used for policy decisions, post-study evaluations be carried out, to assess the application of the results. This, they say, would serve to identify any problems in the practical implementation of policies based on valuations, and enhance the credibility of valuation methodologies.

TOP-DOWN VERSUS PARTICIPATORY VALUATION APPROACHES

An issue dealt with in most of the critiques of the studies from Latin America and the Caribbean is the contrast between Cost-Benefit Analysis (CBA) – seen as 'top-down' – and other more participatory valuation methods, such as Multi-Criteria Analysis (MCA).[11] MCA can take into account the preferences of multiple stakeholders and the trade-offs between, for example, conservation and development. This method is therefore particularly appropriate in the valuation of multiple use resources, such as forests, where an analysis of the interests of different stakeholder groups is an explicit objective.

The exclusive use of CBA in the valuation of mangroves in Nicaragua (by Windevoxhel (1992)) is questioned in Chapter 14, as the CBA was not able to consider the distribution of impacts of forestry policies on groups depending on the mangroves for their subsistence. Furthermore, Fürst et al point out that CBA does not provide a tool for revealing and resolving the complex conflicts of interest between users and government bodies responsible for the management of the mangroves. They therefore recommend the use of additional methodological approaches, such as MCA, to integrate the different preferences of stakeholders and to try and gain some consensus on the design of the most favourable management option.

These criticisms of CBA are reflective of a set of wider concerns about CBA, expressed by proponents of participatory methods. Davies and Richards (1998) list some of these concerns, including:

- the top-down analysis ignores the fact that different stakeholders value the same costs and benefits in different ways, according to their perspectives and objectives;
- the tendency of CBA to ascribe less weight to equity, livelihood and institutional issues, including resource access and control; and
- the lack of transparency makes it easy for economists to 'massage' the data or hide key assumptions in order to window-dress a pre-determined outcome.

However, in the cases where MCA is mentioned, this methodology is seen as a complement, not an alternative to the more traditional economic valuation methods. A single economic value of a resource, produced for example by CBA, can be used as the basis for assessing different stakeholders' preferences on the economic, ecological, and social values of the resource. This can help provide a 'bottom-up' approach to decision-making, rather than, as CBA tends to do, centralizing the valuation in the hands of a few decision-makers.[12]

THE PARTICULAR CASE OF COUNTRIES IN TRANSITION

While many of the issues mentioned so far apply equally to developing countries and CITs, it is worth looking at a few particular characteristics of CITs that affect how valuation methods are being used in these countries. Kasianov and Perelet (1996), in their analysis of the cases from Eastern and Central Europe, list some of the problems facing former 'socialist' countries, and especially the former Soviet Union, which might limit the use and usefulness of valuation methods. These include economic and social problems, political instability, significant environmental problems, undeveloped market relations, and the lack of democratic traditions. On the other hand, as they say, these countries benefit from a strong scientific capability, the availability of natural resources, experience with state development planning (important for environmental regulation) and the predominantly state-ownership of natural resources, which makes it easier – at least in theory – to allocate natural resource property rights efficiently and to use market forces in their management.

In terms of the appropriateness of different valuation methods, Kasianov and Perelet consider the Reproduction Cost Method (RCM) preferable to methods based on WTP. This they say is important in former socialist countries, where environmental needs are given less priority than basic material needs. Thus, survey-based methods will tend to undervalue the natural resources in question, and valuation methods based on technical and data (such as the reproduction cost method) will be more likely to produce estimates nearer the true value of the resources. In contrast, they say, the higher environmental demand in more developed countries makes WTP a valid measurement there. They also cite two other problems with using WTP-based methods in former socialist countries. Firstly, these techniques presuppose well-developed markets and a 'market mentality', neither of which is yet fully established. Secondly, WTP techniques stress individual preferences in the poorly-understood and risk-prone field of the environment, where, Kasianov and Perelet propose, collective precautionary judgement may be more appropriate.

These views on the Reproduction Cost Method are reflected in the cases from Eastern and Central Europe, all three of which include the use of this method, alongside other valuation methods (as shown in Table I.1). However, Kasianov and Perelet also point out one limitation of using RCM in these countries. That is, the fact that the actual prices (in the form of environmental charges or taxes) of natural resources are incomparable with the actual costs of their reproduction. Nonetheless, they report that efforts are now being made to use these techniques to reform and, where possible, raise the efficiency of the existing taxation system, to make these taxes better reflect the true value of the resources involved.[13]

NOTES

1   Contact information for the regional coordinators is provided at the end of this chapter.

2   Georgiou et al (1997) explain the dominance of North American and European economists in the field of valuation as a reflection of the lack of environmental economics education in developing country universities, and the lack of training for agency and government staff.

3   The regional coordinators included: Hugo van Zyl, Thomas Store and Anthony Leiman (Africa); Marian delos Angeles (Asia); Edgar Fürst, David Barton and Gerardo Jiménez (Latin America and the Caribbean); and Pavel Kasianov and Renat A Perelet (Eastern and Central Europe).

4   The following synthesis draws on the analytical work of the following regional coordinators: Hugo van Zyl, Thomas Store and Anthony Leiman (Africa); Edgar Fürst, David Barton and Gerardo Jiménez (Latin America and the Caribbean); and Pavel Kasianov and Renat A Perelet (Eastern and Central Europe).

5   See glossary for explanation of the term 'benefit transfer'.

6   See glossary for brief descriptions of these valuation methods.

7   At the time of the study, one US dollar equalled approximately 250 CFAF (Central African francs).

8   A recent initiative by Environment Canada seeks to make available an inventory of benefit values of biodiversity from a large number of valuation studies around the world, to facilitate the use of benefit transfer. See Filion et al, 1998.

9 Market failure is defined here as the failure of markets to reflect the full social costs of production in the price of traded products and inputs. Government failure (sometimes called 'policy failure') refers to the policy interventions by governments that produce less efficient outcomes than if the markets were allowed to allocate resources. These inefficient interventions may include subsidies, price controls, ownership controls, etc. See Pearce and Warford, 1993, for more details on both market and government failure.

10 Discussions of the different forms of bias in the Contingent Valuation Method are found in the reviews by Fürst et al (Haiti) and van Zyl et al (in their chapter on wildlife viewing in Kenya), and a brief description of the main biases is given in the glossary.

11 See glossary for a brief description of MCA.

12 Davies and Richards (1998) discuss how participatory research methods are increasingly being combined with neo-classical economic methods, in the development of 'participatory economic analysis', in the context of participatory forest management. Other interesting examples of participatory valuation methodologies are found in IIED (1997) and Emerton (1996).

13 See the introductory chapter of Rietbergen-McCracken and Abaza (2000) for a discussion on the economic efficiency of environmental taxes and charges in developing countries and CITs.

REFERENCES

Asabere, P K (1981) The Determinants of Land Values in an African City: The Case of Accra, Ghana. *Land Economics*, vol 57(3), pp 385–397.

Davies, J and Richards, M (1998) Economics and Participatory Forest Management: A Case of Inappropriate Precision or Untapped Potential? Forest Policy and Environment Group, ODI, London.

Emerton, L (1996) Participatory Environmental Valuation: Subsistence Forest Use Around the Aberdares, Kenya. African Wildlife Foundation, Applied Conservation Economics Discussion Paper no 1, Nairobi.

Eskeland, G S (1994) The Net Benefits of an Air Pollution Control Strategy for Santiago, in World Bank, Chile – Managing Environmental Problems: Economic Analysis of Selected Issues. Environment and Urban Development Division, Latin America and the Caribbean Country Department LA2, Washington, DC.

Fallon Scura, L and van't Hof, T (1993) Economic Feasibility and Ecological Sustainability of the Bonaire Marine Park: The Ecology and Economics of Bonaire Marine Park. The World Bank, Environment Department, Divisional Paper no 1993–44, Washington, DC.

Filion, F, Frehs, J and Sprecher, D (1998) Revealing the Economic Value of Biodiversity: A New Incentive Measure to Conserve and Protect It. Paper presented at the Seventh Meeting of the OECD Expert Group on Economic Aspects of Biodiversity, 20–21 January 1998, Paris.

Fürst, E, Barton, D N and Jiménez, G (1996) Case Study Analyses on the Application of Environmental and Natural Resource Valuation Methods in Developing Countries and Countries in Transition to Market Economies: Latin America and Caribbean Substudy. Report for the United Nations Environment Programme by the International Center on Economic Policy for Sustainable Development and Universidad Nacional, Costa Rica, mimeo.

Georgiou, S, Whittington, D, Pearce, D and Moran, D (1997) *Economic Values and the Environment in the Developing World. United Nations Environment Programme.* Edward Elgar Publishing, Cheltenham.

Kanennova, I E and Martynov, A S (1994) Integrated Valuation of Willingness-to-Pay and other Elements of Economic Valuation of the Moscow Region's Biological Resources. Report presented at the IUCN/GEF Conference on Methods of Economic Valuation of Biodiversity, Moscow.

Kasianov, P, and Perelet, R (1996) Applications of Environmental and Natural Resource Valuation Methodologies in Eastern and Central European Region. Report for the United Nations Environment Programme, by the Centre for International Projects, Moscow, mimeo.

Kuik, O J et al (1990) *Assessment of Benefits of Environmental Measures.* Free University Institute for Environmental Studies, Amsterdam.

Mitchell, R C and Carson, R T (1989) *Using Surveys to Value Public Goods: The Contingent Valuation Method.* Resources for the Future, Washington, DC.

Navrud, S and Mungatana, E D (1994) Environmental Valuation in Developing Countries: The Recreational Value of Wildlife Viewing. *Ecological Economics*, vol 11, pp 135–151.

Niskanen, A (1995) Evaluation of Profitability of Forest Plantations in the Philippines Using Conventional and Extended Cost-benefit Analysis. Thesis for the Licentiate degree in Forest Management and Economics, University of Joensuu, Joensuu, Finland.

Pearce, D W, Adger, W N, Brown, K, Cervigni, R and Moran, D (1993) Mexico Forestry and Conservation Sector Review: Substudy of Economic Valuation of Forests. Report by CSERGE, University of East Anglia and University College London, for the World Bank, Latin America and the Caribbean Country Department LA2, Washington, DC.

Pearce, D, Markandya, A and Barbier, E B (1989) *Blueprint for a Green Economy. A report by the London Environmental Economics Centre, for the UK Department of the Environment.* Earthscan Publications, London.

Pearce, D and Moran, D (1994) *The Economic Value of Biodiversity.* Earthscan Publications, London.

Pearce, D and Turner, R K (1990) *Economics of Natural Resources and the Environment.* Johns Hopkins Press, Maryland.

Pearce, D W and Warford, J J (1993) *World Without End: Economics, Environment, and Sustainable Development.* The World Bank, Washington, DC, and Oxford University Press, New York.

Rietbergen-McCracken, J and Abaza, H (eds) (2000) *Economic Instruments for Environmental Management: A Worldwide Compendium of Case Studies.* Earthscan Publications, London.

Ruitenbeek, H J (1991) The Rainforest Supply Price: A Tool for Evaluating Rainforest Conservation Expenditures. *Ecological Economics*, vol 6, pp 57–78.

van Zyl, H, Store, T and Leiman, A (1996) A Case Study Analysis on Valuations of Environmental and Natural Resources in Africa. A Report to the United Nations Environment Programme. University of Cape Town, School of Economics, mimeo.

Windevoxhel, N J (1992) Valoración Económica Parcial de los Manglares de la Región II de Nicaragua. MSc thesis, CATIE, Costa Rica.

Whittington, D, Mu, X and Roche, R (1990) Calculating the Value of Time Spent Collecting Water: Some Estimates for Ukunda, Kenya. *World Development*, vol 18(2), pp 269–280.

CONTACT INFORMATION FOR REGIONAL COORDINATORS

Anthony Leiman (Africa Region Coordinator)
University of Cape Town
School of Economics
Private Bag
Rondebosch 7700
South Africa
email: LEIMAN@socsci.uct.ac.za

Marian delos Angeles (Asia Region Coordinator)
Resources, Environment and Economics Centre for Studies
Unit 3N
#219 Katipunan Avenue
Ext. Blueridge Subdivision
Quezon City
Metromanila
The Philippines
email: reecs@psdn.org.ph

Sergei Tikhonov (Eastern and Central Europe Region Coordinator)
Director
Centre for International Projects
PO Box 165
CIP Moscow
Russia 117292
email: cip@mepnr.msk.ru

Gerardo Jimenez (Latin America and Caribbean Region Coordinator)
Centro Internacional de Politica Economica para el Desarrollo
Sostenible (CINPE)
Universidad Nacional
Apartado 555–3000
CR–3000 Heredia
Costa Rica
email: gjimene@una.ac.cr

PART I

AFRICA CASE STUDIES

1

VALUING TIME SPENT COLLECTING WATER IN A KENYAN TOWN[1]

Hugo van Zyl, Thomas Store and Anthony Leiman[2]

WATER COLLECTION

The state of water provision services in a community can have a significant effect on the quality of life of the inhabitants. Many people in developing countries (and particularly women) spend a significant portion of their day hauling water from sources to their homes. Enhanced access to environment-improving services such as water provision can yield substantial benefits in the form of productive time saved.

Different options for improved water delivery services such as yard taps, handpumps, and standposts result in varying amounts of time saved because they cut out the need to haul water from more distant sources. The choice of system does however involve a trade-off between increased costs and the benefits of time saved. Attaching a value to the time that people spend collecting water thus indicates the economic benefits of improved access to water services, which can then be compared with the estimated costs of such services, to assist decision-making on appropriate service provision.

DESCRIPTION OF THE STUDY

Objectives and Focus

This chapter reviews a study by Whittington et al (1990a), which attempted to value the time that people spend collecting water, using as an example a small town in Kenya.

The Inter-American Development Bank had assumed that time savings should be valued at 50 per cent of the market wage rate for unskilled labour in the local economy. Although they had no empirical basis for this, estimates of the value of time from studies of people's travel mode choices in developing countries had indicated that people typically value travel time savings at less than their market wage rate (Bruzelius, 1979; Yucel, 1975). The relevance of these findings to time savings from improved water access was unknown though, hence the need to determine the value of time spent collecting water, and in so doing test the Inter-American Development Bank's assumption.

Responding to this deficiency, the study presented two methods of estimating the value of the time spent hauling water based on revealed willingness to pay. The study illustrated the application of these two methods in Ukunda – a small town of 5000 inhabitants, situated 40 kilometres south of Mombasa, in Kenya. The following water sources are available to the residents of Ukunda:

* A *pipeline* which runs through the town, and which has only 15 private connections;
* Licensed *water kiosks* which sell water directly to the people; *or water vendors* who buy water from the kiosks and then deliver it from house to house.
* Six *open wells* and five *handpumps* that can be used free of charge by anyone.

Methodology

Both of the methods used in the study were based on discrete choice theory and the aim of both was to estimate values based on the preferences revealed by individuals through their choice of water service. The data were used in a discrete choice theory framework to determine upper and lower bound estimates of the value of time spent collecting water.[3] Given discrete choices, utility (satisfaction) functions for individuals were formulated, based on their revealed preferences (in this case revealed by their actions in purchasing water and their answers to a questionnaire). The utility derived from using the three different water sources was expressed as a function of the attributes of each source.

In the *first part* of the study the following attributes (which varied between sources) were assumed to determine utility: the price of the water, its collection time per litre and its taste. A simplifying assumption is made for the purposes of the calculations, and taste is left out as a determinant of utility, leaving only price and collection time. The household's utility per unit of water can then be obtained.

In the first part of the study the analysis uses discrete choice theory. This works directly with the utility functions instead of through demand functions, which would have been the case if continuous choice theory had been used. The conceptual framework suggested by discrete choice theory is as follows:

Among J exclusive alternatives (in this case, water sources), household h will choose alternative j over alternative i if and only if:

$U_{jh} > U_{ih}$ for $j, i \in J$ and $i \neq j$

Since each of the three water source alternatives differs in the three source attributes (P = price; COL = collection time per litre; T = taste), the additive utility of each of the three water sources is given by:

$U_v = B1P_v + B2COL_v + B3T_v$
[Utility of using a vendor]

$U_k = B1P_k + B2COL_k + B3T_k$
[Utility of using a kiosk]

$U_w = B1P_w + B2COL_w + B3T_w$
[Utility of using a well]

The Bs are parameter values of the indirect utility functions representing the household's preferences. For the purposes of the calculations, the influence of taste is ignored and the assumption is made that the household's choice of source is based solely on collection time and cash price. Dividing the indirect utility functions by B1 gives the household's utility per unit of water:

$U_v/B1 = P_v + (B2/B1)COL_v$

$U_k/B1 = P_k + (B2/B1)COL_k$

$U_w/B1 = P_w + (B2/B1)COL_w$

The Coefficient (B2/B1) is the value of time spent carrying water. Assuming that the alternative with the highest utility (in this case meaning the alternative with the lowest total price per litre including collection costs) will be chosen, with the upper and lower bounds for the value of time spent being calculated as follows:

Household chooses a kiosk:
This implies that $U_k > U_v$ and $U_k > U_w$ which yields an upper bound of $(P_v - P_k)/COL_k$ and a lower bound of $P_k/(COL_w - COL_k)$.

Household chooses a vendor:
This approach reveals two lower bounds of $(P_v - P_k)/COL_k$ and P_k/COL_w. If the household's value of time were less than the higher of

these two lower bounds, it would rationally switch to either the kiosk or open well.

Household chooses an open well:
This approach yields two upper bounds of $Pv/COLw$ and $Pk/(COLw - COLk)$. If the household's value of time exceeds the lower of these two upper bounds, it would have an incentive to switch to either a kiosk or a vendor.

The *second part* of the study is based on a random utility theory approach, which incorporates household characteristics as well as the source characteristics that were used in the first part of the study. Some inconsistencies in observed behaviour are inevitable, and these are assumed captured by a random term which is added to the systematic term in the household's random utility function so that:

$$U_{ih} = V_{ih} + E_{ih}$$

where V is the systematic term and E is the random term yielding the following utility function for household h choosing water source i:

$$U_{ih} = V_{ih} \ (\text{TIME, CASH, TASTE, INCOME, WOMEN, EDUCT})$$

where
TIME   =   Collection time per day including travel time, queue time, and fill time (expected to have a negative influence on choosing a source);
CASH   =   Total amount of money paid for collecting water per day, ie, the cash price times the amount of water consumed per day (expected to have a negative influence on choosing a source);
TASTE =   Household's perception of the taste of water from open wells – equalled to one if the taste is poor, zero otherwise (expected to have a negative influence on choosing a source);
INCOME = Total annual household income (expected to have a favourable influence on choosing a vendor or kiosk as opposed to a well);
WOMEN = Number of adult women in the household (as women collect 75 per cent of the water in Ukunda this is expected to have a favourable influence on choosing a well or kiosk because of the more women available to carry water);
EDUCT =   Number of years of formal education of family members (expected to have a favourable influence on choosing a vendor or kiosk above a well).

Since the distribution of Uih depends on the distributions of Eih, different assumptions about the distribution of Eih will lead to different discrete choice models. Here it was assumed that Ei has a Gumbel distribution so that the probability of choosing a source will have a logit-type function. Note that the independent variables in the random utility function which describe the *source* attributes vary across sources; the independent variables that describe the *household* attributes do not vary across sources (they can therefore be used to explain variations in tastes across households). The standard statistical tool for dealing with the first set of independent variables is a logit model while the standard approach for dealing with the second group is a polychotomous model. McFadden (1973, 1976, 1982) and Maddala (1983) have developed the following conditional logit model to deal with a data structure which includes both groups of independent variables:[4]

$$Ph(j) = \exp(BXjh + \alpha jZh) / \sum_{i=1}^{j} \exp(BXih + \alpha iZh)$$

where it is assumed the household's utility function is additive:

$$Vih = BXih + \alpha iZh$$

The purpose of presenting this discrete choice model was to derive an estimate of the value of time spent hauling water. If the value of time is defined as the marginal rate of substitution between the time spent collecting water and the money paid for the water, it can be calculated from two of the estimated parameters of this model:

$$\text{Value of time} = (B1/B2)$$

Main Sources of Data

The study used the results of interviews with 69 randomly selected households. The interviews, together with direct observations of these households, were conducted by the African Medical Research Foundation in the summer of 1986. The distance and travel times from each household to the available sources were obtained by walking to the sources, and data on the queue times were collected through observation. The study area of south-eastern Ukunda was ideal because several water source alternatives existed in the area, and no obvious choice stood out from the others. Each household was faced with three basic choices: a vendor charging 1.5 Kenyan shillings (ks) (US$0.10) per 20 litres; the nearest kiosk at 0.15 ks per 20 litres; and the nearest open well with no charge.[5] The interviews showed that 43 households (62 per cent) chose a kiosk, 17 (25 per cent) chose vendors and 9 (13 per cent) chose open wells. The interviews consisted of three parts that fulfilled all of the remaining data needs of the study not covered by direct observation.

The first part established basic demographic, occupational and educational data. The second dealt with water quality perceptions, the amount of water collected and the number of trips per day. The third part collected data on family incomes.

Comprehensiveness of the Estimates

The first part of the study showed that, although the upper and lower bounds for the 43 households using *kiosks* were relatively far apart, the vast majority fell between US$0.20 and US$0.50 per hour (standard deviation = US$0.11), yielding an average value of time collecting water of US$0.38 per hour. This figure was very close to the rough estimate for the average household income of this group, which was US$0.35 per hour.[6]

For the 17 households using *vendors*, the average value was US$0.57 per hour – a figure significantly higher than that for kiosks. This figure was also very close to the rough estimate of average household income of this group, at US$0.56 per hour.[7] Both figures tend to suggest that the value of time collecting water is close to the market wage rate and at the very least 50 per cent of the market wage rate.

For five of the nine households choosing *open wells*, the collection time was less for the open wells as opposed to the kiosks and thus this alternative was preferred, assuming water quality does not affect source choice. The remaining four households preferred open wells to kiosks, even though collection time was higher for the wells. This sample was thought to be too small to be significant.

The second part of the study valued the average time spent collecting water by the groups as a whole at US$0.31 per person hour. This was almost 25 per cent higher than the US$0.25 per hour average local wage rate for unskilled labour, and verified the results of the first part of the study, where the value of time spent collecting water was close to the market wage. The result must be seen as an average for all 69 households and not a household specific result derived using 'revealed preference' inequalities as in the first part of the study.

Treatment of Time Aspects

Time aspects were not taken into account as the analysis was cross sectional, focusing on values at one point in time.

Accuracy and Reliability

The model used to generate results in the second part of the study was highly significant, with an adjusted likelihood ratio of 0.51 and the variables TIME and CASH significant at the 1 per cent level. The other variables showed the following levels of significance:

TASTE	0.52;
V-INCOME	0.07;
V-WOMEN	0.09;
V-EDUCT	0.25;
K-INCOME	0.33;
K-WOMEN	0.36;
K-EDUCT	0.11

(V = vendor & K = kiosk).

Taste was thus found to have a low level of significance. Total annual household income and number of adult women in the household were of relatively high significance for households choosing vendors, but much less so for households choosing kiosks. Education level was relatively significant for households choosing kiosks, but much less so for those choosing vendors. The signs of all the explanatory variables were as expected.

The estimates on the value of time were consistent with the data on the average number of women in different groups of households. Because women were collecting about 75 per cent of the water fetched by households in Ukunda, one would expect that households with more adult women, having a greater labour supply for hauling water, would be less likely to purchase water from vendors. This was, in fact, the case. Households using vendors averaged only 0.88 women, while households using kiosks averaged 1.44 women, and households using open wells averaged 1.78 women.

CRITIQUE OF THE STUDY

Methodology

The theoretical underpinnings of the methodologies used are well explained at the outset of the paper, enhancing the accessibility of the study. Discrete choice theory, utility functions, random utility models and the revealed preference approach are all introduced conceptually before they are applied practically.

The study's credibility is strengthened by the use of two methodologies to value time spent. This allows comparison of, and increases confidence in, the results obtained.

Revealed preference approaches have the advantage of being better at avoiding 'human error' such as the various biases that can occur in CVM studies. This advantage is achieved by not eliciting subjective opinions and sticking to observation and straightforward questions.

The water market in Ukunda was found to be highly competitive with no participants making exorbitant profits (Whittington et al, 1989). This also enhanced the reliability of the study. The application of this methodology is not advisable in situations where market prices have been distorted as this would make the derivation of accurate values difficult.

Alternative methodologies that could have been applied to valuing the time spent collecting water include contingent valuation.[8] Other methodologies (elaborated on in the Haitian case study forming part of the Latin American and Caribbean section of this compendium) that could be used to value water services include: consumer surplus calculation based on an estimated demand function; hedonic property value approaches; and cost-savings approaches based on savings from water not purchased from vendors; or expenditure avoided in improving water quality.

Discrete choice or random utility models could also be used in other types of valuation studies. For example, both models are applicable in travel cost and hedonic pricing methodologies.[9] In travel cost calculations where it is difficult to properly account for the values of site characteristics or the effects of variations in site quality on the demand for a site, discrete choice models can be used to explain the choice of sites as a function of their characteristics. However, these models do not explain the total demand for a recreational activity (measured in visitor days), despite their ability to explain choices among sites.

In conventional hedonic models, the assumption is made that each attribute of the housing bundle is a continuous variable. This is clearly not realistic and is dealt with by discrete choice theory. Freeman (1993) defines two types of models: (i) bid rent or random bidding models, which focus on the individual's bid function, based on the probability that an individual will be the highest bidder for a specified bundle of housing attributes; and (ii) random utility models, which focus on the individual's utility function defined on housing attributes, and investigate the probability that a specified bundle of housing attributes will be chosen by the individual. Both types of model can be used to derive the marginal bid or marginal willingness to pay function for individual attributes from an estimate of the bid function or indirect utility function and thus can be used for valuation purposes.

Comprehensiveness of the Estimates

The authors of the study stress that the estimates obtained should be considered preliminary and that further research is needed before generalizations could be made. Firstly, they suggest that a larger sample would increase confidence in the results. Secondly, they suggest that, although general considerations such as the number of women in the household and household education levels were included, an in-depth anthropological investigation should also be carried out to determine whether social, cultural and political factors influence the choice of water source. Lastly, they suggest that more research is needed to determine whether households' valuation of time varies by hour of the day, day of the week, or between seasons.

The inclusion of income and education level differences adds to the credibility of the estimates. Although income level can be seen as a proxy for unemployment, the inclusion of household unemployment in the analysis might have added further to its credibility, given the lower opportunity cost of time spent collecting water for an unemployed person. The value of time may also be affected if the unemployed people engage in subsistence activities.

Treatment of Time Aspects

The analysis presented was a static one, which used cross-sectional data and so cannot be used to predict trends. Attempting to do this would require the use of a more complex time series analysis.

Accuracy and Reliability

As mentioned above, the limited amount of data available resulted in rather broad confidence intervals. Nevertheless, the upper and lower bounds for the estimates in the first part of the study helped present a clear picture of the results and suggested the sources of variation in them. In the second part of the study, the overall model was found to be highly significant, with a high adjusted likelihood ratio.

The testing of the results against the cultural expectation that households with more adult women would have a greater labour supply and would thus be less likely to purchase water from vendors is an interesting inclusion. It serves to confirm expectations and further justify the inclusion of the number of adult women variable in the analysis.

Policy Relevance

If other research shows that the value of time spent collecting water is near the market wage rate in other developing countries, this study will have important policy implications, raising the priority accorded to piped distribution systems in small towns and villages. The study tends to show that the value of time is greater than was previously assumed. It should raise the priority accorded to time saving projects.

Assuming that the relatively unexpected results of the study are correct, it is possible to look for intuitive reasons for the value of time spent collecting water being higher than the average wage rate. For example, there is the possibility that employed people have an increasing marginal value of time not spent at work, because they see it as 'precious' relaxation/leisure time.

Other research has already shown that households using vendors spend approximately 8 per cent of their income on water, while 1–5 per cent of household income is spent on most piped water systems

(Whittington et al, 1989). In the case of households using vendors, water supply is obviously a substantially larger financial burden.

Another factor for policy consideration, which raises the value of piped systems, is the higher degree of health benefits that these systems provide.[10] Whittington (1989) points out that vendors sometimes sell water from polluted sources or polluted containers. Water from open wells also has a higher likelihood of being a health risk.

The major trade-off to be considered in replacing vending and/or kiosk systems with piped systems is the employment that they provide to the local community.

Other studies focusing on rural water supply and sanitation policy have placed a value on improved services in a more direct way, by assessing willingness to pay for these services. In a study by Anjum Altaf et al (1993), household willingness to pay for reliable improved services was shown to be high enough to ensure full cost recovery in a new system. This study also revealed that in the absence of sufficient government investment in services, people tend to find private sector alternatives to meet their water needs, often at high economic and environmental costs. On the other hand, studies by Bohm et al (1993) dealing with water supply, and Whittington et al (1993) dealing with sanitation services, indicated that willingness to pay was not high enough to ensure cost recovery in new schemes. In cases such as these, subsidies might be considered.

LESSONS LEARNED

The lessons learned from reviewing this study include the following:

- bigger sample sizes are ideal, but need not be an overly limiting factor;
- the use of more than one method in an analysis is useful in verifying results, and in picking up influences that one method may have missed;
- the use of upper and lower bounds for values can help to give a clearer picture and add credibility to the results, in the absence of a full sensitivity analysis;
- direct observation of actions, as opposed to pure questionnaire based studies, can provide reliable information that avoids 'human error' such as biases;
- it is useful to express results not only in monetary terms but also in relation to the price of labour;
- the inclusion of unique features of societies or cultures that may affect results, such as the inclusion of the number of women per household in this study, is important for comprehensiveness.

NOTES

1   This chapter reviews, and therefore draws heavily on, Whittington et al (1990a).

2   University of Cape Town, School of Economics.

3   For a comprehensive treatment of this, see Freeman (1993), pp 133–136.

4   See glossary for description of the terms Gumbel distribution, logit model, and polychotomous model.

5   Approximately 5KS=US$1.

6   This figure was calculated using an estimated annual income for households using kiosks of $1250 and assuming 1.5 working adults per household with a working week of 50 hours per adult.

7   This figure was calculated using an estimated annual income for households using vendors of $2000 and assuming 1.5 working adults per household with a working week of 50 hours per adult

8   This method is used by Whittington et al (1990b) in estimating the willingness to pay for water services in Southern Haiti.

9   See Freeman (1993) for details on applications of hedonic models and travel cost models.

10 It is not known whether this is a positive externality or whether people build this consideration into their willingness to pay for piped systems. Assuming people are aware of health benefits, the latter should be the case.

REFERENCES

Anjum Altaf, M, Whittington, D, Jamal, H and Kerry Smith, V (1993) Rethinking Rural Water Supply Policy in the Punjab, Pakistan. *Water Resources Research*, vol 29 (7): 1943–1954.

Bohm, R A, Essenberg, T J and Fox, W F (1993) Sustainability of Potable Water Services in the Philippines. *Water Resources Research*, vol 29 (7): 1955–1963.

Bruzelius, N (1979) *The Value of Travel Time*. Croom Helm Ltd, London.

Freeman, A M (1993) *The Measurement of Environmental and Resource Values: Theory and Methods*. Resources for the Future, Washington, DC.

Maddala, G S (1983) *Limited-Dependent and Qualitative Variables in Econometrics*. Cambridge University Press, Cambridge, UK.

McFadden, D (1982) Econometric Models of Probabilistic Choice, in: Manski, C and McFadden, D (eds) *Structural Analysis of Discrete Data: with Econometric Applications*. MIT Press, Cambridge, MA, USA.

McFadden, D (1976) A Comment on Discriminant Analysis versus Logit Analysis. *Annals of Economic and Social Measurement*, vol 5: 511–523.

McFadden, D (1973) Conditional Logit Analysis of Qualitative Choice Behaviour, in: Zarembka, P (ed) *Frontiers of Econometrics*. Academic Press, New York.

Whittington, D, Lauria, D T, Okun, D A and Mu, X (1989) Water Vending in Developing Countries: A Case Study of Ukunda, Kenya. *Water Resources Development*, vol 5 (3): 158–168.

Whittington, D, Lauria, D T, Wright, A M, Choe, K, Hughes, J A and Swarna, V (1993) Household Demand for Improved Sanitation Services in Kumasi, Ghana: A Contingent Valuation Study. *Water Resources Research*, vol 29 (6): 1539–1560.

Whittington, D, Xinming, Mu and Roche, R (1990a) Calculating the Value of Time Spent Collecting Water: Some Estimates for Ukunda, Kenya. *World Development*, vol 18 (2): 269–280.

Whittington, D, Briscoe, J, Xinming, M and Barron, W (1990b) Estimating the Willingness to Pay for Water Services in Developing Countries: A Case Study of the Use of Contingent Valuation Surveys in Southern Haiti. *Economic Development and Cultural Change*, vol 38 (2): 293–311.

Yucel, N C (1975) A Survey of the Theories and Empirical Investigations of the Value of Travel Time Savings. World Bank Staff Working Paper no 199, The World Bank, Washington, DC.

2

THE RECREATIONAL VALUE OF VIEWING WILDLIFE IN KENYA[1]

Hugo van Zyl, Thomas Store and Anthony Leiman[2]

WILDLIFE VIEWING AND THE THREAT OF POLLUTION

Lake Nakuru National Park (LNNP) in Kenya is one of the few parks in East Africa served by tour operators, with large concentrations of flamingos (greater and lesser). Water pollution in the lake was suspected to be the cause of dwindling wildlife in the park. More specifically, increased farming activities and urbanization in the catchment basin are thought to be having a negative effect on the flamingos and other animals in the park.

Wildlife resources can provide much needed sustainable revenue for developing countries and so it is important to realize the economic potential of these resources. The pollution problem in LNNP is therefore threatening not just the park's attributes, but also its economic potential.

DESCRIPTION OF THE STUDY

Objectives and Focus

This chapter reviews a study by Navrud and Mungatana (1994) which aimed to estimate the recreational value of LNNP and the flamingos, which are the park's main attraction. By estimating how much revenue the park can generate through user fees, the study highlighted an implicit trade-off between different types of economic activity. Although this recreational value is only one part of the total economic value (TEV) of the resource, it offers a valid, if conservative, foundation on which to base entrance fee pricing decisions. More accurate pricing decisions will help the park, and others like it in Africa, to protect wildlife and earn sustainable revenue.

Methodology

Two independent methods, the Travel Cost Method (TCM) and Contingent Valuation Method (CVM), were used to estimate the non-consumptive use value or social benefits of preserving wildlife in LNNP. The use of two methods enabled the validation of their results, by checking for convergence in the estimates. The resulting estimates of recreational values, consumer surpluses and demand functions were recognized and used by the Kenya Wildlife Service as part of a long term pricing policy, initiated by the Tourism and Development Board.

As the estimated TCM values exceeded those of the CVM, the Willingness-To-Pay (WTP) estimates from the CVM provided a lower bound, ie a lower conservative estimate of the TEV of preserving wildlife in LNNP. The TCM values were used as an upper bound on the recreational values. Entrance fee decisions were made with reference to calculated price elasticities. These were calculated from the estimated bounded recreational values of the two samples (non-residents and residents), in relation to actual per capita entrance fees and the annual total revenue of LNNP at the time of the study.

Two sorts of benefit categories were provided by the study. Firstly, non-consumptive use values (ie recreational values) were estimated, demonstrating the social benefits of national parks and wildlife species in particular. Secondly, the study illustrated how developing countries can achieve pricing decisions that will allow them to maximize or at least increase national park revenues.

Travel Cost Method

The Travel Cost Method (TCM) is an indirect, revealed preference valuation method. The amount paid by visitors to travel to a particular recreational activity is used as a proxy for the market price of that activity. The number of visitors, expressed as a visitation rate, is used to illustrate the amount of recreation purchased at those prices. These two variables, the price of travel costs and the visitation rate, can then be used to estimate a demand curve for the recreational activity. From the demand curve, the total value of recreation and the consumer surplus are calculated.

Two separate demand curves were estimated in the study, one for non-residents and one for residents, as it was assumed that the two groups had different preferences for recreation and that foreigners, unlike residents, did not visit only LNNP, but other destinations as well.

Non-residents were asked about the length of their stay in Kenya; the time they had spent in LNNP; and the amount of time spent viewing and photographing flamingos. From this information the recreational values of entire trips to Kenya, of the stay in LNNP and of flamingo viewing were calculated. For residents, the TCM model directly estimated the demand for LNNP and for flamingo viewing.

The demand functions that underpinned the TCM required a set of independent variables that could be used in regression analysis, to identify factors of potential influence on the demand for LNNP (ie the visitation rate). These variables included: the travel costs to the park, household income, and other socio-economic variables such age, sex and education levels. Zonal and individual observation regression models were calculated. The visitation rate based on zonal observations used the following equation:

$$V_j = (USERS_j/POP_j)$$

where:
V_j = per capita visitation rate for zone j;
$USERS_j$ = total number of sampled users from zone j to LNNP in 1991;
POP_j = population of zone j.

The individual visitation rate, based on the probability of participation, used the equation:

$$V_{ij} = [T_i/(USERS_{ij}/POP_{ij})]$$

where:
V_{ij} = rate of visitation per capita for individual i from zone j;
T_i = the number of times the individual i visited LNNP in 1991;
$USER_{ij}$ = the total number of sampled users from zone j that individual i originates from;
POP_{ij} = the population of zone j that individual i originates from.

The zonal visitation rate per capita was used as it allowed for the different population sizes of the zones of visitor origin, population being an important determinant of the demand for recreational services and resources. As the travel costs of non-residents from the same country varied significantly, zones (and zonal populations) were defined according to the total cost of visiting Kenya rather than as simply a function of distance. On the other hand, residents were categorized according to conventional distance zones, as it was more plausible to assume that they travelled to LNNP by car and that there was a constant relationship between travel costs and distance travelled.

In addition to travel costs, travel time costs were added to estimate total travel costs. A commonly used factor of 0.3 of each visitor's wage rate was used to value his/her time spent travelling. This value varied from individual to individual according to data on their personal income.

The opportunity cost of time spent on the recreation site was not, however, included in this study's calculation of total travel cost.

Total travel costs to substitutes for LNNP were also estimated. This was done by asking visitors to name places that could be substitute sites for LNNP, and then estimating the travel costs of visiting those sites. Non-residents' perceptions of quality were estimated by respondents' willingness to extend their stay in the park after their visit. Residents' ratings of the experiences in LNNP, compared to those in other parks, were used as a quality indicator. Individual preferences for different activities in LNNP were obtained, which required rating the importance of flamingo viewing.

The general form of the equation was written as:

$$V_{ij} = f(P, I, A, S, E, P', F, Q, I')$$

where:
P = travel costs(round trip + travel time);
I = income (annual personal income in US$);
A = age (years);
S = sex(0 = female, 1 = male);
E = education (years of education);
P' = travel costs to substitute site;
F = preference for flamingo viewing (1–6, 1 = most and 6= least);
Q = quality of LNNP (dummy variable);[3]
I' = additional household income (ie, annual income of the household in excess of personal income, in US$).

✤ *Contingent Valuation Method*
This method involves directly asking people how much they would be willing to pay for specific improvements in, or to avoid damages to, an environmental public good. It is therefore a direct stated preference technique. The environmental change to be valued in this study was the possible loss of the current recreational value of flamingos in LNNP, due to pollution.

Two types of valuation exercises were carried out. In the first exercise both CVM questions used open-ended WTP questions and were stated as increased trip expenditures. This exercise involved visitors valuing their overall visit to LNNP. The second exercise involved visitors valuing flamingos, independent of the overall recreational value of LNNP. Both Willingness-To-Accept (WTA) and WTP questions were asked in the second exercise, with the latter using a payment card and the former an open-ended question format.

In the first exercise the following questions were asked:

Approximately how large are your personal total costs of this trip to LNNP (or to Kenya, for non-residents)? Include round trip travel costs and accom-

modation, but not food and special equipment (clothes, cameras, binocu-lars) bought for this trip (in US$).

Considering your experience so far on this trip to LNNP, and the total costs of this trip as stated earlier, what is the maximum increase in your total costs you would have accepted before you would decide not to come to LNNP? (in US$).

The following questions were asked in the second exercise:

You stated your total trip costs earlier. What is the minimum reduction in your total trip costs you would accept as compensation should there be no flamingos in LNNP? (in US$).

Flamingos in LNNP are threatened by water pollution and the Kenya Government is engaged in a clean up and pollution control programme for Lake Nakuru. The success of this programme depends on the availability of funds, which currently are in short supply. Imagine that a fund was set up by the World Wide Fund for Nature (WWF) to ensure that flamingos survive here in the park and that all the money collected will be used for this purpose.

Thinking of your experience of seeing the flamingos on this trip and your personal total costs stated earlier, which of the following amounts best describes the maximum amount you are willing to pay per visit, in addition to your personal costs, to ensure that flamingos do not disappear from LNNP? (show payment card). Please tick one.

0   1   5   10   15   20   25   50   100   150   200   US$/visit

The WTA question used an open-ended format to find the compensation that would be necessary should there be no more flamingos in LNNP. The last question in the second exercise was the only one to use a payment card.

Main Sources of Data

The basis of the study was empirical research, involving a relatively small, random sample of 185 visitors. Respondents included residents and non-residents and each group was treated separately to avoid complications and biases. The interviews took place during the peak tourist season (August to December). Each in-person questionnaire lasted approximately twenty-five minutes and included information on socio-economic variables and other information needed for the TCM and CVM techniques.

The existing sources of data used in the study included the annual revenue for LNNP, and the recorded number of visitors to the park in 1991. These were used to compare the actual revenue with the estimated recreational value of LNNP and to calculate the total recreational values of all visitors in 1991.

Comprehensiveness of the Estimates

On a general note, the fact that the study included calculations of the price elasticities for non-residents and residents enhanced the comprehensiveness of the results and made the estimates useful for decision making purposes. The demand for recreation at LNNP by non-residents was found to be price inelastic (–0.169 to –0.842). On the other hand, residents' demand for recreation was price elastic (–1.77 to –1.99).

TCM Estimates

In the Travel Cost Method, separate demand functions were estimated for residents and non-residents, based on zonal and independent observations. This permitted the estimation of recreational values and consumer surpluses for both residents and non-residents.

The recreational value of non-residents' visits to LNNP in 1991 was valued at 10.1–10.6 million US$. Non-residents received net benefits (consumer surplus) of the overall visit to Kenya, of 2.1 million and 2.0 million US$ calculated from the function and the observations, respectively. The total recreational value of residents' visits to LNNP amounted to 3.6–4.5 million US$. Consumer surplus for residents' visits to LNNP was estimated at 0.004–0.005 million US$.

Total non-use (recreational) value of visiting LNNP in 1991 was estimated at 13.7–15.1 million US$ while the recreational value of flamingo viewing was estimated at 5.0–5.5 million US$.

The regression models used for the TCM included not only travel costs, but many other independent variables (including income, and social and cultural variables), which improved its comprehensiveness. Education, additional household income, income and age were significant variables determining visitation rates. The quality of the site and the travel costs to a substitute site were found to be insignificant.

CVM Estimates

CVM results included annual recreational values for residents and non-residents and utilized both WTP and WTA questions (see Table 2.1 for the results of the different question formats). Non-residents were estimated to have higher recreational values than residents. WTA questions gave estimates that were 4 to 4.5 times higher than the estimates from WTP questions. Response rates for the different question formats were also given.

Treatment of Time Aspects

The study attempted to estimate the recreational value of LNNP and its flamingos over a one-year period in 1991, and was therefore a static analysis. No discount rates or time horizons were mentioned explicitly.

Table 2.1 *Results of the Contingent Valuation (CV) questions. Annual Recreational Value in 1991 (in US$)*

CV format	Mean value per visitor (US$)[a]	Aggregate value for all visitors (US$)[b]	Respondents with WTP or WTA=0 (%)	Response rate (%)
WTP-LNNP Increased expenditures	53.25	7,525,929	9.7	99.5
WTP-FLAMINGO Increased expenditures[c]	19.44	2,747,494	9.7	99.5
WTP-FLAMINGO Fund	21.88	3,093,527	19.4	97.3
WTA-FLAMINGO Reduced expenditures	86.97	12,292,558	34.3[d]	75.7[e]

Notes: a Weighted average of resident and non-resident visitors.
b 141,332 adults visited LNNP in 1991. The non-residents were assumed to have a WTP/WTA equal to respondents in the sample.
c 'WTP-FLAMINGO Increased expenditures' is calculated as 36.5 per cent of 'WTP-LNNP Increased expenditures', as this is the average percentage of time which visitors spent observing flamingos in LNNP.
d Average for the sample. 17.9 per cent and 39.3 per cent of the resident and non-residents visitors, respectively, stated WTA =0.
e Average for the sample. 96.6 per cent of the resident visitors replied, while the corresponding percentage for the non-residents was only 66.1 per cent.
Source: Adapted from Navrud and Mungatana, 1994

Accuracy and Reliability

The use of two approaches to valuation in the study allowed the authors to compare the estimates of the two methods using convergent validation.

Accuracy and Reliability of TCM Results
In the TCM, a sensitivity analysis was carried out, using three functional forms: linear, semilog, and loglinear. Different combinations of zonal definitions, independent variables and regression equations, using individual and zonal observations, were carried out. A sensitivity analysis of the definition of zones was carried out to find statistically stable travel cost coefficients.[4] Subsequently, the final parameters were selected to calculate consumer surplus. The 'best' functional forms were chosen based on these second stage benefits (consumer surplus). One way ANOVA tests between the benefits (consumer surplus) estimated from the function and the observations were carried out on each functional form to find the best fit. Criteria such as R^2, the number of independent variables, and the number of significant variables were used where more than one functional form gave consistent estimates. Confidence intervals, adjusted R^2 and the coefficients obtained were shown in tabular

form for the various functional forms for both non-residents and residents.

Accuracy and Reliability of CVM Results

Confidence intervals on the mean WTPs were not constructed, nor was a distribution about the mean estimates derived. The omission of statistics like these makes it difficult to assess the reliability of the WTP estimates. Considering the problems normally associated with the WTA method, the use of the WTP estimate for recreational value is ordinarily expected to be more conservative, but more reliable.

The results of the CVM were subject to qualitative theoretical testing. No statistical tests were carried out to determine the validity of specific relationships of the coefficients, in terms of theoretical expectations.

The authors seemed confident that they reduced *sponsor*, *embedding* and *scenario mispecification* biases.[5] If the authors were correct in this assertion, then the validity of the estimates should be good.

CRITIQUE OF THE STUDY

Methodology

The decision-making method used in the study is based on the estimated bounded values for recreation, extracted from the TCM and the CVM. As the estimates of the TCM were substantially higher than those produced by the CVM, the estimates of the latter were used as conservative values for preserving wildlife. LNNP entrance fee decisions were based on calculated price elasticities for non-residents and residents. Using price elasticities of recreational demand is particularly useful for developing countries that have abundant, undervalued wildlife resources. The fact that the Kenya Wildlife Service used these pricing estimates to increase their entrance fees for non-residents by 310 per cent illustrates the practicality of this decision-making method.

As the authors mentioned, the study only attempted to place a value on the recreational use of LNNP and its flamingos. Non-use values such as bequest and existence values may be of less practical use when considering entrance fee pricing decisions. Therefore, the omission of these benefit categories may actually have enhanced the appropriateness of the study, since the results were used specifically for pricing decisions and not for international transfers etc. The relevance of correct pricing decisions is highlighted by Norton-Griffiths' and Southey's (1995) study on the opportunity costs of biodiversity conservation in Kenya. They conclude that, with increasing pressure on land-use, the opportunity cost of conserving wildlife parks is becoming greater. They argue that, considering the global nature of benefits from Kenya's conservation efforts, the international community should contribute more to maintain conservation areas. They insist that increased entrance fees may not be adequate to cover these rising opportunity costs and that international transfers may be necessary to help Kenya 'catch up' until it can carry the burden itself. Studies being undertaken for such a purpose should ideally also include option, bequest and international external values.[6]

The use of two independent methods provided a check on the validity of the methods. In addition, it captured a wider spectrum of variables that can affect the demand for the resource. Mitchell and Carson (1989) point out, though, that a convergent validation only contributes to the credibility of both methods and does not prove the accuracy of either.

CVM Methodology

The CVM used open-ended WTP and WTA questions. Both non-residents' and residents' mean WTA were significantly higher than their WTP, with the non-residents' value being highest. WTA questions gave estimates approximately four times higher than the estimates from WTP questions. The authors' explanation for this large discrepancy is that there were no close substitutes for LNNP and its flamingos. This makes the hypothesized change, suggested in the WTA model, irreversible and respondents' WTA will therefore be high. According to Turner (1993), this result is common when evaluating environmental goods of this nature and the discrepancy should be viewed as theoretical backing for the internal consistency of the CVM.

Although the differences in the WTP and the WTA estimates may reinforce the theoretical basis of the CVM, Mitchell and Carson (1989) believe that WTA is the incorrect measure for valuing decreases in the level of provision of a large class of public goods. Turner (1993) also notes that it is inappropriate to use a WTA measure when valuing an environmental good that has public or collective right properties. Therefore, the authors' apprehension as to the reliability of the WTA estimates in this study seems justified.[7]

It is also suggested that if the WTA measure is used, a referendum-type CV format should be utilized. Turner (1993) proposes that payment cards should not be used, due to the existence of anchoring bids, which may cause bias in the estimates and hence affect the accuracy of the estimate.[8]

The use of open-ended questions in the CVM is not elaborated on. Turner (1993) notes that close-ended or dichotomous formats may produce estimates larger than the true WTP, while open-ended formats will lead to estimates lower than the true WTP. With this in mind it is suggested that both question formats be used to obtain a useful envelope of true evaluation.

There is no mention of a pre-test for the CVM questionnaire. If a pre-test is not carried out, the questionnaire may not be understandable, readable or clear. This can cause problems when evaluating the validity of the CVM.[9] This is discussed further below, in the section on accuracy and reliability.

TCM Methodology

The non-residents' demand functions based on zonal observations contradicted basic consumer theory, as the visitation rate grew as distance increased. To overcome this problem individual observations were used. These individual observations take into account different incomes, travel costs, age etc. within each zone. Although Turner (1993) points out that there is no agreement in TCM literature on the validity of zonal versus individual observations, there are a number of problems with the zonal measure. These include the fact that individual-specific information can not be included, the intra-zonal variation is lost, and a questionably high R^2 is produced, as variations are caused by the different definitions of zones. Thus, the use of individual observations for non-residents seems to be justified.

As the zonal travel cost parameters for residents were not significantly different from zero at the 5 per cent level, individual observations were also used. Since most resident visitors came from areas close to the park, their travel costs did not vary significantly from zone to zone. There has been some discussion on this issue (Turner, 1993; Gibson, 1978; Parson, 1991). However, it is not clear whether or not the issue of endogeneity of the price of a trip is relevant here.

There is little elaboration on the definition of total cost used in the TCM. The way in which actual travel costs, travel time, and on-site time costs are defined may influence the resulting estimates. For non-residents this did not seem to be a problem as travel costs were specified according to the total costs incurred in visiting Kenya. For residents travelling by car three measures are possible: petrol costs only, full car costs, or perceived costs as estimated by respondents (Turner, 1993). Each of these measures can produce significantly different results, with the first one being the most reliable (Bateman, 1993). This is because full car costs include overheads such as insurance and depreciation, which may overstate travel costs. The third measure is unreliable since some respondents may include the above mentioned sunk costs while others will not have considered them relevant to the visit. The first option shows the marginal cost associated with the visit.

For travel time costs the authors use a factor of 0.3 of the visitors' hourly wage rate. This assumes that visitors have negative utility for travel time to LNNP or Kenya. This may not necessarily be the case for many visitors who could have zero opportunity cost for travel time. Perhaps a question asking whether visitors were self-employed would have overcome this. Turner (1993) suggests that utility weighting be applied to travel time costs.[10]

The authors chose to omit the on-site costs of recreation. Contrary to the authors' assertion that this omission is negligible, Turner (1993) suggests that 'tests be carried out as per Bojö (1985) to obtain some estimate of the magnitude of the consumer surplus estimation error likely if time costs are ignored'.

Comprehensiveness of the Estimates

As mentioned earlier, the CVM did not attempt to elicit TEV. The estimates depict only the recreational values of LNNP and its flamingos. Considering that the estimates were used for policy decisions on entrance fee pricing, it is reasonable that the other values were not researched. Had the study been used for other policy decisions, more comprehensive estimates might have been needed. It is important to keep cost and credibility considerations in mind when dealing with developing countries that have budget constraints and lack experience in interpreting the results of environmental valuations.

The inclusion of residents and non-residents' consumer surpluses is good and has made it possible to determine the respective price elasticities of recreation for LNNP. Norton-Griffiths and Southey (1995) highlight the importance and general lack of this information in a developing country like Kenya. Demand elasticity information is essential if revenues from parks are to be improved and the full benefits of conservation realized.

Ordinary visitor statistics of LNNP did not include information such as nationality, length of stay, and socio-economic variables such as age, sex, educational level and income. Although there was little the authors could do about this, it meant that they could not check the representivity of their sample. Thus, the comprehensiveness may be reduced, as it is not possible to determine whether the income, social and cultural considerations included were in fact representative of the population of users. This is a lesson for park boards in general.

The authors did not discuss the income effect in the estimation of recreational values and consumer surpluses in the TCM. One of the classic problems of consumer surplus measures is the income effect. As the TCM produces a marshallian demand curve (ie one that does not hold income constant) this effect may be problematic for measuring large changes in prices. If however the income elasticity of demand is unitary, this problem is not an issue. On the other hand, this lack of elaboration may be due to the fact that the TCM results were not used in the final estimations of partial TEV and consumer surplus, as they were deemed unreliable.

Treatment of Time Aspects

The authors do not include a discount rate in their calculation of the recreational value of conserving LNNP and its flamingos. They state that WTP is the correct format to use when valuing decreases in the provision for those public goods that require an annual payment to maintain a given level of a good. Presuming that preservation of this kind would involve high initial costs but would produce long-term benefits, a discussion on the issue of social time preference would have been warranted.

Accuracy and Reliability

Reliability is defined as, 'the extent to which the variance of a response or estimate is a result of random sources of noise'(Mitchell and Carson, 1989). Thus, the standard error of the mean revealed WTP estimate is the measure of reliability. Reliability can be improved by increasing the sample size and by improving the sample design (Freeman, 1993). Confidence intervals describe the reliability of calculated estimates as a measure of the true value.

Reliability of the CVM
The CVM used a sample size of 58 and 127 for resident and non-resident visitors respectively. According to Mitchell and Carson (1989), CVM samples need to be large.[11] The sample used in this study does seem unusually small. In addition, considering that the visitor statistics did not include information about nationality, length of stay, or socio-economic variables like age, sex, education and income, it is unclear as to how representative the sample used was. Reliability problems of this sort are especially common where the sample size is small and heterogeneous (Mitchell and Carson, 1989).

Validity of the CVM
The measure of validity is schematic error, which may be improved by altering the design of the CVM. Three types of validity are important when assessing the validity of WTP estimates, namely content, criterion and construct validity.

Content validity assesses whether or not the CVM questionnaire asks the 'right questions in an appropriate manner' and whether the WTP measure is 'what respondents would actually pay for a public good if a market for it existed'(Turner, 1993). Although content validity is not regarded as a serious problem, pre-testing and pilot surveys can help reduce it. The authors make no mention of these kinds of procedures.

A comparison of the CVM estimates with the true recreational value would test for criterion validity. Mitchell and Carson (1993) suggest that if a created market exists for the public good being valued, it is possible to compare the resulting prices with values obtained from the CVM. This is difficult to do, since it would require conducting experiments using parallel or simulated markets for the good in question. This may not have been undertaken because it increases the cost of the study and there may not be parallel markets for LNNP.

According to Turner (1993), two variants of construct validity exist: theoretical and convergent validity. The first confirms whether or not the CVM estimates conform to theoretical expectations. In this case, the price elasticity estimates conformed to the prior expectations, with elasticities for non-residents being low and those for residents being high. Statistical tests can be performed on WTP values to assess the theoretical validity of the estimates. This is done by 'regressing some form of the WTP amount on a group of independent variables believed to be theoretical determinants of people's willingness to pay for the good being valued' (Mitchell and Carson, 1989). The sizes and signs of the resulting coefficients are then analysed in a theoretical context. Turner (1993) also suggests that simple t-tests be carried out to determine the significance of these coefficients. Thus, the validity of the WTP estimates could have been enhanced by regressing WTP on significant independent variables.

Considering convergent validity, the study restricted the CVM to estimates of recreational value, thus excluding existence, option and bequest values. This actually made the benefits measured more comparable, since the TCM can not capture the above-mentioned benefits either. However, contrary to theoretical expectation, the CVM produced smaller estimates than the TCM. This is surprising since CVM has the potential of capturing non-use values, although similar results have been observed in other comparative studies. Furthermore, the fact that the TCM yields an uncompensated consumer surplus, while the CVM produces a compensated measure, could explain why the TCM value is greater. This difference is dependent on the income elasticity of demand. The difference between the two measures is zero only when this elasticity is equal to one (unitary). These issues are not mentioned in the paper. The difference in size between the TCM and CVM estimates may also be a reflection of the way the questions were set.

The CVM study estimated the aggregate annual recreational value for LNNP at 7.5 million US$. On the other hand, the estimated TCM value was between 13–15 million US$. The two estimates were 50–60 per cent within each other. This is consistent with other convergent validity studies that have been carried out (Cummings, Brookshire and Shultz, 1986).

The WTA scenario did not work well, particularly with non-residents. This format, which involved asking what amount of compensation visitors would accept for the absence of flamingos, produced a large number of non-responses. As mentioned earlier, this may affect the reliability of the estimates, as the sample was already small. The authors acknowledged the problems with the WTA format and passed the estimate off as being unreliable.[12]

Alternatively, a close-ended WTP format could have been used as a back up. The reason for this suggestion is that the exclusion of a close-ended question format in the CVM exercise does not allow for a validity check on the WTP estimates. Kealy and Turner (1993) found that for a public good, different types of question format used can lead to significantly different WTP values. Typically, close-ended formats lead to higher values than open-ended formats. Instead of using only the payment card and open-ended formats, exercises using close-ended and open-ended formats might have produced a more useful envelope of estimates. However, it is realized that the WTA is the logical back up to WTP and that using a close-ended format may require more interviews and thus more resources. Also the use of an open-ended format allows a project to proceed even when only small sample numbers are available.

Open-ended questions may also produce a high number of protest bids and non-responses (Mitchell and Carson, 1989). This seems to be problematic in cases like this one where the sample is already small.

The format used by the authors may have been subject to various biases.[13] The use of the open-ended format contains more information on the respondents' value of the good in question (Mitchell and Carson, 1989). It also enables the use of relatively straightforward statistical techniques. However, as mentioned before, it is often difficult for respondents to conceptualize a value for an environmental good, so such open-ended questions can result in non-responses and protest zero responses. Table 2.1 shows that the response rate was only a problem for the WTA question format, where the response rate was only 75.7 per cent. Considering that the CV survey was not all that complex and did not involve valuing an amenity that people were completely unfamiliar with, this result is not surprising. However, the open-ended results may be subject to *strategic* bias. By relating the WTP and WTA questions to increased expenditures, instead of to entrance fees, the motivation for strategic behaviour by respondents may have been reduced.

The use of the payment card may induce biases that arise from the ranges used on the cards. On the other hand, the card can circumvent strategic behaviour.

Part whole bias seems to have been minimized by the authors taking various precautions. Firstly, they asked respondents to value the recreational value of LNNP and subsequently asked them to value the flamingos, thus overcoming geographical part whole bias. In addition, both the WTA and WTP questions were related to the visitors' total expenditures of their trip. This, combined with the fact that the questions only attempted to elicit use values, may have prevented benefit part whole bias.

Reliability of the TCM
The estimation techniques used were not mentioned in the paper, making it difficult to assess the extent to which truncation bias may be present. Perhaps the authors could have estimated their benefit measures using both Ordinary Least Squares and Maximum Likelihood estimation techniques. This would have given an indication of the reliability of the estimates.

The choice of the functional form is a contentious issue. However, it seems as though comprehensive treatment of the choice of functional form was carried out. Turner (1993) suggests the use of either the Mann-Whitney U test or a Wilcoxon signed ranks test, to test for the most consistent functional form.

The lack of elaboration on travel costs (money expenditure necessary to reach a site) may cause reliability problems, as different definitions can produce significantly different consumer surpluses.

The omission of on-site costs may also cause reliability problems. The omission may have produced an underestimation of consumer surplus. Since no theoretical backing is presented on this omission, a test such as that described earlier should have been carried out. This would have given an indication of whether or not the omission is significant. Furthermore, a sensitivity analysis could have been carried out using different values of wage rates.

Validity of the TCM
Firstly, the use of two separate demand equations for non-residents and residents is good. Since many non-resident visitors originate from developed countries, it must be assumed that these two groups have different preferences and income levels.[14]

Theoretical and statistical testing carried out on the zonal and individual travel cost equations showed that zonal observations, for both residents and non-residents, were invalid. Since there is no agreement as to which form is superior, this type of validity testing is important.

LESSONS LEARNED

This review of the study by Navrud and Mungatana (1994) reveals several lessons for the valuation of wildlife resources and the methodology of other studies of this kind. The lessons learned include:

Lessons on Valuing Wildlife Resources

- Wildlife resources in developing countries may be significantly undervalued. In other words, large consumer surpluses may exist, especially when many visitors are non-residents.
- The study found that flamingos are the single most important species for recreation in LNNP. Therefore, measures to preserve them will enhance or at least sustain its revenue-raising capacity in the future. Valuation exercises on specific attributes in parks can highlight their importance in influencing the demand for recreation.
- These resources represent a potential source of significant, sustainable revenue for developing countries.

- A general lesson for park board authorities in Africa is to collect as much socio-economic data on visitors as possible. This may aid future research on valuation, and reduce the costs of these studies.
- Price elasticity information is essential when using the results of valuations for policy decisions.
- With rising opportunity costs of conservation in developing countries, it is important that foreigners pay according to the benefit they receive from wildlife resources. The use of elasticity information is therefore essential for these kinds of policy decisions.
- The use of the two methods enhances the reliability of the estimates and provides a conservative estimate for the total economic value of LNNP and of the flamingos. Both methods can be used to bound the value, and to contribute to pricing policies.
- If possible, post study surveys should be carried out to observe how demand reacts to the policy decisions taken, based on the study.

Lessons Learned on the CVM Methodology

- Whenever CVM studies are used for policy purposes, it is useful to have some form of validity test (such as a test for convergent validity).
- CVM studies must address bias problems explicitly.
- Although cost considerations are always an important part of valuation studies, samples must be of a significant size for the generation of reliable estimates, particularly if the results are to be used for policy purposes.
- Pre-test and pilot surveys can help to enhance the reliability and validity of the study.
- Caution must be exercised when using WTA question formats, to ensure they are phrased appropriately.
- A careful assessment of the choice of question formats must be undertaken before each study. It is important to note that WTA formats may produce unreliable estimates, which represent an opportunity cost. More comprehensive and reliable results may be produced if complementary elicitation methods are used together.

Lessons Learned on the TCM Methodology

- When valuing amenities that are used by both foreigners and residents, two separate demand functions should be estimated.
- Both zonal and individual observations should be used, to determine which gives more reliable estimates.
- Researchers should be careful in the definition of travel costs, travel time, and on-site time costs.
- Comprehensive statistical analysis should be undertaken for the selection of the best functional form.

NOTES

1 This chapter reviews, and therefore draws heavily on, Navrud and Mungatana (1994).

2 University of Cape Town, School of Economics.

3 This dummy variable of the quality of LNNP was based on non-residents' willingness to extend their stay in the park. Residents' rating of their experiences in the park, compared to other parks, were used as a proxy for site quality. All residents rated the park to be of high or very high quality.

4 Statistically significant travel cost coefficients remained almost constant in different zonal definitions. This was done by gradually increasing the class boundary of the zones of origin.

5 See glossary for a brief explanation of these biases.

6 Norton-Griffiths and Southey (1995) give off-site value of erosion and watershed protection as examples of domestic external values while values of carbon sequestration and biodiversity would be international external values.

7 See Mitchell and Carson (1989), Freeman (1993), and Turner (1993) for comprehensive discussions on other studies addressing this issue.

8 See glossary for brief explanation of this bias.

9 More specifically, this may cause content validation problems.

10 Respondents would be asked to rate their enjoyment of travel time only. An inverse index can then be constructed ranging from 1 for those who hate travelling, to 0 for those who prefer travelling to visiting.

11 Mitchell and Carson (1989) provide a table of sample sizes needed for various confidence intervals, relative errors and per cent differences between true and revealed WTP estimates.

12 Generally, CVM literature seems to support the finding that WTP is a more reliable estimate when valuing environmental goods where there are no clearly defined property rights (Mitchell and Carson, 1989; Freeman, 1993; Turner, 1993).

13 See glossary for brief descriptions of different kinds of biases.

14 A table showing where the non-residents came from is given in Navrud and Mungatana (1994).

REFERENCES

Bateman, I J et al (1993) Recent Experiments in Monetary Evaluation of the Environment. Environmental Appraisal Group, University of East Anglia, UK.

Bojö, J (1985) Kostnadsnyttoanalys av fjällnära skogar – fallet Vålådalen (Cost-Benefit Analysis of Forest Harvesting versus Preservation of the Vålå Valley), Stockholm School of Economics (with assistance from Lars Hultkrantz).

Cummings, R G, Brookshire, D S and Schultz, W D (eds) (1986) *Valuing Environmental Goods: A State of the Arts Assessment of the Contingent Valuation Method*. Rowan and Allen, Totowa, New Jersey, USA.

Freeman III, A M (1993) *The Measurement of Environmental and Resource Values: Theory and Methods*. Resources for the Future, Washington, DC.

Gibson, J G (1978) Recreation Land Use. In Pearce, D W (ed) *The Valuation of Social Cost*. Allen and Unwin, London.

Kealy, M and Turner, R W (1993) A Test of The Equality of Closed-Ended and Open-Ended Contingent Valuations. *American Journal of Agricultural Economics* vol 75: 321–331.

McConnell, K E (1992) On Site Time in Demand for Recreation *American Journal of Agricultural Economics* vol 74: 918–925.

Mitchell, R C and Carson, R T (1989) *Using Surveys to Value Public Goods: The Contingent Valuation Method*. Resources for the Future, Washington, DC.

Navrud, S and Mungatana, E D (1994) Environmental Valuation in Developing Countries: The Recreational Value of Wildlife Viewing. *Ecological Economics* vol 11: 135–151.

Norton-Griffiths, M and Southey, C (1995) The Opportunity Costs of Biodiversity in Kenya. *Ecological Economics* vol 12: 125–139.

Parson, G R (1991) A Note on Choice of Residential Location in Travel Cost Demand Models. *Land Economics* vol 67: 360–364.

Turner, R K (ed) (1993) *Sustainable Environmental Economics and Management. Principles and Practice*. John Wiley and Sons, Chichester, UK.

3

Determinants of Land Values in Accra, Ghana[1]

Hugo van Zyl, Thomas Store and Anthony Leiman[2]

Land Values

The issue addressed in this chapter is that of land values and their determinants. While not primarily an environmental issue, the value of land does have important impacts on the environment. In a market system, it is the price of land that is the rationing mechanism, allocating it between competing alternative uses. The failure of this allocative function can lead to problems in the urban environment such as: overcrowding, traffic congestion, haphazard or uncontrolled development, pollution and urban blight. These problems are particularly acute in developing countries experiencing rapid urbanization. An analysis of the determinants of land values can highlight the sources of failure in the allocative function of land prices. A clear understanding of these determinants can assist land use planners and public policy decision-makers in the formulation and implementation of land use policies.

As the capital of Ghana, Accra has experienced rapid urbanization as a result of population growth and migration from rural areas.

Description of the Study

Objective and Focus

This chapter reviews a study by Asabere (1981) on the determinants of land values in Accra, the capital of Ghana. This study was chosen as it was the only example found of the hedonic pricing technique, an important valuation methodology.

The study identifies the negative externalities that exist in low-income residential housing areas, including environmental externalities such as overcrowding, pollution, and sanitary problems. Furthermore, the study highlights what effect the condition of the beaches has on property values in Accra. These can be seen as surrogates for environmental factors.

Methodology

The hedonic model used in the study was a value equation, which incorporated variables representing both the demand and supply side of the market. The variables included were:

- access variables, including distance to the Central Business District (CBD), measured using a simple linear distance to CBD model; distance to the sea, measured using a similar linear distance model; and presence of a major or class-A road;
- government zoning variables, including the different zones of high class residential, middle class residential, low class residential, commercial and industrial;
- culturally rooted variables, including land tenure effects such as land ownership (stool/shrine or individual); the interest attached to land (freehold or leasehold); and ethnic clustering (three different groups: Gas, Zongos and mixed);[3]
- time of sale variables, referring to the dates at which the land transaction took place;
- site services variables, which include access to a residential access road, proximity to mains water and electricity lines, and the extent of site clearing; and
- variables of lot size.

The equation used was:

$$SP_i = B_0 \exp [B_1 dCBD_i + B_2 dSEA_i + B_3 ROAD_i + B_4 COM_i + B_5 HRES_i + B_5 MRES_i + B_7 LRES_i + B_8 IND_i + B_9 MOS_i + B_{10} STOOL_i + B_{11} INDV_i + B_{12} GA_i + B_{13} ZONGO_i + B_{14} MIXED_i + B_{15} INT_i + B_{16} SS_i] A_i^{B17}$$

where:
The Bs are parameter values;
SP_i = selling price of a lot i in Ghanaian Cedis (2.75 Cedis = US\$1.00);
$dCBD_i$ = the distance in miles of lot i from the CBD (ie, the Accra Central Market);
$dSEA_i$ = the distance in miles of lot i from the sea;
$ROAD_i$ = a dummy variable assigning 1 if lot i is located within a quarter mile of the nearest class A road, and 0 if the distance to the road is greater than a quarter of a mile;

COM_i = a dummy variable assigning 1 if lot i is located in a commercial zone and 0 for all other zones;

$HRES_i$ = a dummy variable assigning 1 if lot i is located in a high residential zone and 0 for all other zones;

$MRES_i$ = a dummy variable assigning 1 if lot i is located in a middle residential zone and 0 for all other zones;

$LRES_i$ = a dummy variable assigning 1 if lot i is located in a low residential zone and 0 for all other zones;

IND_i = a dummy variable assigning 1 if lot i is located in an industrial zone and 0 for all other zones;

MOS_i = month of sale of lot i. Fractions of months are included based on 30 day months. Sales extend from MOS=.443 to 60, or from January 1974 to December 1978;

$STOOL_i$ = a dummy variable assigning 1 if lot i is sold by a chief and 0 if sold by other-than chief;

$INDV_i$ = a dummy variable assigning 1 if lot i is sold by a private individual and 0 if sold by other-than private individual;

GA_i = a dummy variable assigning 1 if lot i is located in a predominantly GA area and 0 for other locations;

$ZONGO_i$ = a dummy variable assigning 1 if lot i is located in a Zongo area and 0 for otherwise;

$MIXED_i$ = a dummy variable assigning 1 if lot i is located in a mixed ethnic or heterogeneous areas and 0 for a homogeneous area;

INT_i = a dummy variable assigning 1 if lot i is sold with a freehold interest and 0 if it is sold with leasehold interest;

SS_i = a dummy variable assigning 1 if lot i had site services at the time of sale and 0 if it had none;

A_i = area of lot i in thousand square feet.

The hedonic model was estimated by taking natural logarithms on both sides of the above equation and using ordinary least squares. Three estimations were made for periods: (i) January 1974–December 1975; (ii) January 1976–December 1978; and (iii) for the whole period January 1974–December 1978. The analysis was divided up in this way in an attempt to capture the potential impact of the artificial price suppression that was experienced under the rule of a military dictatorship in the 1974–75 period. All three models were applied using all the variables, to make it possible to identify and exclude the insignificant variables from the final estimations of the models.

Based on the third model, two bid rent curves were constructed. The first assumes the lot was sold at the end of 1974, while the second assumes the lot was sold at the end of 1978. Further assumptions made included: the lot is located half a mile away from the sea, and more than a quarter of a mile away from the nearest A-class road; it is zoned for middle class residential, located in a GA area, sold by a chief, has no site services and has an area of 8000 square feet.

Main Sources of Data

The data were collected by Asabere in 1979. The principle source of data was the records held by the Bank for Housing Construction in Accra. This consisted of up-to-date records on property transactions carried out through the bank and included: lot sale price, time of sale of lot, lot size, location, type of improvements on and to the lot, type of interest attached to the land, type of seller, zoning classification, estimated value of the lot, etc. In addition, data on self-financed property transactions from real estate brokers were included. These data were compared with data from the Department of Lands, which keeps similar information on all land transactions that involve title transfers. Where details diverged or transfers were not believed to be bona fide, the information was excluded from the sample. Plot maps provided distance information. Other information such as that used for stool lands and other land tenure information was obtained through interviews with divisional chiefs, elders, and some authorities of both the University of Ghana, Legon, and the University of Science and Technology, Kumasi. The data covered a five-year period from January 1974 to December 1978 and included 211 observations.

Comprehensiveness of the Estimates

The study focused on determining the *relative* coefficient magnitudes of the variables that were deemed significant in influencing land values. Thus, no specific attributes of land values were isolated and valued. If an environmental good had been included it would have been possible to determine its value using more comprehensive hedonic techniques.[4]

The study made use of a large number of variables, and was thus a comprehensive analysis. The results of the three regression equations were as follows:

In model 1 (Jan 1974–Dec 1975) the following variables were found to be insignificant and thus excluded from the final run: $dCBD_i$, $ROAD_i$, $MRES_i$, IND_i, SS_i, $INDV_i$, and INT_i. The specification $(1/MOS_i)$ was the best fit of the model. The signs of the remaining variables were as expected and the adjusted coefficient of determination was 0.65.

In model 2 (Jan 1976–Dec 1978) the following variables were insignificant and thus excluded from the final run: $MRES_i$, IND_i, SS_i, $INDV_i$, and INT_i. The signs of the remaining variables were as expected and the adjusted coefficient of determination was 0.49.

In model 3 (Jan 1974–Dec 1978) the following variables were insignificant and thus excluded from the final run: $MRES_i$, IND_i, $INDV_i$, and INT_i. The signs of the remaining variables were as expected and the adjusted coefficient of determination was 0.53.

In all the above three models the levels at which the omitted variables were not significantly different from zero were not included.

Table 3.1 shows the results of the three models. By analysing the signs and magnitudes of the various coefficients, one is able to see which variables affect the urban land market. Legislative market distortions occur from government zoning practices and rent controls, while socio-political distortions result from traditional land tenure systems and ethnic clustering.

Table 3.1 *Land Value Regressions for Accra*

Variable	1974–75 Model 1	1976–78 Model 2	1974–78 Model 3
$dCBD_i$	–	$-0.113^†$	-0.129^{**}
		(-1.533)	(-2.2015)
$dSEA_i$	0.108^*	0.307^{***}	0.325^{***}
	(1.918)	(4.416)	(5.431)
$ROAD_i$	–	0.866^{***}	0.707^{***}
		(5.104)	(5.011)
COM_i	1.367^{**}	$0.487^†$	0.629^{**}
	(3.420)	(1.343)	(2.159)
$HRES_i$	$0.421^†$	0.309^*	0.282^*
	(1.591)	(1.709)	(1.854)
$MRES_i$	–	–	–
$LRES_i$	–	-0.359^{**}	-0.268^{**}
		(-2.083)	(-2.024)
IND_i	–	–	–
MOS_i	–	0.021^{***}	0.018^{***}
		(3.631)	(5.905)
$1/MOS_i$	1.069^{***}	–	–
	(4.774)		
$STOOL_i$	-0.288^{**}	$-0.215^†$	-0.203^*
	(-2.137)	(-1.516)	(-1.901)
$INDV_i$	–	–	–
GA_i	-1.123^{***}	-0.411^{**}	-0.463^{**}
	(-4.553)	(2.132)	(-2.879)
$ZONGO_i$	-0.846^{**}	-0.423^{**}	-0.438^{**}
	(-3.074)	(-2.073)	(-2.347)
$MIXED_i$	–	–	–
INT_i	–	–	–
SS_i	–	–	$0.140^†$
			(1.316)
$1n\ A_i$	0.416^{***}	$0.161^†$	0.201^{**}
	(3.603)	(1.563)	(2.389)
CONSTANT	1.539^{***}	2.785^{***}	1.826^{***}
	(2.479)	(4.377)	(3.985)
R^2	0.65	0.49	0.53

Notes:
* significant at 90 per cent level of confidence
** significant at 95 per cent level of confidence
*** significant at 99 per cent level of confidence
† significant at 90 per cent level of confidence using one tail test
– excluded from that model
Source: adapted from Asabere, 1981

Treatment of Time Aspects

The analysis was performed using data obtained over a five year period, January 1974 to December 1978. The time period was further divided into three separate periods, to capture effects such as political trends in the property market.

Accuracy and Reliability

Data used in the study were double-checked with the Department of Lands records and conflicting data were excluded. The division of the model into three time sections enhanced the reliability of the model by taking important political trends into account. The results of the three models showed relatively high coefficients of determination after the variables deemed to be insignificant were excluded from the final runs.

Confidence levels of the variables, varying from significant at 90 per cent level using a one tail test to significant at the 99 per cent level, were stated. In addition, those deemed not significant were highlighted.

CRITIQUE OF THE STUDY

Methodology

The hedonic pricing model (HPM) used in the study attempted to identify the main determinants of land values in Accra, without isolating or valuing any specific environmental attribute. Nevertheless, it is felt that some valuable lessons can be learnt from this study.

There is no decision making method or benefit category included in the study. The sizes and signs of the regression coefficients of the various variables were used to indicate their potential significance in influencing land values.

As the study did not carry out the full HPM procedure, the following is a brief description of the usual HPM procedure, highlighting the steps that could be added if an HPM study were to be undertaken to value an environmental amenity.

The following principal procedures are used in the HPM: (Adapted from Winpenny, 1995)

1   Define and measure the attributes;
2   Specify the hedonic price function;
3   Collect data (cross-sectional data or time series data);
4   Use multiple regression analysis to find the coefficients of the attribute in question;
5   Derive the demand curve for the specific attribute.

Step one was adequately carried out in the study and has already been discussed in the methodology section. The second step involved specifying the variables that could influence the price of property (in this study explicit environmental attributes were not tested for, but they could easily be included). The functional relationship between the price of vacant lots and the chosen variables was of the double log form. This is useful if elasticities are to be calculated though this was not elaborated on in the study. The choice of the functional form is important in the estimation of benefit measures. In this case, the functional form of the equation was imposed at the outset, though a number of different functional forms might have been used and analysed.[5]

This study utilized time series data, in step three, to capture the effects of the different political regimes on property prices that existed in the city. Cross-sectional data are preferred if an environmental attribute is to be isolated and valued, as time series data are likely to capture changes in tastes, other structural factors or trends that may invalidate the estimates.

Step four involved using the Ordinary Least Squares estimation procedure. More recent HPM studies make use of a Maximum Likelihood procedure. The attribute 'distance from the CBD' was isolated and correlated to property values. Implicit prices of this variable were expressed as two bid rent curves.

If an environmental amenity is to be valued, step five involves second stage estimation procedures (something not done in the study), involving the determination of the demand of households for the attribute in question. This is done by regressing the implicit price of the amenity against the socio-economic characteristics of individuals. Once the demand curve is estimated it is possible to measure the consumer surplus gained or lost from increases or decreases in the attribute. However, this entails making assumptions about households' preferences and tastes for the attribute, which are often highly questionable (Pearce and Turner, 1990). Therefore this final stage is often omitted in the HPM.

A study by North and Griffin (1993) illustrates this fifth step, in their estimation of the WTP for improved water supplies of residents of the Bicol region in the Philippines. This involved isolating a specific site characteristic, for instance proximity to a mains water supply and then deriving a demand function for this specific attribute.

Comprehensiveness of the Estimates

Like many other HPM studies, this study could not capture non-use values, as it measured only the use values of attributes of particular sites. As a demand curve was not estimated, no consumer surplus measures were included in the study. Clearly before this could have been done, additional data (especially on household income) would have had to be available.

An interesting feature of the study was its highlighting of the institutional functioning of the urban land market and the distortions created by various policies. In particular, it showed that governmental zoning modified market outcomes.[6] High-class residential areas showed a positive land value effect, while low-class zones experienced a negative effect on values. The author attributes this to the existence of negative externalities that flow from other sources such as industry in these areas.

The study also captured the effects of various political eras.[7] This example is especially important for researchers using the HPM in developing countries in Africa where there has been much political change.

Another distortion highlighted by the study was that of land transfer by benevolent chiefs, charging subsidy prices. Under quantity restrictions, this practice leads to various unrecorded costs that may have offset the subsidies provided by the traditional leaders. These costs include long waiting times, dubious deals, cuts taken by the various middlemen involved, and litigation expenses.

Ethnic clustering was also significant in the determination of land values. Obviously distinct enclaves of ethnic clustering must be present for this variable to be included. This is also an important consideration to be taken into account when using the HPM in developing countries in Africa.

The results of the study show that a land market exists, albeit an imperfect one. The inclusion of a broad range of social and cultural considerations makes the study useful for other researchers, as it provides some information on what variables to include in the HPM.

Treatment of Time Aspects

Since no values of environmental attributes were estimated in the study there is little to comment on regarding discount rates, time horizons or treatment of irreversibilities.

Accuracy and Reliability

Reliability

The study analyses the value of vacant lots. Considering that the sample size is quite small (211 observations), there is a risk of bias in the sample. For example, the possibility that there were relatively few vacant lots near the city centre and more towards the outskirts of the city may cause the coefficient estimates to be unreliable.

The data used were based on market data, which are preferred (Freeman, 1993). This obviously enhances the reliability of the data used in the study.

Validity

In general, the hedonic pricing method is based on a number of fairly demanding assumptions. However, since the study does not value a specific attribute it is not subject to many of these common assumptions.[8]

The issue of multi-collinearity is particularly relevant in HPM studies (Turner, 1993; Freeman, 1993). The author seems to have a good theoretical basis for the selection of each of the variables included in the study. No statistical tests were carried out to test for multi-collinearity.

The validity of the bid-rent curve is questionable since the study did not collect any socio-economic data on the households involved in the sample. Therefore, there is no information on whether the households were alike in their preferences and utility functions. If they were not, which is highly plausible, the validity of the bid-rent curves is questionable. If the households' preferences differ, then each will have different WTP for being near to the CBD. Thus the demand for this specific attribute will not coincide with the bid rent function.

LESSONS LEARNED

This review of the HPM study on land values reveals some valuable lessons for other applications of this method, and for possible improvements in the land use planning in Accra.

Lessons for HPM Applications

- Cities in developing countries that are experiencing rapid rural-urban migration may be plagued by the same kinds of urban problems as those described in this paper. A hedonic methodology can help identify distortions that have been created in the property market.
- Variables used in the analysis should be reflective of the sociological and cultural circumstances of the residents.
- The inclusion of environmental variables to measure environmental quality could improve the analysis.
- A broad spectrum of variables should be included to improve accuracy and comprehensiveness.
- The choice of functional form used in regression analysis should be explicitly validated.
- Special treatment must be given to unusual circumstances that affect the property market such as the military dictatorship episode in this study.
- Hedonic pricing is a relatively straightforward method that can be taken further than its use in this study in the determination of values.
- Recent developments in hedonics and other methods should be applied.

Lessons for Land Use Planning in Accra

- Access could be improved by building more access roads and upgrading the transport system.
- Decentralization could direct development away from the congested CBD.
- Improvements could be made to beaches.
- The town planning process should take basic demand and supply analysis into consideration before zoning, to avoid distortions in the allocation of land.
- Low residential zones need to be upgraded and protected from negative externalities.
- Instead of nationalizing land, policy measures should concentrate on the problems associated with the supply and demand sides of the market.
- Government rent controls were partly responsible for low maintenance and low rate of construction in the low residential zones.
- Minimum lot area zoning can have positive results.
- More research on property markets is needed in developing countries.

NOTES

1   This chapter reviews, and therefore draws heavily on, Asabere (1981).

2   University of Cape Town, School of Economics.

3   Stool or Shrine land refers to land belonging to the traditional tribal authorities in Ghana. Ga and Zongo are the main ethnic groups in Accra.

4   For summaries of such studies, see Bateman (1993) and Freeman (1993).

5   Freeman (1993) notes that the linear, quadratic, the log-log, the semi log, the inverse log, the exponential and the Box-Cox transformation functional have been used in HPM. He also gives an overview of how the best functional form may be chosen.

6   Governmental zoning regulates the form of development to be undertaken by any zone by imposing constraints on its use, height, and minimum environmental standards.

7   For instance, Col. Kutu Akyeampong overthrew the democratically elected Busia government in 1972 and embarked on an artificial price suppression policy, which may have kept land prices low.

8   See Turner (1993) for a list of these assumptions.

REFERENCES

Abelson, P (1995) *Project Appraisal and Valuation Methods for the Environment, with Special Reference to Developing Countries.* Macmillan, London.

Asabere, P K (1981) The Determinants of Land Values in an African City: The Case of Accra, Ghana. *Land Economics* vol. 57 (3): 385–397.

Freeman, A M (1993) *The Measurement of Environmental and Resource Values: Theory and Methods.* Resources for the Future, Washington, DC.

North, J H and Griffin, C C (1993) Water Source as a Housing Characteristic: Hedonic Property Valuation and Willingness-To-Pay for Water. *Water Resources Research* vol 29 (7): 1923–1929.

Pearce, D W and Turner, R K (1990) *Economics of Natural Resources and the Environment.* Harvester Wheatsheaf, London.

Turner, R K (ed) (1993) *Sustainable Environmental Economics and Management: Principles and Practice.* John Wiley and Sons, Chichester, UK.

Winpenny, J (1995) *The Economic Appraisal of Environmental Projects and Policies: A Practical Guide.* OECD, Paris.

4

Measuring the Costs of Rainforest Conservation in Cameroon[1]

Hugo van Zyl, Thomas Store and Anthony Leiman[2]

Rainforest Conservation Costs

In many parts of the developing world, rainforests are being converted to other land uses such as agriculture, forestry and fuelwood gathering, which are seen as more beneficial than conservation. Countries such as Cameroon simply cannot afford to conserve large areas of rainforest. In order to promote the conservation that the international community often calls for, conservation must be viable and some form of compensation to developing countries may be required. Monetary transfers and debt-for-nature swaps have been widely propagated as means of promoting rainforest conservation in developing countries. A method is therefore needed to help determine the appropriate allocation of scarce international funding between specific rainforests.

Description of the Study

Objective and Focus

This chapter reviews a study by Ruitenbeek (1991), which developed the idea of the 'rainforest supply price' (RSP) as a way of aiding decisions on the allocation of funding for rainforest conservation. The RSP is basically a monetary measure of the compensation that a developing country should be given by the rest of the world in the form of transfers to conserve a particular rainforest.

The area for which the RSP was calculated was Korup National Park in Southwest Province, Cameroon. At the time of the study, the

Government of Cameroon and external funding agencies were formulating a development plan for the area, which was meant to complement the conservation goals of the park. Interest from the international aid and conservation community was centred on the park because of its significance as a biodiversity reserve. It is the oldest remaining rainforest in Africa and is characterized by a very high species richness. It is home to over 1000 species of plant and 1300 animal species, including 119 mammals and 15 primates. Of the total species in the area, 60 occur nowhere else and 170 are listed as endangered or vulnerable. Land-use pressures including timber production, fuelwood gathering, hunting, trapping and forest farming have increased the pressures on the rainforest. This has led the World Wide Fund For Nature (WWF) to initiate a conservation programme in the area, focused on the management of a 12,600 hectare area with a 300,000 hectare buffer area.

Methodology

A conventional Cost-Benefit Analysis (CBA) was used to calculate the RSP. Formally, the net present value (NPV) of *compensation* must be equal to or greater than the NPV of the net *loss* attached to the conservation of the forest instead of its best alternative use. Thus:

$$\text{PV of compensation} = \text{PV of (net benefit of best alternative use}$$
$$- \text{net benefit of conservation)}$$

The compensation that would be paid to Cameroon is calculated for every year that a given hectare of rainforest is conserved. Two scenarios: *without the compensation project* and *with the project* were hypothesized for the CBA.

The *without project* scenario is written as a vector:

$$E = \{E0, E1, E2, Et\}$$

where Et is the area (in hectares) of undisturbed rainforest in any given year t.

The *with project* scenario is written as:

$$E = \{E'0, E'1, E'2, E't\}$$

where $E't$ is the area of undisturbed rainforest in any given year t.

A conservation project would then generate some change in the amount of undisturbed rainforest, where:

$$\Delta E = E' - E = \{E0' - E0, E1' - E1, E2' - E2,..., Et' - Et,...\}$$
$$= \{\Delta E0, \Delta E1, \Delta E2,..., \Delta Et,...\}$$

ΔE is referred to as the 'protection scenario', as it represents the amount of rainforest conserved compared to some base scenario without a conservation project. ΔEt was thus the area, in year t, that would remain undisturbed as a direct consequence of the conservation project.

In calculating the RSP, the yearly value selected will be that which is just enough to bring the total NPV of the project plus the transfers to zero. Using simple cost-benefit conventions, this results in the condition that:

$$0 = \sum_{t=0}^{\infty} (1 + r)-t \cdot (Bt - Ct) + \sum_{t=0}^{\infty} (1 + r)-t \cdot \text{RSP}\Delta Et \qquad (1)$$

where Bt is the stream of local benefits at shadow prices (excluding transfers) to the host country as a result of the rainforest conservation project, Ct is the stream of local costs expressed using shadow prices, and r is the real discount rate. The first term on the right hand side is the NPV of the project in the absence of transfers. Assuming that the RSP is a constant payment for each hectare saved in any given year, equation (1) can be rearranged to give:

$$\text{RSP} = \sum_{t=0}^{\infty} (1 + r)-t \cdot (Bt - Ct) / \sum_{t=0}^{\infty} (1 + r)-t \, \Delta Et$$

Up to this point in the calculation of the RSP the study assumed that rainforests can be treated equally, and that, for example, conserving a hectare of rainforest in Brazil is of no greater or lesser value than conserving a hectare in West Africa. The RSP relies on the idea that some area unit of rainforest (in this case a hectare) can be considered a common numerical indicator of an ecosystem's quality. The literature is quite divided on this issue, with some authors favouring population and species number counts over area. Regardless of what may be decided to indicate rainforest quality, a hedonic pricing technique can be introduced to adjust the RSP accordingly. If you let δ be a dimensionless index for rainforest quality, normalized such that $\delta = 1$ for a standard hectare-year for some standard forest, then we can define a hedonic rainforest supply price RSP^h as RSP/δ.

The starting point of the RSP calculation in the study was a detailed CBA of the conservation project, undertaken from the perspective of the Government of Cameroon. A simple cost-benefit analysis based on production function analysis was used.[3] The benefits were defined as the stream of local benefits at shadow prices (excluding transfers) to Cameroon as a result of the rainforest conservation project and the costs as the stream of local costs at shadow prices. The actual key analytical criteria and shadow prices were selected through discussions with the planning officials in the Cameroon government, to ensure consistency with other projects being evaluated in the country.

Costs included forgone benefits from commercial logging and forgone traditional uses mainly relating to the prohibition of hunting (although other peripheral residents will be able to make traditional use of the forest if it is conserved). All estimates of changes in local incomes for hunting, gathering, fishing and farming were based on a detailed survey of 357 households conducted in 1988. Capital infrastructure costs and running costs were also estimated.

Benefits included tourism benefits based on conservative estimates. The CBA further attempted to value a number of local environmental functions associated with the forest using a damage function approach. The main functions valued were: fisheries protection, flood control, and soil fertility maintenance. Global benefits of conservation, notably 'biodiversity value' and 'climate control value', were not included in the analysis.[4]

Fisheries protection relates to the forest's role in ensuring the survival of the fish resource. Without the forest, the ecological balance in the adjacent mangroves would be disturbed to such an extent that many of its commercial species could be lost. The link between the forest and the offshore fishery was not established and thus only the effect on the onshore fishery was measured. This was justified further by the fact that any commercially harvestable offshore fish dependent on the mangrove for breeding would primarily be found outside Cameroonian waters.

The *flood control function* relates to the increased chance of flooding without the forest. As rainforests disappear, the peak and trough levels of surface water flows become more pronounced. In a high rainfall area such as Southwest Province in Cameroon, the potential for flooding increases with deforestation. While it was impossible to predict exactly when a devastating flood might occur, the CBA here estimates the *expected* net present value of benefits. As a first approximation it was assumed that the expected value loss of flooding in any year t is:

$$\text{flood control benefit} = Nfc(Ad/A)(Yfc / T)$$

where Nfc is the number of people expected to be affected by a flood event, and Ad/A is the proportion of the deforested area of the forest to the total originally forested area. Yfc is the per capita income in the region lost due to the flood event. The flood event is assumed to occur every $T = 5$ years. For calculating the NPV benefit, it was assumed that $Nfc = 20,000$, which corresponds to the population in the Korup rural development zone as well as about 8000 people living along the river courses between Korup and the coast (excluding those in the mangrove estuaries). The income loss is estimated to be that corresponding to all livestock income and one season of cash crop income, as the flooding would likely occur in July or August and the major harvest occurs in October.

The *fertility maintenance function* was a measure of the forest's contribution to the maintenance of soil fertility and was measured in terms of potential agricultural product losses. Although soils in the area are generally not of very high quality, the rainforest does contribute to some maintenance of soil fertility through various mechanisms. The benefits were broadly estimated based on the assumption that agricultural productivity would drop by 10 per cent without the forest. This loss would commence in 2010 and manifest itself fully by the year 2040.

Main Sources of Data

A more detailed CBA undertaken from the perspective of the Government of Cameroon was used as the source of figures for the RSP calculations.

Comprehensiveness of the Estimates

The RSP was calculated by dividing the required transfer of 1,852 million CFAF by the present value of the protection scenario, 513,800 ha-years.[5] Thus, as shown in Table 4.1, the RSP for Korup was approximately 3600 CFAF/ha/year or 10.60 ECU/ha/year.[6] This implies that if the rest of the world were to give Cameroon anything above 3600 CFAF for each hectare protected in any given year, Cameroon would have an incentive to protect the park. This transfer payment need not be made in equal annual instalments, as any programme of transfers with an NPV in excess of 1852 million CFAF would be adequate.

Treatment of Time Aspects

The first step in the evaluation of the conservation project defined the impacts that the project would have, compared with the status quo case. Without conservation, normal exploitation of the biological and forest resources will eventually result in complete elimination of the primary forest between the years 2010 and 2040.

The infrastructure and programmes mobilized by the Korup Project showed no immediate conservation benefits. This was because it takes time for restrictions to be implemented and for the forest to recover. In the very near term, no protection will be afforded because the population currently living in the park will continue their activities. After about 5 years, restrictions on these activities would effectively protect 20,000 ha of forest area that otherwise would have been lost. Only by 2010 would major protection benefits be realized, corresponding to the imposition of logging restrictions. The study finds that 315,000 ha that would have been lost without the project would be protected in perpetuity under the project. The cost benefit streams also reflect the protection

Table 4.1 *Summary of Korup National Park Cost-Benefit Analysis*

Cost or Benefit Items	Net present value (million CFAF)
Social Costs	
Total capital costs, excl. Roads	−1988
Total capital costs, roads	−1022
Total long-term operating costs	−2381
Labour adjustment for direct costs	961
Lost timber value	−353
Lost forest use	−223
Total costs	−5051
Social benefits	
Sustained forest use	354
Tourism	680
Fisheries protection to Cameroon	1770
Control of flood risk	265
Soil productivity maintenance	130
Total benefits	3199
Net benefits	−1852
Present value of net protected area	(hectare years) 513,800
Supply price	(CFAF/ha/yr) 3605

Note: all values are expressed in 1989 constant terms, with discounting conducted at an 8 per cent discount rate. Calculations are based on cost and benefit streams in Table 4.3 in the Appendix. Capital costs of the roads included 33 per cent of the budgeted costs, corresponding to that estimated to be incremental to those expenditures which would be incurred in any event. A labour adjustment was applied to correspond to Cameroonian planning practice, to value labour in this region at 50 per cent of the market wage.

scenario, with costs such as infrastructure costs and losses in hunting income being experienced early, while major benefits associated with environmental functions are realized from 2010 onwards. Hence the sensitivity of the results to the discount rate.

The CBA showed that the NPV of the project to Cameroon at an 8 per cent rate of discount was *negative* at 1852 million CFAF. Cameroon would thus need an incentive of 1852 million CFAF to pursue the park initiative at a discount rate of 8 per cent.

Accuracy and Reliability

A sensitivity analysis undertaken at a discount rate of 6 per cent yielded a *positive* NPV of 319 million CFAF. The benefit and cost streams at shadow prices correspond to a real internal rate of return of 6.2 per cent from Cameroon's perspective.

A further sensitivity analysis illustrated the effect of excluding the protective benefits of the forest to the onshore mangrove fisheries. Essentially this exclusion doubled the negative net social cost of the project.

International comparisons of transfers for rainforest conservation were undertaken to see if the estimated RSP was realistic. Six specific transfers that occurred between 1987 and 1989 involving debt-for-nature swaps and fund raising campaigns to conserve specific rainforests were investigated. The results of the comparisons range widely from 15 ECU/km²/year to 1600 ECU/km²/year. The Korup RSP falls near the middle of this range at 1000 ECU/km²/year.

CRITIQUE OF THE STUDY

Methodology

The scope of the study is clearly stated from the outset – to find allocation criteria to distribute limited conservation funds between rainforests in developing countries. If a more in-depth analysis of the value of a rainforest were to be attempted,[7] the study could be expanded to include such values as biodiversity, climate control, existence and local amenity value. These values would be potentially relevant in making requests for transfers from the international community, as they represent positive international externalities.

Although there are no examples of *biodiversity valuation per se*,[8] in developing countries, the literature on the subject continues to expand.[9] Valuations such as the one done for the Korup rainforest often focus on valuing other functions such as flood control and ecotourism that are likely to benefit biodiversity conservation. There have been attempts to elicit willingness to pay responses for biodiversity in developed countries. They have however largely been limited to 'charismatic' species and ecosystems (Pearce and Moran, 1994).

In the case of the *climate control value* of forests, research undertaken after the Korup study has made it possible to assess the minimum global economic damage (excluding catastrophic events) caused by global warming linked to rainforest burning. An average value of $20 of damage per tonne of carbon released is suggested by Fankhauser (1994). Assuming an average of 200–300 tonnes of carbon released per hectare of primary and secondary forest burnt, an average 'climate control' value can be calculated for forest areas.

The measurement of *existence value* would be possible with the use of CVM. *Amenity value* of the rainforest to local inhabitants could also be measured, using questionnaire techniques. In the case of the Mantadia National Park in Madagascar, 91 per cent of the local inhabitants indicated that primary forests were 'more fun' than secondary forests, indicating a higher amenity value (Munasinghe, 1993).

Estimates of changes in local incomes from hunting, gathering, fishing, and farming were based on a detailed survey of 357 households conducted by Ruitenbeek in 1988. This sample size is relatively large and contributed to the sound methodology. Also, the CBA included changes in input costs or opportunity costs incurred in deriving income. For example, lost hunting revenues were partially offset by decreased hunting costs and, in the case of Korup, increased hunting levels at other locations outside the protected area.

Aylward and Barbier (1992) suggest a number of caveats to the ecological assumptions used by the RSP study, including the assumption that the fishery will be a total loss if the Korup forest is removed. This is not ecologically substantiated and is not likely to occur, according to Aylward and Barbier. In addition, the rationale for assuming that the damage function produces linearly increasing costs to fishery production as the absolute area deforested increases is also questionable in their view. It may be that the amount of deforestation and concurrent degradation of the protection function causes little damage up to some threshold amount of degradation, at which point considerable damage is incurred. Aylward and Barbier derive a final caution from Pearce (1990), who cautions against assuming that deforestation itself leads to the loss of functions such as flood control or fishery maintenance. Instead it is the ensuing land-use that is all important in determining the extent of damage to the protection function.

Comprehensiveness of the Estimates

The study attempts to estimate the costs and benefits accruing to Cameroon only. International externalities are not valued and therefore the study captures only the national use-value of the Korup rainforest. No attempt is made to estimate other possible values of the forest to local inhabitants such as the gratification of living in or around the forest.

Important suggestions are made on how transfers should be paid. Korup is categorized as a project with a 'social' nature that runs the risk of being neglected in a developing country budget as it generates few revenues. To counter this it is suggested that payments be made on an ongoing basis as opposed to a lump sum at the beginning of the project. Direct payment of the operating expenses of the park would be another way to ensure that a large part of funds reach their intended destination.

The international comparison for similar forest conservation transfer payments, primarily debt-for-nature swaps, puts the RSP into perspective. The broad range established shows the variability in transfer payments. Not all of the transfer payment amounts were arrived at based on valuations. It can however be argued that these figures represent a form of willingness to pay and thus a form of valuation on the part of the international community for global values (ie existence, biodiversity and climate control values) associated with the rainforest in question.[10]

Pearce and Moran (1994) estimate the carbon sequestration benefits of rainforests to be in a range between $1000 and $4000 per hectare, based on Fankhauser's findings. They go on to state that global values of this kind are not a priority for developing countries and are only relevant if the issue of appropriability is resolved. This further justifies the author's exclusion of these values from the RSP.

For a similar study within Africa, it is worth looking at Kramer et al's study (1995) in Madagascar, in which a similar valuation was conducted to assess the opportunity costs to local residents of forgone benefits from forest products and agriculture. The assessment was done using a two-part survey of 351 households in 17 villages within a 7.5 km radius of the park boundary. The first part of the survey valued the opportunity cost using socio-economic questions to construct cash flow models that estimated income losses from no longer having access to the park area. The second part used a contingent valuation question on how much each villager would be willing to accept as compensation for not being allowed to use the park area. The cash flow models showed an NPV of $566,000 while the contingent valuation produced a figure of $673,000, using a 10 per cent discount rate and 20 year time horizon.

In the Korup park study the net present value of tourism benefits was estimated at US$1.66 million using conservative estimates and an 8 per cent discount rate. The Madagascar study employs a more comprehensive approach using a CVM questionnaire and a travel cost survey[11] and arrives at an NPV figure of US$2.16 million over 20 years at a 10 per cent discount rate.

Accuracy and Reliability

Ruitenbeek recognized that the lack of comprehensive data for some costs and benefits led to subjective judgements representing best estimates at the time. He did not however feel that any of the figures ran the risk of being large overestimations. Indeed, since global benefits were excluded, one could argue that the figures presented in the study were underestimations.

The sensitivity analysis on the protective benefits of the forest to the onshore mangrove fishery illustrated the importance of environmental variables. The sensitivity analysis could have been extended to include flood protection, and soil fertility maintenance.

Treatment of Time Aspects

The study places a strong emphasis on the effects of time on the manifestation of benefits and cost. The values of the three environmental functions valued in the study are only really manifested after 2010. The losses from timber production are also only long-term considerations. The benefits from gathered and farmed products from the forest are also felt in the long term due to the long-term conservation of Korup. In the short term there are no conservation benefits from the park, only the short-term costs of setting it up and the immediate restrictions on hunting.

The results of the study rely heavily on the use of the appropriate discount rate. If the discount rate is dropped from the 8 per cent used to 6 per cent, the results for the amount of transfer required drop into a negative range. Thus if a discount rate of 6 per cent was used, no transfer would be required at all. Some indication of the degree of confidence in the discount rate would have been useful.

The well-documented debate over the 'correct' social discount rate continues.[12] At one extreme the argument has been made for a 0 per cent discount rate. At the other, a discount rate equal to the standard opportunity cost of capital has been argued for, often accompanied by calls for a safe minimum standard of environmental stocks and quality to ensure a degree of sustainability. A more recent contribution by Weitzman (1994) argues that the assumption of a constant discount rate assumes some stationarity over time, which is inappropriate for a world moving towards ever increasing environmental concern. Bearing in mind that the question of the 'correct' discount is far from resolved, it is vital for studies to include discount rate sensitivity analysis. The often highly significant influence that the rate has on results serves to further emphasize the necessity of sensitivity analysis.

The inclusion of the costs and benefits over time is an important part of the study report (see Table 4.3 in the Appendix). A static analysis would not have been complete.

LESSONS LEARNED

This review of the Ruitenbeek study yields some valuable lessons, both for conservation funding policy, and for the methodologies of similar valuation studies.

Lessons on Policy Implications

In conservation efforts for rainforests and other environments, it is important to recognize that their wise use has been hampered not only by a lack of information on their value, but by other factors such as policy-induced distortions. In Brazil, Indonesia and Zaire policies such as agricultural subsidies, tax breaks and settlement programmes have created an incentive structure that favours the over-exploitation of forest environments (Barbier et al, 1991).

The necessity of some form of transfer payment to justify the conservation of the Korup National Park is illustrated by the study. It serves to highlight the point of view of the Cameroonian government, while showing the international community what is required for conservation to make economic sense. The methodology used in the study can provide guidance on the optimal allocation of limited conservation funds worldwide.

Determining the amount of transfers needed does not necessarily mean that funds will be allocated in an effective or equitable manner. The inclusion of suggestions on how and to whom transfer funds should be distributed could have further enhanced the policy relevance of the study. However, this was covered to some extent by the suggestion that the funds be paid over time and directly to the park to help cover costs.

Apart from arguing for economic incentives for conservation provided by transfer payments, the study advocates policies aimed at integrating conservation with local development initiatives. This integration has proven vital to the success of conservation, particularly in developing countries.

Lessons on Methodology

- Non-use values including global benefits can have a significant effect on the overall value of an environment and should be included if possible.
- Valuation studies with small budgets and information constraints can still be effective, particularly if they focus on aspects relevant to decision makers.
- When discounting, the reasons and assumptions behind the selection of a particular rate are important. This shows the importance of a sensitivity analysis.
- Care must be taken to investigate and explicitly state the ecological assumptions used in damage function analysis.
- The method of transfer payment should be geared to have the best chance of ensuring continuation of programmes. Combinations of different payments such as lump sums and debt for nature swaps can be used together.
- The income distributional effects of alternative plans or policies are particularly important in a developing country with a skewed income distribution. Investigation or at least recognition of this issue is important.

APPENDIX

Table 4.2 *Benefit Categories for Protected Areas*

Benefit categories	
1 Recreation/tourism	5 Education and research

2 Watershed values
   Erosion control
   Local flood reduction
   Influence on stream flows
	6 Consumptive benefits
	   Timber
	   Wildlife products
	   Non-timber forest products (eg,

3 Ecological processes
   Fixing and cycling of nutrients
   Soil formation
   Circulation and cleansing of air
     and water
   Global life support
	edible plants, herbs, medicines,
	    rattan, building materials, rubber)
	7 Non-consumptive benefits
	   Aesthetic
	   Spiritual
	   Cultural/historical

4 Biodiversity
   Gene resources
   Species protection
   Ecosystem diversity
   Evolutionary processes
	Existence value
	8 Future values
	   Option value
	   Quasi-option value

Source: Dixon and Sherman (1990)

Table 4.3 *Summary of Korup Project Cost and Benefit Streams (CFAF millions, at constant 1989 values)*

	1989–1995	1996–2009	2010–2039	2040–∞
Direct costs (at market prices)				
capital and running costs	2338			
infrastructure costs	3685			
operating costs		280/yr	280/yr	280/yr
Opportunity costs (at shadow prices)				
lost timber value			147/yr	
lost forest use	0–34/yr	34/yr		
Direct benefits (at shadow prices)				
sustained forest use		0–132/yr	132/yr	
tourism	3–24/yr	24–48/yr	48/yr	48/yr
fisheries protection			54–1628/yr	1628/yr
flood control			8–244/yr	244/yr
soil fertility maintenance			4–120/yr	120/yr

Notes:
Summaries of direct costs for 1989–1995 are period totals obtained from the Korup National Park Master Plan (WWF-UK 1989). Direct costs include capital costs of park infrastructure (895), park vehicles and equipment (79), roads and airstrips (3350), labour (690), administration (205), compensation payments (256) and a contingency (548). The amount entering the CBA, however, is only 3272 million CFAF: costs related to compensation payments are purely pecuniary and are thus excluded; and a portion (67 per cent) of the road costs would be spent in any event because of other regional operatives.

Opportunity costs for lost timber value include those associated with a commercially marginal timber resource having an undiscounted net standing value of about 4400 million CFAF, which would otherwise have been harvested over a 30-year period commencing in 2010.

Lost forest use corresponds to the subsistence income to the region's residents, associated with restrictions on selected hunting, trapping, gathering and farming activities.
Direct benefits include, over a longer term, sustained gathering incomes to local residents, as well as the benefits arising from three environmental functions of the rainforest. Fisheries protection benefits are the net changes in income to Cameroonian fishermen in the downstream mangrove area. Flood control benefits are the estimated value of agricultural products, which would otherwise be lost due to declines in soil fertility. Tourism benefits are a conservative estimate of the net revenues from incremental wilderness-based tourism and scientific research.

ACKNOWLEDGEMENTS

We would like to thank the following people for their contributions to this case study: Sue Lane, Dale Whittington, Xinming Mu, Robert Roche, Ståle Navrud, Eric Mungatana, Paul Kwadwo Asabere, H. Jack Ruitenbeek, Anders Ekbom, Jan Bojö, Charles Perrings, Michael 't Sas-Rolfes and the authors of the other regional sub-studies in this compendium for their comments.

NOTES

1   This chapter reviews, and therefore draws heavily on, Ruitenbeek (1991).

2   University of Cape Town, School of Economics.

3   For details on production function analysis, see Freeman (1993).

4   See Table 4.2 in the Appendix for a comprehensive list of possible benefit categories for protected areas, taken from Dixon and Sherman (1990).

5   CFAF = Central African franc.

6   ECU = European Currency Unit (soon to become the Euro). Approximately 1.1ECU = US$1.

7   The 'Total Economic Value of Forests in Mexico' (Pearce et al, 1993), analysed in the Latin America and the Caribbean section of this compendium attempts a more comprehensive valuation including carbon storage, biodiversity, option and existence value.

8   The main reasons often given for this are the complexity of the concept, and a lack of information on the measurement and functions of biodiversity.

9   See, for example, Wilson, 1988; Randall, 1991; and Pearce and Moran, 1994.

10 See the analysis of Pearce et al (1993) presented in the Latin American and Caribbean section of this compendium for a discussion on this.

11 The study on the recreational/tourism benefits of Lake Nakuru National Park in Kenya, presented earlier, also used these methods.

12 See Lind (1982), Fisher and Krutilla (1975), Freeman (1993).

REFERENCES

Alyward, B and Barbier, E B (1992) Valuing Environmental Functions in Developing Countries. *Biodiversity and Conservation* vol 1: 34–50.

Barbier, E B, Burgess, J C and Markandya, A (1991) The Economics of Tropical Deforestation. *Ambio* vol 20 (2): 55–58.

Dixon, J A and Sherman, P B (1990) *Economics of Protected Areas: A New Look at Benefits and Costs.* Island Press, Covelo, CA, USA.

Fankhauser, S (1994) The Social Costs of Greenhouse Gas Emissions: An Expected Value Approach. *The Energy Journal* vol 15 (2).

Freeman, A M (1993) *The Measurement of Environmental and Resource Values: Theory and Methods.* Resources for the Future, Washington DC.

Fisher, A C and Krutilla, J V (1975) Resource Conservation, Environmental Preservation and the Rate of Discount. *Quarterly Journal of Economics* vol 89 (3): 358–370.

Kramer, R A, Sharma, N and Munasinghe, M (1995) Valuing Tropical Forests: Methodology and Case Study of Madagascar. World Bank Environment Paper no 13, The World Bank, Washington, DC.

Lind, R C et al (1982) *Discounting for Time and Risk in Energy Policy.* Resources for the Future, Washington, DC.

Munasinghe, M (1993) Environmental Economics and Biodiversity Management in Developing countries. *Ambio* vol 22 (2–3): 126 – 135.

Pearce, D W and Moran, D (1994) *The Economic Value of Biodiversity.* Earthscan Publications, London.

Pearce, D W (1990) An Economic Approach to Saving the Tropical Forests. LEEC paper DP 90–06, International Institute for Environment and Development, London, UK.

Pearce, D W, Adger, W N, Brown, K, Cervigni, R and Moran, D (1993) Mexico Forestry and Conservation Sector Review Substudy of Economic Valuation of Forests. Report prepared for the World Bank by CSERGE, University of East Anglia and University College London, UK.

Randall, A (1991) The Value of Biodiversity. *Ambio* vol 20 (2): 64–67.

Ruitenbeek, H J (1991) The Rainforest Supply Price: A Tool for Evaluating Rainforest Conservation Expenditures. *Ecological Economics* vol 6: 57–78.

Weitzman, M L (1994) On the 'Environmental' Discount Rate. *Journal of Environmental Economics and Management* vol 26: 200–209.

Wilson, E O (ed) (1988) *Biodiversity.* National Academy Press, Washington DC.

WWF-UK (1989) *Korup National Park Master Plan.* WWF, Yaounde.

PART II

ASIA CASE STUDIES

5

EVALUATION OF THE PROFITABILITY OF FOREST PLANTATIONS IN THE PHILIPPINES[1]

Marian delos Angeles, Herminia Francisco and Anssi Niskanen[2]

REFORESTATION EFFORTS IN THE PHILIPPINES

From 1970 to 1990, the Philippines experienced severe depletion and degradation of its forest resources, with its dipterocarp forests cut at a rate of 199,100 ha per year.[3] The log export boom, which took place from the 1960s up to the early part of the 1970s, contributed to this major loss of the country's old growth forest resources. Subsequent logging operations and forest conversion resulted in a massive decline of second growth forest in the late '70s to early '80s. By the 1990s, only about one million hectares of old growth forest remained undisturbed, with even fewer secondary forests considered to be in good condition. The large upland population in the forest zone is responsible for the conversion of forest land to other land uses, primarily to agriculture. Recent statistics claimed that there were about 10 million ha of intensively managed land and 9.4 million ha of extensively managed areas within the forest zone (DENR, 1990; ALMED, 1993; and Uitamo, 1995). The resultant problems of forest depletion and degradation are evidenced by a shortage of timber and non-timber forest resources and a loss of critical environmental functions, which in turn has been linked to soil erosion and sedimentation, loss of biodiversity, and global warming. Non-use values of the forests, such as bequest and existence values, have also been lost.[4]

To respond to this situation, the government, together with other concerned sectors of society, introduced reforestation activities and agroforestry systems in the forest zone. The lead agency in these efforts has been the Department of Environment and Natural Resources (DENR). Since the 1980s, the DENR has undertaken massive reforestation projects throughout the country, supported by loans from the Asian Development Bank (ADB) and the Overseas Economic Co-operation Fund (OECF). Participants in these projects include communities, local government bodies, individual upland families, and industries. Reforestation contracts allow those involved to manage, protect, and benefit from the reforested areas over a period of 25 years. The contract is renewable for a second term of 25 years. All these efforts aim to reverse forest degradation by making it profitable for stakeholders to invest in forest management and plantation. The performance of these programmes to date and their likely future success have not yet been fully assessed.

DESCRIPTION OF ORIGINAL STUDY

Objective and Focus

This chapter reviews a study by Niskanen (1995), which aimed to evaluate if tree plantations do indeed promote economic development by providing sufficient financial and economic returns from the reforestation investment. The study also sought to assess what the socio-economic and environmental-economic impacts of tree planting in Luzon (the main island of the Philippines) would be.

The study assessed the profitability of alternative forest management options, from the point of view of both the private entity involved and society. It then illustrated how traditional cost-benefit analysis can be expanded to include other non-efficiency concerns, such as equity and environmental protection. These extensions translate into what Niskanen termed socio-economic profitability and environmental-economic profitability analyses.

Methodology

The basic decision-making framework used was cost-benefit analysis. Of the seven land management options considered, six are reforestation options, while one represents the dominant agricultural practice of corn monocropping. The various options included revegetation with either *Acacia auriculiformis*, mahogany, corn, or a combination of these. Both corporate and community management systems were considered.

Niskanen initially subjected all the land management options to a financial cost-benefit analysis. This type of analysis relies on the use of market prices and is limited to cash transactions. The next stage involved an economic analysis, using shadow prices.[5]

The study then computed the socio-economic profitability of the various land use options. Income distribution was included in the analysis, by using a social shadow wage rate. This wage rate reflects society's marginal willingness to pay for non-educated labourers. A lower social shadow wage rate *vis-à-vis* the economic shadow wage rate (without considering income distribution) would indicate a bias towards labour-intensive development projects. If society equally favours the objectives of economic efficiency and income distribution, the social shadow wage rate will be equal to the economic shadow wage rate.

Under this type of cost-benefit analysis, the impacts on the poor were weighed against the impacts on the average consumers. The present value of weighting was then added to the economic profitability analysis.

The study then carried out an environmental-economic profitability analysis for all the land use options. It valued three environmental impacts of plantation forestry, namely, erosion control, nutrient consumption by trees, and carbon sequestration. The study measured the benefits of soil erosion control in terms of the on-site and off-site costs avoided. Two methods were used in estimating the on-site costs – the replacement cost method and the change in productivity approach. Off-site costs of soil erosion, measured using the loss of earnings method, used data obtained in one large watershed in the Philippines. The shadow project method followed by Nabuurs and Mohren (1993) measured the carbon sequestration impact of forest plantation. The replacement cost method valued the nutrient lost during harvesting.

The following section discusses in more detail the various valuation methods used in the study.

Replacement Cost Method

This method used economic parity prices to determine the value of the amount of fertilizers needed to replace the nutrients lost because of soil erosion. The study used the estimates of sheet and rill erosion obtained by David (1988) using the modified universal soil loss equation. While the author recognized the importance of temporal and spatial differences in the impacts of soil erosion, the analysis was constrained by a lack of data on these factors.

Change in Productivity Method

This approach calculated the value of potential timber yield lost, due to soil erosion and land degradation. It assumed that as the topsoil diminishes, tree growth slows down and eventually stops, up to the point when all the soil is lost. The on-site cost of soil erosion and land degradation is therefore calculated as the sum of the net present values (NPV) of timber yield forgone during the active soil loss period, and the yields forgone after the entire topsoil is lost.

Niskanen noted that there are serious limitations to this method *vis-à-vis* the replacement cost method. The most serious limitation is the absence of reliable data on growth and yield in many plantations and natural forests in the country. However, it was also noted that the replacement cost method does not represent a true measure of society's willingness to pay for erosion control.

Loss of Earnings Method

The study followed the approach used by Cruz et al (1988) in estimating the off-site cost of soil erosion. A dam in the study area, built for both hydroelectric generation and irrigation, had a sediment trap to catch some of the sediment flow. The study adopted the assumption used by David (1988) that only 3 per cent to 6 per cent of the quantity of sediments passes through the gate of the reservoir. The study also assumed a sediment delivery ratio of 40 per cent and a 95 per cent trap efficiency of the reservoir.

Using the loss of earnings method, the study determined the impacts of soil erosion on electricity generation and irrigation for agriculture. Data used included the volume of water in the active storage capacity of the reservoir, the annual electricity production capacity, the volume of a ton of sediment, and the price of electricity. The study computed the production forgone due to a reduction in, or the complete loss of, irrigation water.

In addition, the study estimated the opportunity cost of constructing a large non-productive sediment pool to prevent the adverse effects of sedimentation.

Shadow Project Method

The study calculated the carbon sequestration impact of forest plantations based on the method followed by Nabuurs and Mohren (1993) to estimate carbon sequestration on Albizia spp plantations established on tropical wastelands. Carbon sequestration in biomass is seen as an opportunity for the reduction of carbon emissions from industrial factories and power plants worldwide. The method is based on an assumption that carbon sequestration in different parts of trees (trunk, foliage, etc) can be estimated when the annual trunk volume increment is known, and is also based on a general understanding that the total mass of foliage and live branches has a high correlation with the stem diameter (Evans, 1992).

Main Sources of Data

The study relied on secondary data for most of the information on quantities and prices. The DENR provided the basic cost data for corporate contract reforestation and for community-managed projects. The National Statistics Office and the Department of Agriculture were the sources of data on corn cultivation. Data on timber prices were difficult to secure, as timber markets are quite imperfect. The prices were therefore rough approximations, based on various sources. The lack of data in many cases led the author to make many simplified assumptions, which are spelled out in the report.

The author was quite open about admitting that there are major inaccuracies in the study. He points out that production functions and price information were based on many assumptions and not on detailed research information or market-based interactions. Growth and yield information for plantation forests was inadequate, as were the data on prices of goods, factors of production, and market distortions. The study estimated growth and yield based on slope gradient and establishment methods. Furthermore, the study excluded many environmental impacts of reforestation projects, due to data constraints. The effects that remain unvalued, such as improved watershed protection, decreased pressure on natural forests and impacts on biodiversity, may be significant enough to alter the results of the analysis.

Comprehensiveness of the Estimates

The study is definitely more comprehensive than most studies on the same subject matter, in the sense that it not only covers the valuation of environmental impacts, but also quantifies equity considerations as well. While most studies stop at correcting for market distortions using border prices as a basis, this study considers non-marketed services of the forest such as erosion control and carbon sequestration functions. Furthermore, the analysis incorporates society's objective of income distribution using the social shadow price of labour.

Treatment of Time Aspects

Discounting takes account of differences in the time value of resources. The study adopts a discount rate of 12 per cent. The author tested for the effects of varying discount rates in the profitability estimates, using a sensitivity analysis.

Accuracy and Validity

The study followed two basic principles to increase the reliability and credibility of the estimates. Firstly, the report describes clearly the methodology followed and all assumptions made in the valuation and estimation activities. Secondly, the study uses conservative figures in key economic data such as yield and prices, so as not to overemphasize the impacts of plantation forestry.

Furthermore, the study performed a sensitivity analysis for all the types of cost-benefit analysis performed. It tested for the sensitivity of financial profitability to varying levels of tree growth and timber yield and price. Results point to the lowest value of the mean annual increments needed to realize positive NPV.

In the economic analysis, the variables considered were the opportunity cost of land and the shadow price of timber. The shadow wage rate drives the sensitivity analysis for the socio-economic profitability analysis. For the environmental-economic analysis, the key variables considered were the shadow prices of soil erosion and carbon sequestration. The analysis also considers the effect of tree growth, timber yield, and the discount rate on the net present value of carbon sequestration.

No formal tests of validity were performed in the study. The author nevertheless draws attention to the consistency of the financial and economic profitability estimates with those derived in similar studies in the country. The lack of comparable socio-economic and environmental-economic studies in the Philippines limits further validation by the author.

Main Findings

The reforestation options were less profitable, in financial terms, than the usual practice of corn monocropping. A limitation to this conclusion is the assumption that corn yield does not decline over time. The low profitability of reforestation options is attributed to poor growth and yield of the tree species. Outcomes of the reforestation options will change, given better growth and yield, and higher timber prices. As a solution, the author recommends the intercropping of some agricultural crops during the first few years of plantation establishment. An improvement in timber prices by at least 50 per cent will make tree plantation monocultures more profitable than plantations with intercrops.

The low financial profitability of reforestation is also caused by the high real rate of interest used in the calculations. These high interest rates are the product of the capital-scarce economy, where the financial market is highly regulated. In the short term, this finding may indicate the need for the provision of low interest credit or direct government subsidies to private enterprises.

Market distortions also make private financial returns on reforestation unattractive. Adjustment for market distortions in tradable inputs and outputs improves the economic profitability of the various land use options. Similar adjustments for non-tradable factors of production such as labour and land have the opposite effect. In general, however, the *economic* profitability estimates from reforestation are higher than the *financial* profitability results. This means that when viewed from society's perspective or when economic prices are used, reforestation options are more attractive than when evaluated from the perspective of the private entity involved.

The returns to labour, measured in NPV terms, are higher for small-scale reforestation with intercropping, than for the large-scale reforestation options. This finding follows largely from the assumption made by the author that in the small-scale management options, the income from the sales accrues to the owner of the land. So, while income from sales in corporate contract reforestation options does not benefit local communities, the communities *do* benefit from the community contract reforestation options. Given these assumptions, it is therefore not surprising that the estimated labour incomes of non-educated workers is higher in the community contract reforestation option than in corporate contract reforestation. In fact, this situation is the basis for the current preference for community-based forest management, whenever it is feasible.

The NPV derived from the environmental-economic profitability of reforestation was higher than the NPV derived using only economic profitability. Accounting for nutrient consumption lowers the economic profitability of the enterprise. Carbon sequestration and erosion control benefits, in contrast, improve the profitability estimates.

Fast-growing species, with a short rotation period, result in better erosion control, higher sequestration, and higher nutrient consumption. The positive environmental effects achieved due to fast growth were thought to partly compensate for the negative environmental effects of the short rotation. Furthermore, the difference between estimates of economic and environmental-economic analyses increases with the increasing slope of the forest land.

Higher NPVs are consistently obtained from plantations using Acacia, due to its higher growth rates. Furthermore, steeper sloping sites generate lower NPVs.

The profitability analysis was performed for sites with varying slope categories: gently sloping, moderately sloping, and steeply sloping sites. For gently sloping sites, the economic profitability recorded higher NPVs than financial profitability because of the positive adjustments for border and domestic distortions. Socio-economic profitability, in turn, had generally higher NPVs than economic profitability, if equitable income distribution is stressed more than economic growth. If the two objectives of equity and efficiency are given equal importance, there would be no difference in socio-economic and economic profitability. Finally, environmental-economic profitability for almost all land options (except for corporate mahogany reforestation with intercropping and corn cultivation) was higher than economic profitability.

In the moderately and steeply sloping sites, the environmental-economic profitability obtained the highest NPVs for all the land management options, except for corn cultivation.

CRITIQUE OF THE STUDY

The study provides a clear illustration and explanation of how traditional cost-benefit analysis can take into account other concerns of society. The socio-economic financial analysis illustrated how the welfare of low-income groups can be given more weight. The environmental-economic profitability analysis shows how to incorporate the valuation of benefits from soil erosion control and carbon sequestration. The study also provides a clear methodological discussion of how to undertake extended cost-benefit analysis. In the process, all the assumptions are clearly spelled out, in contrast to the often unclear exposition of many studies.

The study made both practical and methodological contributions to our understanding of the profitability of forest plantations. On the practical side, the study has provided policy makers with a basis on which to make decisions that go beyond the economic efficiency objective, to include other concerns such as income distribution and the environment. Acacia and mahogany forest tree species are found in most reforestation projects in the country, managed either by communities or corporations. The study's findings therefore could be quite useful to the country in its forest rehabilitation efforts. As such, the findings should be disseminated to the potential users of the information (eg DENR policy makers, programme managers, reforestation contractors, etc). It is not clear from the study report the extent to which such dissemination has already been carried out.

Recommendations on Methodology and Follow-Up

Efforts to disseminate the results should be incorporated into a validation-cum-extension exercise, to check the consistency of the research results, based on the experience of those involved in the reforestation efforts on the ground. Reports on the outcomes of the validation-cum-extension activities should then be disseminated.

The study provides good reference material for students of cost-benefit analysis and valuation methods, particularly with the clear explanations given of the steps taken to incorporate income distribution elements and environmental concerns into the traditional economic analysis.

One point which could probably be improved in the study report is the general use of the term 'profitability' for all types of analysis. The use of this term seems most appropriate for financial analysis, where the private entity's concern is profit. Society's concern is the optimal use of its resources, better income distribution, and protection of the environment. The use of the term profitability is thus not appropriate for the other types of analysis performed in the study. It would have been sufficient to call the other analyses simply economic analysis, socio-economic analysis, and environmental-economic analysis.

Limitations of the Study

The Choice of the Discount Rate

The study explained that the choice of the discount rate is a critical factor in any cost-benefit analysis, yet it failed to explain the reasons for its choice of the 12 per cent discount rate. It simply states that 12 per cent is chosen as this figure is often used as a lower estimate by financing institutions for developing countries (Pearce et al, 1990).

The study noted that the estimates are in fact quite sensitive to the discount rate used, and changes in the discount rate could change the conclusions of the study. For example, the study found that the environ-mental-economic profitability of community contract reforestation was *higher* than the economic profitability with a 12 per cent discount rate, but *lower* with a 16 per cent discount rate. It also showed that only corn cultivation was profitable at a 16 per cent discount rate, whereas all options were profitable at 8 per cent.

The Choice of Valuation Method for On-Site Effects

Two valuation methods were applied to put a monetary value on the on-site effects of soil erosion: the replacement costs and the change in productivity methods. The results illustrated that these two valuation methods could result in quite different outcomes. This variability could be expected due to the different conceptual framework implied by the two methods – replacement cost focuses on re-establishing previous conditions and change in productivity focuses on losses due to changes from previous conditions.

The study author cited that, in general, the replacement cost method tends to give the upper limit estimates of the economic costs of soil erosion while the change in productivity approach tends to give the lower limit estimates, since the latter method values the diminished production potential of the site.

The Assumption of Constant Corn Yields Over Time

A critical assumption that could have resulted in the favourable profitability of corn production was that the yield of corn does not decrease over time. The author recognized this limitation, but data constraints prevented him from making a more realistic assumption. Although it is obvious that the growth and yield in upland farming practices will decline over the years, there are few empirical measure-ments of the actual levels of this decline. The difficulty of predicting declines in yield is also due to the ever-changing climatic, biological, and human influences, which can affect crop productivity.

The Off-Site Costs of Soil Erosion

The total off-site costs of erosion were significantly lower than the national average, because the study included only losses in irrigated agricultural production and electricity production. It would have been useful to state the reasons for excluding other factors and to give an outline of how these additional factors could have been measured.

It must be pointed out though that the nation-wide off-site cost estimate of Saastamoinen (1994) is hardly a good basis for comparison, since it was based on many simplifying assumptions that are not clearly explained. As Niskanen (1995) himself pointed out, Saastamoinen's study is based largely on what the author calls educated guesses.

The Treatment of Administration Costs

For simplicity, administration costs were excluded from the profitability analyses. This decision is hardly justified, since there is a large difference between the administration costs of community-based managed projects and those of corporate-managed projects. In the Philippines, a large part of the administration costs in community-based forestry management projects are borne by the government, but from society's perspective these are real costs and should be accounted for.

The Productivity of Grazing Land

In the economic analysis, the study assumed that the alternative use of the land would be extensive grazing. The author actually pointed out that some tracts of land may be unsuitable for either pasture or agricultural cropping. In these cases, the value of the land will be close to zero and reforestation of these sites will be economically more profitable than reforesting pasture or agricultural land. Furthermore, the study found out that any land valued at more than P400/ha would make reforestation with mahogany unprofitable.[6]

This part of the analysis shows how critically certain assumptions can influence the outcome of the analysis. By assuming a low marginal productivity of grazing land without any intervention, the NPV that results from the incremental production from the project would be high. The analysis is not clear about whether this assumption of low land productivity was translated into lower reforestation benefits, compared with reforestation on more fertile land. As an alternative, the author translated the low productivity of land into a higher cost of production, thereby allowing the yields to be maintained at levels similar to those obtained for reforestation in agricultural sites.

The Economic Analysis

The author states that the study's economic analysis differs from traditional economic analysis in the sense that it uses export and import parity prices for tradable goods instead of using border prices directly. This claim has no basis at all, since correct economic analysis always adjusts the border prices for transport and distribution charges to derive export and import parity prices. Even basic textbooks on project analysis show that one should use parity prices rather than border prices.

The study does indeed differ from most other studies, but this is due to the treatment of income distribution and environmental impacts in the analysis. The strongest point of this study is its detailed discussion of how socio-economic profitability analysis and environmental-economic analysis are carried out. While there is plenty of literature available on how to perform cost-benefit analysis, and on case study applications of this type of analysis, this study combines the 'how to do it' discussion with an illustration of how the steps were actually carried out.

NOTES

1 This chapter reviews, and therefore draws heavily on, Niskanen 1995.

2 Resources, Environment and Economics Center for Studies, Inc.

3 Dipterocarp forests are forests dominated by trees of the Dipterocaraceae family, comprising important timber species such as the red and yellow merantis (*shorea* spp).

4 See glossary for brief descriptions of these non-use values.

5 The shadow prices of tradable inputs and outputs represent market prices adjusted to remove transfer payments and the shadow price of foreign exchange. For tradable inputs, the shadow prices correspond to export and import parity values, while for non-tradable inputs such as land and labour, the shadow prices correspond to their opportunity costs.

6 P = Philippine pesos; approximately P25.51 = US$1.

REFERENCES

Agricultural Land Management and Evaluation Division (ALMED) (1993) Crop Development and Soil Conservation Framework for Mindanao Island. Bureau of Soils and Water Management, Department of Agriculture, Quezon City, Philippines.

Cruz, W D, Francisco, H A and Conway, Z T (1988) The On-Site and Downstream Costs of Soil Erosion in the Magat and Pantabangan Watersheds. *Journal of Philippine Development* XV (1): 85–111.

David, W P (1988) Soil and Water Conservation Planning: Issues and Recommendation. *Journal of Philippine Development* XV (1): 47–84.

Department of Environment and Natural Resources (DENR) (1990) Masterplan for Forestry Development. DENR, Quezon City, Philippines.

Evans, J (1992) *Plantation Forestry in the Tropics*. Clarendon Press, Oxford.

Nabuurs, G J and Mohren, G M J (1993) *Carbon Fixation through Forestation Activities*. Institute for Forestry and Nature Research, Wageningen.

Niskanen, A (1995) Evaluation of Profitability of Forest Plantations in the Philippines Using Conventional and Extended Cost-benefit Analysis. Thesis for the Licentiate degree in Forest Management and Economics, University of Joensuu, Joensuu, Finland.

Saastamoinen, O (1994) Offsite Costs of Soil Erosion and Watershed Degradation in the Philippines: Sectoral Impacts and Tentative Results. Philippine Institute for Development Studies, Discussion Paper no 94–18.

Uitamo E (1995) Changes in Land Use and Land Cover in the Philippines Since the Sixteenth Century. Unpublished manuscript, Faculty of Forestry, University of Joensuu, Finland.

6

HEALTH EFFECTS AND THE VALUE OF AIR POLLUTION REDUCTION IN TAIWAN[1]

Germelino Bautista,[2] Anthony Ygrubay,[3] Daigee Shaw,[4] and Marian delos Angeles[5]

HEALTH EFFECTS OF AIR POLLUTION

The results of air quality monitoring indicate that pollution in most Taiwanese cities is severe. The major pollutants present at levels above the Pollution Standards Index are suspended particulates, carbon monoxide, ozone, and sulphur dioxide. Industrial development, the increase in population and the rise in vehicular traffic are the main sources of pollution in major metropolitan areas.

DESCRIPTION OF ORIGINAL STUDY

Objective and Focus

This chapter reviews a pioneering study on air pollution in three cities in Taiwan. The study, documented in Shaw et al (1996) and Alberini et al (1996), estimates the benefits of reducing health-threatening air pollutants. The study has both an academic and policy orientation. It is the first study to administer an epidemiological survey and a contingent valuation survey to the same group of respondents, thereby providing considerable information for environmental valuation. Its valuation of air quality and health improvements and its assessment of the empirical relationship between acute respiratory symptoms and chronic diseases, air pollution and other suspended risk factors, are noteworthy contributions to the literature on health and environmental economics.

The study also aimed to provide inputs for policy formulation in Taiwan. In light of the lack of epidemiological data available to link pollution to health effects in Taiwan, and the dependence of policy makers on foreign studies, the main motivation behind the research was to generate information on the local health impacts of air pollution, which could guide the Environmental Protection Administration (EPA) in their implementation of the amended Air Pollution Control Act.

Methodology

The framework of the study is based on the relationship between health status (ie the nature and severity of individual illnesses) and several variables, including: ambient pollution levels; individual responses to the threat of illness which may take the form of aversive and mitigating activities or expenditure outlays; and other conditions affecting health outcomes, such as the person's general health status or the presence of chronic conditions. Unlike previous research, which used chronic illness as a dependent variable to indicate health status, this study uses instead short-term respiratory illnesses or acute pollution-related symptoms.

The study specifies a probit function[6] where a person's short-term health status (coded as 1 if any of the 15 symptoms considered is present; 0, otherwise) depends on:

- a set of environmental conditions (air quality readings on four pollutants, and humidity and temperature levels);
- non-environmental variables, such as defensive activities and socio-demographic variables;
- the probability of being a smoker; and
- the probability of having a chronic disease.

The probit function is specified in a simultaneous equation model, where the propensity to have a chronic disease and the propensity to smoke are also dependent variables. The chronic disease variable (coded as 1, if any of the following five chronic diseases have been diagnosed: asthma, bronchitis, emphysema, heart trouble, and high blood pressure; 0, otherwise) is endogenously dependent on environmental variables (operationalized in terms of the average levels of PM-10 and SO_2, temperature, and humidity) as well as non-environmental factors such as defensive activities, such as the use of an air conditioner or dehumidifier, and regular exercise. The propensity to smoke (coded as 1, if smoking regularly; 0, otherwise), is also endogenously dependent on environmental conditions, such as exposure to pollution at work, and on non-environmental exogenous variables (including age, gender, performance of regular exercise, and whether or not the respondent is a student).

The choice of a simultaneous equation model allowed the researchers to account for the potential endogenous effects of smoking and chronic disease, and this resulted in greater coefficient estimates of critical variables than those obtained from an ordinary probit model. Since the pollutant variables were measured in different units, they were transformed into logarithms to draw out policy implications. Using the coefficient of each transformed pollutant variable, which measures the percentage change in the probability of having an acute respiratory illness given a 1 per cent change in its concentration, the study identifies which of the three pollutants (PM-10, SO_2, O_3) are positively related to the likelihood of experiencing acute symptoms. By comparing the elasticities of the pollutants at their respective ambient air quality standard levels, the study also shows which particular pollutant is more health-damaging.

The elasticities also helped the researchers determine the total health effects of an improvement in air quality. Given the probability that someone living in any of the three study sites (Taipei, Kaohsiung, and Haulien) would succumb to an acute respiratory illness in a year, an improvement in air quality or a percentage decrease in air pollution is expected to reduce the probability of sick days. The following conditions were posited in order to determine the total health benefits or the decrease in the total number of person-days of illness. In the first three conditions, the level of each air pollutant was reduced, one at a time, by 50 per cent across the three cities, while in the fourth condition the levels of all the pollutants were reduced simultaneously by 50 per cent. In the last condition, the pollution levels in Taipei and Kaohsiung were reduced to the level of Haulien, the least polluted city.

The experiment suggests that a pollution control policy would effect an improvement in air quality. The value of such a policy would be calculated as the resulting reduction in the total number of sick person-days times the individual's willingness to pay (WTP) to avoid acute illnesses.

The WTP for marginal air quality improvement is conceptually defined as the product of the reduction in sick time associated with the decrease in pollution, on the one hand, and the marginal cost of sick time, on the other. The latter may be represented by the aversive or mitigating expenditure outlays to reduce the time of illness. Thus, the WTP for a marginal environmental change is equal to the product of the resulting reduction in sick time and the avoided cost of an additional day of illness. The WTP to avoid illness may also be formally represented as consisting of the sum of the value of lost time, the change in averting and mitigating expenditures (ie the private cost of illness or the lower bound of WTP) and the value of the discomfort suffered.

Main Sources of Data

In order to generate these variables, various data sources were tapped. Information on the exposure and ambient pollution levels came from the nearest EPA monitoring stations, which were less than 750 metres away from the respondents. A background survey provided information on health status, the presence of chronic respiratory illness, exposure to air pollution, lifestyle (diet, smoking, exercise), and socio-economic and demographic variables which may affect health outcomes. A separate contingent valuation (CV) survey involved 1,285 respondents who generated information on their WTP to avoid the latest episode of acute symptoms, as well as the aversive and mitigating actions they had taken. Categorized as subsample I in the study, 864 out of these contingent valuation respondents were also involved in an epidemiological survey. This epidemiological survey was conducted over a 92-day period to record the daily health status of all 864 respondents, the presence and duration of any one of the 15 air pollutant-related symptoms, and their severity as reflected in the activities, medical visits, and medication taken by the survey participants. The rest of the respondents in the CV survey did not have any diary experience and were simply asked to evaluate their most recent illness.

With regard to the procedures in the contingent valuation study, the respondents were first asked to state the most recent acute illness episode and respond to questions regarding the duration and severity of their illness, and the associated costs and efforts to alleviate the symptoms. They were then asked whether they would pay a stated amount to avoid the illness. In order to test for starting point bias, the stated amount came from a predetermined structure of bids, and was followed by two or three follow-up bid questions.[7] A range of WTP values was thus elicited from the respondents.

The relationship of the respondents' WTP to their characteristics and their illness episodes was specified by a statistical model representing the logarithm of WTP as a linear function of the respondent and illness characteristics. The respondents' characteristics included income, 'taste' for good health, and baseline health condition. 'Taste' was operationalized in the study in terms of the number of years of education and the dummy variables on whether the respondent exercised regularly or was a smoker. Two dummy variables, on whether the respondent suffered from serious lung disease, or from a non-lung related chronic illness, defined the baseline health condition.

The characteristics of the illness episode referred to its duration and severity. Following US studies, which distinguish illnesses by their symptoms, duration was measured by the number of days between the time the first symptom appeared and the time the last symptom subsided. Severity, on the other hand, was defined by the number of symptoms experienced and two dummy variables, on whether or not the episode was a cold, and whether the respondents experienced loss of work days, bed disability, or restricted activity days (RADs). Severity was also associated with mitigating activities which were represented by two dummy variables: a visit to a doctor or the purchase of medicine. This implies that as the duration of the illness lengthens and becomes more severe, entailing greater discomfort and more RADs or medication, the WTP to avoid illness increases.

The information collected through the various surveys was supplemented by data from the EPA on ambient air quality. A comparison was made between the results from the basic data generated and the valuation that would have occurred through the use of benefit transfer estimates where the WTP values were obtained from US research.

Comprehensiveness, Accuracy, and Reliability of the Estimates

The results of the WTP equations for subsample 1 show that the WTP values are reliable. Over successive rounds of bidding, the responses of those who also participated in the epidemiological survey have been stable, with no evidence of a starting point bias. As expected, WTP also changed with the characteristics of the illness episode and of the respondent. The Hausman test for differences in coefficients between rounds of responses resulted in coefficients that are not significantly different.[8] The findings suggest that the responses of subsample I meet the criteria of internal validity.

The WTP equations for subsample II, however, yielded results that were in sharp contrast to those for subsample I. The responses were unreliable and unstable across successive follow-up questions. WTP did not vary as expected with illness episodes or respondent characteristics, and some of the estimated coefficients changed significantly from one round to another. This suggests that these respondents did not have well-defined values for WTP. The study posits the explanation that the respondents in subsample II were not familiar with the commodity being valued, or had poor recall of their most recent short-term illness.

The composition of subsamples I and II must have differed. Subsample I was certainly more homogeneous, as the close monitoring of acute morbidity in the epidemiological survey resulted in 79 respondents who had reported illnesses lasting longer than 30 days being excluded from subsample I. This monitoring was not possible in subsample II. Moreover, unlike the subsample I respondents who were involved in reporting their daily short-term health status, sample II respondents were probably not as concerned with evaluating their health condition and did not give as much thought to the loss of days and the costs associated with their most recent short-term respiratory illness. In other words, their non-involvement in the epidemiological survey meant that subsample II respondents did not have the same perspective and learning experience as had subsample I respondents. The value of the epidemiological survey may lie in orienting and training participants for contingent valuation, hence ensuring its success.

CRITIQUE OF THE STUDY

There are a number of reasons for the unreliable and unexpected results from the analysis of subsample II data. When asked about their recent illness, it is possible that some respondents did not understand the instruction to recall their 'most recent short-term illness episode, such as a cold or flu, or even a day of coughing'. It may be the case that symptoms like coughing, phlegm, eye irritation or headaches are considered part of their normal everyday experience. As reflected in their responses, they were thinking of more serious respiratory illnesses, which required going to a doctor and buying medication. While they could not recall the duration and number of symptoms, they remembered the more severe illnesses because these inflicted discomfort and required efforts to seek relief from a doctor or medication. It is interesting to note that the severity of the illness and mitigating action were significant predictors of WTP. The significance of a serious respiratory disease in determining the likelihood of WTP suggests that individuals gave more attention to more serious illnesses than to recent short-term respiratory symptoms when they formed their WTP.

Alberini's finding that sample II respondents tended to recall more significant past illnesses rather than their more recent short-term illness confirms Shaw's model, where acute respiratory disease is a function of chronic illness. The respondents' focus on chronic illness, even if instructed by researchers to look more at acute symptoms, reflects the value given to a persistent chronic illness, *vis-à-vis* acute symptoms. This implies that in the minds of ordinary people, valuation applies more to chronic diseases than to acute symptoms. Moreover, it may have methodological implications because respondents may not register symptoms that are ignored in the conduct of their daily lives.

Probably since the study focused on short-term illnesses and was geographically confined to a radius of less than 750 metres from the EPA monitoring station, it confined its operational definition of aversive behaviour to the possession of air-conditioners and humidifiers. If this concept refers to the avoidance of exposure to pollution, however, it must also include efforts to spend less time within the polluted area, if not to relocate. Had these aversive activities been included in the study, the relative value of pollution-related illnesses would have been greater. Moreover, the inclusion of such forms of human behaviour would have provided a better understanding of the variables affecting health status.

The use of the diary in the survey process was certainly helpful in producing robust statistical results in the contingent valuation study. But the improvements in estimation were obtained at a high cost. There are many alternative ways of achieving similar results at a lower cost. For instance, Alberini's analysis using estimates of the WTP in Taiwan to predict the WTP of a US household yielded estimates that are comparable to similar CV studies conducted in the US. Similarly, the predictions of Taiwan WTP from two US studies fell within 95 per cent confidence interval of the median WTP of subsample I. Alberini is, therefore, implicitly putting forward benefit transfers as a less costly alternative.

A major contribution of the study is the comparison made between the results of the detailed estimation of local residents' valuation of health risks using the contingent valuation method, and the estimates obtained through a benefits transfer approach. The results of this comparison are shown in Table 6.1 below.

Table 6.1 Willingness to Pay to Avoid a Head Cold: USA vs Taiwan (September 1992, US$)

Study (95% confidence intervals in brackets)	No RAD		With RAD		Household income	
	USA	Taiwan	USA	Taiwan	USA	Taiwan
Tolley et al, 1986 (one day of severe head congestion and throat irritation)	–	–	40.32	28.01	40,583[a]	
Loehman et al, 1970 (one day of head congestion, eye, ear and throat irritation)	8.91	7.08	19.15	15.23	28,675[b]	
Taiwan CV Survey (one day and average number of symptoms; doctor not visited)		17.48 [13.62– 34.6]		23.97 [11.46– 23.50]		28,260[a] 22,800[b]

Notes:
a Mean household income.
b Median household income. Predictions for Taiwan from the US study were obtained by mulitiplying the US figures by the ration of median household income of the Taiwan-based sample to median household income of the US-based sample. If mean household income but not median household income was reported in the US study, predictions for Taiwan were formed using the ratio of mean household incomes.

NOTES

1   This chapter reviews, and therefore draws heavily on, Shaw et al (1996) and Alberini et al (1996).

2   Ateneo de Manila University.

3   Resources, Environment and Economics Center for Studies, Inc.

4   Academia Sinica, Taiwan.

5   Resources, Environment and Economics Center for Studies, Inc.

6   See glossary for a brief explanation of probit functions.

7   See glossary for a brief explanation of starting point bias in contingent valuation surveys.

8   The Hausman test is a test for whether or not the estimates from two different estimating procedures differ significantly from one another.

REFERENCES

Alberini, A et al (1996) What is the Value of Reduced Morbidity in Taiwan? In: Mendelsohn, R and Shaw, D (eds) *The Economics of Pollution Control in the Asia Pacific.* Edward Elgar, Aldershot.

Loehman, E and De, H D (1982) Application of Stochastic Choice Modeling to Policy Analysis of Public Goods: A Case Study of Air Quality Improvements. *The Review of Economics and Statistics* vol 64 (3): 474–80.

Shaw, D et al (1996) Acute Health Effects of Major Air Pollutants in Taiwan. In: Mendelsohn, R and Shaw, D (eds) *The Economics of Pollution Control in the Asia Pacific.* Edward Elgar, Aldershot.

Tolley G, Babcock, L, Berger, A, Bilotti, G, Blomquist, M, Brien, R, Fabian, G, Fishelson, C, Kahn, A, Kelly, D, Kenkel, R, Krumm, T, Miller, R, Oshfeldt, S, Rosen, W, Webb, W, Wilson and M Zelder (1986) 'Valuation of Reductions in Human Health Symptoms and Risks.' Report for US EPA Grant #CR–811053–01–0 US Environmental Protection Agency, Washington DC.

7

ENVIRONMENTAL CONSIDERATIONS IN THE ENVIRONMENTAL IMPACT ANALYSIS OF THE KATUNAYAKE EXPRESSWAY IN SRI LANKA

V Sivagnasothy[1] and David S McCauley[2]

BACKGROUND

Environmental Considerations in Development Project Design

The use of Environmental Impact Assessments (EIAs) to identify the potential environmental consequences of development projects is now widespread in Asia, and the quality of this analysis is improving steadily. Most countries of the region now have legislation requiring EIAs, and this legal authority often includes not only the right to demand the redesign or cancellation of projects if serious problems are identified, but also to insist on public participation in their review. The EIA requirements have also forced a more interdisciplinary look at project design, at least in its latter stages. After an initial emphasis placed by EIA practitioners on *qualitative* assessment, greater attention is now being given to *quantifying* the health and environmental damages associated with the construction and operation phases of development projects.

What EIAs generally have not done, however, is to place monetary values on the positive or negative impacts identified. This has complicated the process of decision making. Despite the range of analytical techniques commonly used in the EIA process, there is no economic common denominator for assessing the relative importance of various damages or for estimating a project's net benefits.

The fundamental premise underlying the effort to better understand the potential environmental impacts of development projects is that the full costs to society from such investments have not been adequately considered in the past. The call for the application of EIAs to development projects grew out of a realization that traditional project appraisal approaches often overlooked many potentially costly environmental damages. In recent years the field of environmental economics has developed rapidly, and much of its attention has focused on the valuation of environmental benefits and costs associated with development projects and policy options. It would seem the time has now come for these two parallel efforts – environmental impact assessment and 'extended' cost-benefit analysis – to be linked, so that environmental considerations can be more fully incorporated into the standard practices of project evaluation, beginning at the earliest design stages.

There is a vibrant body of literature now available within the field of environmental economics, which provides valuation techniques to accomplish this monetization and 'extend' conventional cost-benefit analysis to include the often overlooked environmental impacts (see, for example, Dixon et al, 1996; or OECD, 1995). The increased attention to economic valuation of environmental impacts by development banks and others has created a strong demand for further training in this field (McCauley, 1995), and both governments and funding agencies are now seeking to widen the application of such approaches (ADB, 1996).

The Sri Lanka Case Study

This chapter presents a case study on the incorporation of environmental considerations into project economic evaluation (cost-benefit analysis) based on the valuation of environmental and land use impacts ignored in the original project appraisal. It covers most of the key environmental issues associated with highway projects, including changes in air, water and noise pollution, land conversion, and damages incurred from actual construction of the road, such as the collection of road materials. As such it offers an opportunity to examine how both the design and decision-making framework of highways projects can be improved through a better economic accounting of environmental impacts.

This case study is a limited illustration of how a new perspective and certain associated tools may be applied to projects of this type. Because the case is drawn from actual experience in Sri Lanka, there are shortcomings in the available data and thus in the analysis conducted. However, this provides a realistic example of how project designers and economic analysts, who are interested in better understanding the values associated with environmental benefits and costs, will have to approach this task.

Except where explicitly stated, all cost and benefit data presented relate to the economic rather than the financial analysis of the project.

All figures are expressed in constant 1991 Sri Lankan Rupees (US$1 = approximately SLRs 50). In most cases, the information used in re-examining the conventional cost-benefit analysis has been drawn from either the project feasibility studies or the environmental impact assessment (JICA, 1984; RDA, 1991; RDA, 1993). After a review of the original economic evaluation, a reappraisal is made based on some key adjustments to the original methods as well as the inclusion of several additional environmental and other benefits and costs excluded from the conventional analysis. Conclusions have been drawn, both for the project at hand and more generally for similar projects, on the basis of the findings and analytical challenges encountered in this analysis.

DESCRIPTION OF THE PROJECT

Rationale for a New Highway Linking Colombo City and Airport

Sri Lanka's economy has grown at an average of around 5 per cent annually during the 1990s. This growth has been largely driven by the export of garments and other products from the light manufacturing sector. The Sri Lankan Government is committed to providing the necessary infrastructure to support continued growth based on this expanding export sector, including good transportation to and from its air and sea ports.

With this as background, a highway project was proposed to link the country's only international airport (Katunayake International Airport) to its primary shipping port and capital, Colombo. Katunayake Airport is the main entry point for air travellers, including all tourists, as well as air freight into the country. The nearby Colombo Sea Port – located adjacent to the capital city – handles 90 per cent of Sri Lanka's shipping cargo. About 95 per cent of the freight handled by these two ports also travels by road. In addition, the Katunayake Export Processing Zone and Ekala/Ja-Ela industrial areas located near the airport are among the most important economic assets to the country, providing continued strong growth in foreign exchange earnings as well as income and employment generation based on the manufacture and assembly of a widening range of export products.

The existing road between the urban and port areas of the City of Colombo and Katunayake Airport is Highway A3. This road is already approaching what has been described as its limiting capacity due to heavy congestion, and the situation can only be expected to deteriorate further in future years. Travellers on the current two to four lane undivided highway are subject to a mixture of heavy vehicles, public and private buses, private cars, three-wheel public transport vehicles, motor cycles, animal drawn carts, and pedestrians, all competing for road space. Speeds and fuel efficiency vary greatly as vehicles are forced to adjust to rapidly changing road conditions, and Highway A3 is the scene of many accidents.

The Katunayake Expressway and Design Alternatives

The construction of a new Colombo-Katunayake Expressway to provide an alternative to Highway A3 was characterized by the Government's Road Development Authority as one of the nation's highest priority infrastructure investments, vital to the nation's future economic development plans. The idea of a new highway or an upgrading of the existing road had been discussed in various forms since the mid-1980s. The Expressway proposal, which finally emerged, called for a 30-kilometre high-speed (100 km/hr) road link from the Colombo Port area to the Katunayake Airport region. The basic consensus design grew out of various pre-feasibility studies, and called for two traffic lanes in each direction, separated by a central median with a barrier and a surfaced shoulder for emergencies. The highway was to be toll-controlled and restricted to high speed and heavy vehicles only, with no pedestrian route along the alignment and only a limited number of intersections for vehicle access.

The proposed route and dimensions of the middle 25 kilometres of the highway were decided during the pre-feasibility stage, so the principal design alternatives finally considered were narrowed down to two issues: (i) the lane/road width; and (ii) the route of the beginning and ending sections of the highway. To ease the analysis, this paper looks only at the case involving a lane width of 3.5 m and overall road width of 25 m, which showed a higher net economic benefit in the conventional analysis. As for the alternative routes, on the Colombo end of the highway the choice was between links with one of two bridges crossing the Kelani River to provide access to the capital: the New Kelani Bridge and the Japan-Sri Lanka Friendship Bridge. Because of far greater costs from the dislocation of existing industry and other infrastructure associated with the latter option, primary attention was focused on the New Kelani Bridge link. On the Katunayake end of the Expressway there were two off-ramp options, and the choice of a more direct connection with the Katunayake Free Trade Zone was again made on cost-effectiveness grounds.

CONVENTIONAL COST-BENEFIT ANALYSIS

Anticipated Benefits of the New Expressway

Two types of economic savings constituted the anticipated benefits from construction of the new Expressway, namely, lower vehicle operating costs and reduced travel time for Expressway users. In addition, the project evaluation considered 'indirect benefits' from anticipated links to regional development, though these were not included in cost-benefit calculations.

Benefits from Reduced Vehicle Operating Costs (VOCs)
The calculation of savings in VOCs from construction of the new highway was made by firstly estimating VOCs per kilometre for six types of vehicles: cars; medium and large buses; and light, medium and heavy trucks. Table 7.1 shows the ten components of VOCs and their estimated economic values (expressed in Sri Lankan Rupees per 1000 km) for each of the six vehicle types.

Table 7.1 *Elements of Vehicle Operating Costs (VOC) Calculation*

Cost Items	Vehicle Type	Cost per 1000 km by vehicle type (SLRs)
Fuel and oil	Passenger car	6410
Tyres	Medium bus	6505
Spare parts	Large bus	7722
Workshop labour	Light truck	7087
Depreciation	Medium truck	7534
Interest	Heavy truck	11,018
Crew charges		
Insurance		
Licence fees		
Overheads		

Forecasts were then made of future traffic demand for the existing Highway A3 and the new Expressway. This was based, in part, on a regression relating Sri Lanka's GDP growth to 1981–1990 data on the number (and types) of vehicles using the New Kelani Bridge, the main entry point from Colombo to the new Expressway. Predicted GDP growth figures for the years 2000 and 2010, as estimated by the Government's Finance Department, were used to forecast traffic volumes by vehicle type in each year, based on the relationship between growth in national income and traffic levels. Forecast traffic growth rates were 4.2 per cent for 1991–2000 and 5.1 per cent for 2000–2010. The Frater Method of constructing future Origin–Destination (O–D) Matrices was used, based on a survey of motorists using the New Kelani Bridge and Highway A3, to judge the proportion of this increase that would be expected to use the new Expressway, based on an estimate of future inter-zonal trip demand for the two years 2000 and 2010. A key assumption used in modelling traffic flows was that travel times at minimum speeds (where limited by road capacity) would be twice those at design/maximum speeds.

A model utilizing all of these data predicted traffic volumes along the Colombo–Katunayake corridor and the division of this traffic between

Highway A3 and the new Expressway (assuming no toll was charged for use of the new road). The forecast demand may be seen in Table 7.2 presented in a with-project and without-project framework. The baseline 1990 Colombo–Katunayake volume on Highway A3 was estimated to be around 28,000 vehicles per day. With construction of the new Expressway, total traffic volumes on the Colombo–Katunayake corridor were predicted to more than double by the year 2000 to around 60,000 vehicles per day and to increase by a further 50 per cent by the year 2010 to roughly 90,000 per day. Assuming that no toll is charged (this assumption will be examined later), approximately 44 per cent of the vehicles (26,700 per day) would use the new Expressway in the year 2000, while 57 per cent (52,620 per day) would use the new road in the year 2010.

Table 7.2 *Projected Traffic Demand in With-Without Project Scenarios in the Colombo–Katunayake Corridor Assuming No Toll (vehicles per day)*

	1990	With 2000	Without 2000	With 2010	Without 2010
Existing Highway A3	27,670	34,075	44,725	40,000	82,025
New Expressway	0	26,700	0	52,620	0
Total	27,670	60,775	44,725	92,620	82,025

This information on predicted future traffic volumes on the Expressway by vehicle class was combined with the per kilometre VOCs for Highway A3 and Expressway use to compile total VOCs for each road in the years 2000 and 2010. The difference between the sum of these VOCs and the VOCs for Highway A3 use alone (in the without-project case) constituted the net savings in VOCs attributable to the Expressway's construction. These methods are commonly used to predict traffic volumes and to calculate the benefits of highway projects. The estimated benefits amounted to some SLRs 1.168 billion in the year 2000 and SLRs 2.261 billion in 2010 (or about US$23 and US$45 million, respectively, for the two years).

Benefits from Reduced Travel Time
In calculating benefits associated with the faster trips offered by the new Expressway, five factors were considered for each of three vehicle types (cars, medium buses and large buses):

- average income (of two groups, car owners and non-owners);
- working hours;
- trip purpose;
- an adjustment for business versus non-business trips (the opportunity cost of the latter was assumed to be zero); and
- average vehicle occupancy.

On this basis, estimates of the value of travellers' time (based on forgone earnings) were made. The benefits estimation was limited to vehicle passengers to avoid double counting with reduced crew/driver costs from the VOC calculations.

The savings in travel time between the with-project and without-project scenarios by vehicle class were estimated using the road use demand forecasts given previously in Table 7.2. The difference between the sum of the value of time saved on the Expressway and Highway A3 in the with-project case compared to the without-project case constituted the net benefit of time savings (costs avoided from lost earnings) attributable to the Expressway's construction. These amounted to SLRs 1.24 billion for the year 2000 and SLRs 2.30 billion for 2010. The time saved in a one-way trip on the Expressway versus using Highway A3 amounted to between 20 and 30 minutes.

Because of concern over the ability of passengers to capture the full benefits of such small amounts of time saved, the annual benefit figures adopted for use in the benefit-cost analysis were only 10 per cent of the total estimated amount (SLRs 124 and SLRs 230 million for 2000 and 2010, or about US$2.5 and US$4.6 million, respectively, in the two benchmark years).

Other Benefits

In addition to these two forms of direct benefits, there were several others mentioned in the project appraisal (but not valued). These were: decreased traffic accidents; decreased freight damage and costs of packing and crating; reduced driver fatigue and increased comfort of transport; and relief of traffic congestion on Highway A3. In particular, failure to value the benefits from decreased congestion on Highway A3 would appear to have resulted in a considerable underestimation of the project's benefits. No explanation was given as to why these benefits were not valued or included in the project's economic evaluation. A number of 'indirect' benefits were also mentioned, without being valued, in the project analysis. These included: development impacts on industry, tourism, commerce, and marketing in the immediate areas around interchanges; reduced urbanization pressures and expanded area available for residential environments; promotion of interregional communication; and increased land values.

Estimated Project Costs

The major cost items for the project were broken into three categories: construction; routine operation and maintenance; and periodic maintenance (repaving every 10 years). These costs are given in Table 7.3. Adjustments were made to the figures to subtract transfer payments (taxes and duties), and the resulting estimated economic costs are shown. Total construction costs were estimated to be SLRs 5.5 billion (or around

US$110 million), with annual maintenance costs of SLRs 19.3 million (US$387,000) and 10-year maintenance costs of around SLRs 179 million (or approximately US$3.56 million). These estimated costs are consistent with the engineering design for the project and their calculation followed established norms for estimating such costs. It is worth noting that land acquisition costs, as calculated in the study, represented only about nine per cent of construction costs.

Table 7.3 *Estimated Project Economic Costs for Construction and Maintenance of the Katunayake Expressway (SLRs millions)*

Construction	Cost	Per cent of total cost
Land acquisition	586.40	8.9
Earth work	1835.90	28.0
Highway paving	925.10	14.1
Bridges	1201.20	18.3
Engineering services	317.20	4.8
Miscellaneous	843.50	12.8
Contingencies	856.40	13.0
	6565.70	100.0
Minus Taxes and Duties	1020.90	
Total Economic Construction Costs:	*5544.80*	

Annual Operation and Maintenance	Cost	Per cent of total cost
Surface maintenance	7.83	33.6
Surface cleaning	5.69	24.4
Electricity	7.67	32.9
Miscellaneous	2.12	9.1
	23.31	100.0
Minus Taxes and Duties	3.96	
Total Economic Annual O&M Costs:	*19.34*	
10-Year Periodic O&M Costs:	**196.56**	**100.0**
Minus Taxes and Duties	17.61	
Total Economic Periodic O&M Costs:	*178.95*	

Net Benefits

The estimates of project economic benefits and costs show the flow of these benefit and cost streams over the project evaluation life of 36 years. The following assumptions were made in calculating these figures:

- A construction period of six years;
- All values expressed in constant 1991 SL Rupees;
- A project life, following construction, of 30 years;
- No toll charged for using the Expressway;

- Benefit streams for years intervening and preceding 2000 and 2010 estimated by interpolation;
- Expressway 'saturation' in 2010, so annual benefits constant after this point; and
- Opportunity cost of capital equals 12 per cent.

At the assumed 12 per cent discount rate, the project was shown to have a Net Present Value (NPV) of some SLRs 3.309 billion (equivalent to roughly US$66 million), an Economic Internal Rate of Return (EIRR) of approximately 19 per cent, and a Benefit-Cost Ratio of about 2.0.

Sensitivity Analysis

A relatively standard sensitivity analysis was performed to examine the effects of changes in the benefit and cost streams, or changes in the assumed project life. There was no specific testing of other underlying assumptions nor were there any validation tests performed on the methods used to estimate benefits and costs. The sensitivity analysis found the following impacts on the Economic Internal Rate of Return (in per cent):

Condition	EIRR
Original estimated benefits and costs	18.89
Benefits reduced by 10%	17.85
Benefits reduced by 20%	16.58
Costs increased by 10%	17.97
Costs increased by 20%	17.01
Costs increased by 20% and benefits decreased by 10%	16.82
Costs increased by 20% and benefits decreased by 20%	14.71
Project life reduced from 36 to 20 years	18.50

Based on the results of the project economic appraisal and sensitivity analysis, the Katunayake Expressway was accepted into the Government of Sri Lanka's public investment programme, and arrangements were made with an interested foreign donor for construction financing.

THE ENVIRONMENTAL IMPACT ASSESSMENT

Scope of the Environmental Assessment

Government acceptance of the project, however, was provisional. Because of the scale and nature of the project, it was placed on the 'prescribed list' of development projects for which an Environmental Impact Assessment (EIA) is required under Sri Lankan law. The terms of reference for the study approved by the Central Environmental Authority, which regulates EIAs, specified only a qualitative assessment of the project's environmental impacts. The potential impacts to be examined included: noise pollution; the highway's potentially adverse consequences on natural systems; and its impacts on air and water quality. The terms of reference made no mention of potentially beneficial environmental impacts. As there were to be no quantitative measures of environmental impacts, there obviously was no requirement that the EIA attempt to place monetary values on the environmental costs or benefits identified.

Negative Environmental Impacts

The EIA divided its findings into two categories, according to the timing of the impacts' cause: those associated with (i) the project's construction; and (ii) the operational phases (RDA, 1993). The following adverse environmental impacts were identified and were deemed significant enough to warrant some mitigatory actions on the part of the project proponents:

- *Noise Impacts* (construction and operations)
- *Air Quality Impacts* (construction and operations)
- *Water Quality Impacts*
  - interruption of flow paths (construction and operations)
  - contamination from highway runoff (operations)
  - long-term leaching from embankments (operations)
- *Community Impacts*
  - destruction of property (construction)
  - severance of communities (construction and operations)
  - destruction or disruption of agricultural lands (construction and operations)
  - disruption of transport links (construction and operations)
  - impacts on public health (construction)
- *Ecological Impacts* (construction)
  - natural ecosystems disruption
  - cultivated lands disruption
- *Extraction and Transport of Highway Construction Materials:* sand, soil, rock (construction)

Environmental Benefits

Although the EIA provided no detailed discussion of potentially beneficial environmental impacts, a record was provided which indicates that some were at least considered during the study. In the list given below, the first item – environmental improvements due to reduced traffic on the existing highway – represents an important benefit that was clearly overlooked in the original cost-benefit analysis. Most of the remainder are either non-environmental, were covered in the original project appraisal, or do not lend themselves easily to valuation for the purposes of cost-benefit analysis. The lack of any analysis of project benefits in the EIA is apparently a result of its not having been required within the study's terms of reference (reflecting a common bias toward negative impacts in EIAs). The following potentially positive impacts were listed in the EIA document:

- improved environment around Highway A3;
- reduced pressure on Highway A3;
- more efficient links between the airport and Colombo;
- safer travel;
- improved fuel efficiency;
- economic boost to the Export Processing Zone and surrounding industrial areas; and
- potential development opportunities at intersections.

EIA Conclusions

For each negative impact identified, a mitigation measure was specified. No cost estimate or cost-effectiveness analysis was provided for the proposed measures, nor was any sensitivity analysis included to examine the effects that these additional costs would have on the economic rate of return of the project if they were internalized. All mitigation measures were combined into a general plan of action with an accompanying monitoring schedule to be followed by the project proponent. However, without quantitative predictions of environmental damages, these requirements were largely based on the need to meet national pollution and natural resources management standards. The EIA's recommendations were approved by the regulatory authorities, and the project was given a green light to proceed on environmental grounds.

EXTENDED PROJECT ANALYSIS

With/Without Analysis

A principal shortcoming of the original cost-benefit analysis was its failure to consistently approach the evaluation from a 'with or without project' standpoint. This accounts for some, though not all, of the overlooked benefits and costs. In particular, the original study failed to take account of environmental benefits associated with the decrease in traffic growth on the existing Highway A3 (though the VOC and time savings calculations appear to have been done properly). To conduct a simple 'extended' analysis, taking better account of all benefits and costs – including anticipated environmental impacts – it is necessary to refer back to the with-and-without framework presented earlier. The basic predicted traffic flows on the old and new roads in the 'with' and 'without' project cases were given in Table 7.2. These form the basis of a clear comparison between the two scenarios.

Without-Project Baseline
To estimate the net benefits from the project, it is essential to first understand clearly the baseline conditions and likely trends that would occur if the project were not undertaken. Much of this information was collected during the original project analysis but only partially used. Taking into account the original benefit and cost estimates and the range of potential environmental impacts identified in the EIA, the following conditions and variables characterize the without-project scenario and mostly relate to the situation on or along the existing Highway A3:

• There are no costs associated with project construction (economic costs of building the Expressway, lost agricultural production, displacement of communities, water pollution, or loss of natural systems).
• There are no costs associated with operation and maintenance of the Expressway.
• No major improvements are made to Highway A3, but annual and periodic costs for maintaining the existing road are estimated at one-third of the applicable costs associated with the Expressway (SLRs 4.28 million annually and SLRs 59.1 million every 10 years, or roughly US$86,000 and US$1.18 million, respectively).
• There are minimal negative environmental impacts from economic development along the proposed route of the Expressway during the 36-year project period.
• Baseline 1990 traffic levels on Highway A3 are estimated at about 28,000 vehicles per day and are expected to grow by 62 per cent to around 45,000 per day in the year 2000 and by a further 83 per cent to around 82,000 in 2010 (with no further growth to the end of the 36-year project period, because Highway A3 would be 'saturated' beyond 82,000 vehicles per day).
• Travel time and vehicle operating costs for Highway A3 users increase to a maximum in the year 2010 when the complete capacity of the road is reached (due to congestion).
• Although traffic speed will be greatly reduced, Highway A3 is already described as approaching its 'limiting capacity', and so noise and air pollution are expected to increase roughly in proportion to the expanded number of vehicles (though no valuation of these costs along Highway A3 is made).

With-Project Scenario
All computed estimates of the original economic cost-benefit analysis are maintained in the with-project scenario. These values cover construction, operation and maintenance costs, as well as benefits from reduced

vehicle operating costs and time savings. The estimates are based on Expressway traffic of approximately 27,000 vehicles per day in the year 2000, and about 53,000 in the year 2010 (assuming that no toll is charged for using the Expressway). Fundamental to many of the revised cost-benefit estimates is the with-project projection that traffic levels on Highway A3 will continue to rise even with the new Expressway (though at a slower rate, because of the new alternative route). The projections and implications are:

- Highway A3 traffic is projected to increase from a 1990 level of 28,000 vehicles per day by a further 23 per cent over 10 years to around 34,000 per day in the year 2000 and by another 17 per cent to around 40,000 in the year 2010.
- No major improvements are made to Highway A3, and the annual and periodic costs for maintaining the existing road are estimated at one-fourth of the applicable costs associated with the Expressway (SLRs 3.21 million annually and SLRs 44.3 million every 10 years, or a saving over the without-project case of roughly SLRs 1.07 and SLRs 14.78 million, respectively).
- Savings in Vehicle Operating Costs and travel time must take into account not only for those using the Expressway, but also for those users facing less traffic on Highway A3.
- Noise and Air Pollution on Highway A3 can be expected to increase roughly in proportion to the additional number of vehicles.

Noise and Air Pollution

The potential for health and environmental damages from increased noise and air pollution must be a strong consideration in the economic evaluation of any highway project. Although not included in the original cost-benefit analysis for the Sri Lankan Expressway, the potential for noise and air pollution problems was clearly noted in the EIA. Unfortunately, there was no attempt to place quantitative estimates on the types and amounts of air pollution to be produced from the new Expressway or to be reduced along the old road, and there was only a limited attempt to quantify the impacts from changes in noise levels.

Construction Phase
The EIA did not estimate the number of people or properties likely to be adversely affected by construction phase air and noise pollution, but it did identify these as a problem to be addressed. In areas of greatest construction noise generation – from, for example, the collection and crushing of highway materials – the levels were projected to exceed 125 dB(A), where an increase in noise level of 10 dB(A) or more or in excess of 75 dB(A) should be considered significant. A distance of between 119–132 metres is needed to reduce noise at 125 dB(A) to an acceptable

level. The project proponent was required through the EIA's recommendations to reduce such noise pollution and/or to take steps to protect the public. The approach taken in the EIA for particulate matter and other air pollution from the construction phase was roughly the same as for noise pollution. The proponent was instructed to take appropriate mitigatory measures to ensure that air pollution levels remained within national standards.

Operational Phase

It is possible to estimate the value of damages from noise and air pollution along the new expressway route. Although there is no comprehensive database on property values in the region, which could be used to more clearly separate out the effects of air and noise pollution on land values, a rudimentary Hedonic pricing method is employed on the basis of the EIA's findings (and a limited survey in the region of the new Expressway). This indicates that the prices of property partially reflect the surrounding environmental quality. It should be noted that no attempt was made to establish dose-response functions between changes in air and noise pollution levels and human health, although this would be an alternative approach for estimating the value of damages associated with these types of negative environmental impacts.[3]

Pre-project noise levels in the proposed path of the Expressway are clearly low. Although no air quality data are available for the region, it can also be safely assumed that air pollution levels are well within Sri Lankan standards in the area surrounding the new Expressway's proposed path. Through interviews with land valuers and residents, it was established that a 10 per cent reduction in the property value for the zone of adverse noise pollution would constitute a lower bound estimate for this negative impact from the presence of the new Expressway. As there are no good data available on air pollution or its links to property values, we have assumed that the localized decrease in air quality levels associated with the zone of the new road will be coupled with the noise impacts to be captured within this 10 per cent reduction. Localized air pollution impacts would be expected to be the most significant because of good wind dispersion in the Expressway region during at least nine months of the year. For Highway A3 (considering the slower rate of traffic growth), it is assumed that the loss in property value has already taken place, and that there will be no major adjustments attributable to Expressway construction.

The EIA estimated that, in addition to land use conversions (see below), roughly 700 properties (370 in the Eastern section and 330 in the West) would be adversely affected by noise pollution (and, no doubt air pollution too, although this was not mentioned in the EIA). The pre-project value of these properties is computed using the data compiled to estimate the losses from land conversion. The EIA estimated that each of the affected 700 properties comprises approximately 30 perches of land (0.077 ha) with 600 square feet of structures.[4] Using a calculated average land value of SLRs 3.9 million/ha and a structure value of SLRs 400/sq ft (assuming semi-permanent dwellings), the pre-project value of the property along the proposed highway path to be adversely affected by noise and air pollution is estimated to be SLRs 406 million (or US$8.12 million). Assuming a 10 per cent loss in value, the cost associated with noise and air pollution from the new highway can be estimated to be approximately SLRs 40 million (or US$800,000). It should be noted that the use of this valuation technique assumes a one-time loss (in year 3) associated with the two types of pollution. Use of a cost-of-illness approach or other method might better capture the value of longer-term health-related damages associated with the pollution (and should be applied to the reduced pollution along both Highway A3 and the proposed Expressway path). For this reason, the estimated value using this rudimentary Hedonic pricing approach represents a lower bound on these costs.

Land Conversion

The original economic analysis included limited compensation costs associated with acquiring land (residential, agricultural and wetlands) in the Expressway's path. This amounted to some SLRs 586 million (or roughly 9 per cent of construction costs). It was assumed that property values as estimated by the Sri Lankan Government's Valuation Department reflected the competitive market prices of these lands, taking into account their productive potential and highest valued uses. However, these values and the extent of land to be affected were both criticized in the EIA for being too low (and the issue of appropriate compensation for land subsequently became the single most important issue in finally determining whether the project was to be approved). Based on re-estimates from data presented in the EIA and limited additional information to support their revaluation, costs can be recalculated for the loss of agricultural lands as well as residential/commercial property.

Loss of Agricultural Productivity
According to EIA estimates (average of upper and lower bounds), approximately 180 hectares of agricultural land – previously used for coconut, paddy (wet rice), rubber, and home gardens – would be converted to highway surface and right-of-way, as follows:

Land Use	Area (ha)
Coconut	50
Paddy	25
Rubber	5
Home Gardens	100
Total	180

A valuation of these lands based on an estimate of lost productivity (because of their conversion from agricultural to highway use) can be carried out as an alternative to the assessed value calculations used in the original cost-benefit analysis. Agriculture Department data were used to estimate annual net returns and a stream of annualized net returns was computed for each land use type as follows (see also Table 7.4):

- *Coconut:* Yield per hectare estimated to be 9,800 nuts; a market price of SLRs 3 per nut was used; the cost of production was estimated at SLRs 3000 per acre; so the value of forgone annual net earnings from coconut production would be SLRs 1,102,500.
- *Paddy:* Yield per hectare per crop estimated to be 4 753 kg, with two crops per year; market price of SLRs 6.5 per kg; cost of production SLRs 19,600 per ha; so the value of forgone annual net earnings from paddy production would be SLRs 1,054,725.
- *Rubber:* Yield per hectare per year estimated to be 690 kg; market price of SLRs 29.3 per kg; cost of production SLRs 14,150 per ha; so the value of forgone annual net earnings from paddy production would be SLRs 2,940,000.
- *Home Gardens:* Net income per hectare per year estimated to be SLRs 29,400; so the value of forgone annual net earnings from home garden production would be SLRs 2.94 million for all areas lost.

Total losses of agricultural earnings from the lands to be displaced by the new Expressway would thus amount to some SLRs 5,127,560 per year. For the purposes of the extended cost-benefit analysis, it is assumed that these losses would be phased in equally over the first three years of the project's construction period and would continue for each year of the project life. The present value of this stream is approximately SLRs 41.6 million (or US$832,000).

Table 7.4 *Lost Agricultural Productivity from Construction of Katunayake Expressway (Monetary Values in SLRs)*

Item	Coconuts	Rice	Rubber	Home Gardens	Total
Area (ha)	50	25	5	100	180
Yield (nuts or kg/ha)	9800	4753	690	–	–
Price (per nut or kg)	3	7	29	–	–
Production per cost	7350	19,600	14,150	–	–
Net income per ha	22,050	42,189	6,067	29,400	–
Annual income lost	1,102,500	1,054,725	30,335	2,940,000	5,127,560
Present Value of forgone Agricultural Income (32 years)					41,592,687

Value of Non-Agricultural Land and Structures to be Converted
The value of built-up lands lying in the Expressway's path was assumed
to be SLRs 10,000 per perch, based on EIA estimates. The total non-
agricultural land area to be converted as a result of the project was
estimated in the EIA as shown in Table 7.5.

Table 7.5 *Estimated Non-Agricultural Land to be Converted*

Size range of land parcels (perches)	Average size (hectares)	Number of land parcels of this size	Estimated total area
0–10	0.013	515	6.60
10–40	0.06	736	47.00
40–60	0.255	240	61.20
160+	0.500	77	38.50
Total			153.31

Using averages for each category, the extent of land to be acquired was
estimated to be 153.3 hectares. Valued at SLRs 10,000 per perch (or SLRs
3.9 million per ha), the loss (taken in year 3) would amount to approximately SLRs 598 million (or around US$12 million).

As for the structures on these lands, the original project economic
analysis dealt with the displacement of all structures, by estimating the
areas to be converted in the Expressway's proposed path and asking the
Sri Lankan Valuation Department for estimates of the compensation
required. The structures were divided into four categories of dwellings:
fine house; common house; small house; and shanty. The total compensation level used for all land and structure losses in the original project
economic analysis totalled SLRs 586.4 million (or approximately US$11.73
million), including an unspecified amount for agricultural lands.

The EIA suggested that this would not adequately account for the
losses to be suffered because of underestimated values and the likelihood
that additional lands would need to be converted. With a corridor width of
100 m for the Expressway (actually the 'upper bound' considered, though
quite reasonable given the style of highway planned), it was predicted that
1568 residential and/or commercial properties would be affected (94.3 per
cent residential). In the recalculation, the original estimated market values
were again used: SLRs 610 per square foot for permanent buildings; SLRs
400/sq ft for semi-permanent buildings (average of 'common' and 'small
house' rates); and SLRs 152/sq ft for temporary buildings. A value of SLRs
250/sq ft was used for buildings under construction. The proportion of
buildings affected, by category, was estimated to be: permanent (55 per
cent); semi-permanent (17 per cent); temporary (15 per cent); and under
construction (13 per cent). Using these figures, a weighted average value
per square foot for all structures was computed to be SLRs 487. The EIA
also estimated the distribution of structures affected in relation to floor
area, as shown in Table 7.6.

Table 7.6 *Estimated Structures to be Affected*

Range of floor area (square feet)	Average floor area (square feet)	Number of structures of this area	Total floor area
0–500	250	557	139,250
500–1000	750	403	302,250
1000+	1500	608	91,200
Total		1568	1,353,500

On this basis, the weighted average value per square foot (SLRs 487) was applied to the aggregate area of all affected structures (1,353,500 square feet) to obtain a total value of approximately SLRs 660 million (or US$13.2 million) for structures to be lost (taken in year 3). The total recalculated costs associated with the conversion of both agricultural and non-agricultural lands is: SLRs 41.6 million as the present value of forgone agricultural production; SLRs 660 million for lost commercial/residential structures; and SLRs 598 million for the land upon which these structures rest. This totals approximately SLRs 1.3 billion (or approximately US$26 million) – more than double the original estimate.

Water Pollution and Change in Fishery Productivity

The EIA raised a number of questions concerning water quality changes during both the construction and operation phases, and their possibly adverse effects on human health and the productivity of aquatic systems. The EIA noted that the Expressway would cross the two key tributaries to Negombo Lagoon, a major estuary on the West Coast of Sri Lanka and source of a valuable fishing economy. Although the project proponents maintained in the feasibility studies that these two waterways would be unaffected by the new highway, the EIA did raise several issues, including: the potential for erosion and runoff from construction site surfaces carrying soil, silt, oil products, construction chemicals, and cement (wash down); changes in community sewage patterns possibly leading to shallow groundwater contamination and related health problems; effects on fishery productivity or contamination of fish (affecting their value) due to toxic pollutants; and the creation of stagnant pools which could serve as breeding grounds for disease-carrying mosquitos (malaria and dengue fever being very real concerns in Sri Lanka).

Of these water pollution issues raised, the only potential damage with costs amenable to quick estimation with available data is the change in fishery productivity. To be properly undertaken, even this valuation exercise would require a reasonably clear dose-response function linking water pollution damages to changes in fishery production. In the absence of such information, the potential damage to the Negombo Lagoon fishery was examined based on an assessment of the extent to which fishery production appears to rely on a steady flow of good quality water emanating from the lagoon's two main tributaries. The EIA indicated that the Negombo lagoon estuary ecosystem is maintained by the regular inflow of fresh water into the marsh at the deltas of the two tributaries.

The gross earnings from the lagoon fishery are in the order of SLRs 100 million per year (US$2 million). Thus even a one per cent reduction due to reduced water quality – beginning in the fourth year and then recurring throughout the remaining 32-year project life – would amount to a significant environmental cost associated with the project. The estimated loss of SLRs 1 million per year represents a plausible value for environmental damages from changes in water quality resulting from the project, especially considering that other potential costs from increased water pollution identified in the EIA have not been valued.

Alternative Method for Calculating Project Benefits

It was assumed from the start that the new Expressway would be a toll road, even though toll free traffic flow estimates were used in all economic analyses. Though no contingent valuation was conducted to estimate willingness to pay for use of the new highway at alternative toll levels, a model was developed using the estimated benefits from the project (and other factors) to predict Expressway (and Highway A3) use under alternative average toll levels.

The introduction of a hypothetical toll for the Expressway allows an alternative method to be used, to estimate benefits based on willingness to pay for use of the new road. In fact, the project proponents wasted an ideal opportunity to gather such information during project design. A detailed survey was conducted of Highway A3 users to calculate the Origin-Destination matrices used in projecting demand for the Colombo–Katunayake corridor. It would have been a relatively simple additional measure to ask about the level of toll that users would be willing to pay for a new expressway. Such expressions of willingness to pay would have internalized the users' anticipated gains from both time savings and reduced VOCs, as well as other anticipated benefits. It could have been used as an alternative means for projecting near-term demand for and benefits from the new Expressway.

Because of the interdependence of these estimates and the original benefits estimates, extreme care must be taken in using the available 'demand' figures to rethink the calculation of project benefits. However, such projections offer an attractive alternative to the VOC and time savings approaches to benefits estimation, because they allow for a direct calculation of the social surplus (consumer and producer surpluses) generated by construction of the Expressway. There is an additional problem in this case because of economies of scale in providing the road's services. But if the marginal cost of road service provision is assumed to be fixed and is estimated based on the project's cost figures (and if the demand projections can be believed), the consumer surplus can be estimated by measuring the difference between the marginal cost per vehicle of providing the Expressway service and the implied demand for this service at all prices.

Using the feasibility study's 'demand' figures, and assuming a roughly estimated fixed cost of SLRs 5 per vehicle, the undiscounted consumer surplus in the year 2000 would amount to approximately SLRs 500 million (or US$10 million) and the corresponding value for the year 2010 would be SLRs 2.125 billion (or approximately US$42.5 million). No attempt has been made to recalculate the present value streams of benefits based on these figures, but it is worth taking account of the possibilities presented by such an approach – especially since any toll road project will need to generate demand estimates in order to evaluate the project's financial viability. It is interesting to note that these estimates of benefits based on consumer surplus are much lower for the year 2000, but only slightly lower for the year 2010, than those used in the original cost-benefit analysis. The annual VOC benefits estimated for the year 2000 were SLRs 1.168 billion and time savings were estimated to be SLRs 124 million. The corresponding figures for the year 2010 were SLRs 2.261 billion and SLRs 230 million, respectively. This would appear to reflect some inconsistencies in the data used to estimate the economic versus financial viability of the project.

Summary of Project Evaluation Extensions

In extending the original cost-benefit analysis for the project, we have replaced the SLRs 548 million land compensation costs with the following recalculated and newly identified and valued economic costs associated with the project (one-time costs or present values in parenthesis):

- Noise and air pollution (SLRs 40 million).
- Conversion of agricultural lands (SLRs 4.6 million per year, with present value of SLRs 41.6 million).
- Conversion of non-agricultural lands (SLRs 660 million) and structures (SLRs 598 million).
- Water pollution (present value of SLRs 8.1 million).

Several other environmental impacts were identified but not valued in the extended analysis. The EIA pointed out the possibility of significant negative impacts associated with the collection and transport of highway building materials: rock, earth and sand. Particular concern was raised over the mining of significant volumes of river sand for the project and the potential effects of this activity on river turbidity, scouring rates, groundwater recharge, and delta formation. Project proponents were asked to ensure that such adverse impacts were minimized through appropriate mitigatory measures, but these were not clearly specified nor costed (ie, it is not clear if such costs have been internalized in the feasibility study's figures). It remains unclear how much these costs, whether they remain external or are internalized, would affect the project's economic viability. The other potentially significant negative environmental impact identified but not valued was the loss of biologically diverse wetlands, but it did not appear that the route chosen for the Expressway would likely result in a major loss of such ecosytems. There is also an unvalued benefit associated with lower health costs or perceived welfare gains from reduced risk of highway accidents (costs to equipment are partially covered by the VOC calculations). Though an estimate of accident probabilities on Highway A3 might well have been feasible, based on alternative use levels, the full project benefits (including the Expressway) would have been difficult to calculate because there are no comparable divided highways in Sri Lanka to help predict the frequency and severity of accidents on the Expressway in a with-project versus without-project framework.

Results of Extended Cost-Benefit Analysis

When the streams of benefits and costs associated with all of the additional direct impacts identified and valued are built into the project economic analysis, the following results emerge as compared to the original cost-benefit analysis:

	Net Present Value	EIRR (%)
Original CBA	SLRs 3,309 million	18.96
Extended CBA	SLRs 2,342 million	16.12

In the absence of information concerning alternative investment opportunities, it is not possible to say whether this revised project appraisal indicates whether the project should still be considered viable on economic grounds. The EIRR is still in a range where the project cannot be rejected outright, even with the additional environmental and land conversion costs built into the project appraisal. This investment opportunity still must be compared with other options, subject to budget constraints on public funds.

CONCLUSIONS

Comparing the Conventional and Extended Cost-Benefit Analyses

Based on the limited recalculations made in this case study, the results of the conventional and 'extended' cost-benefit analyses differed only on the basis of some additional costs identified and incorporated into the analysis. Several questions were raised, however, about the underlying assumptions used for benefits estimates in the conventional cost-benefit analysis. Based on the demand estimates used in testing the project's financial viability (to examine revenues generated by alternative toll rates for the new highway), it appears that the VOC and time savings estimates may have been overstated. On the other hand, there may well have been some undercounting of benefits from reduced traffic on the existing Highway A3, though it was difficult to determine the exact methods used in the project appraisal in the absence of a clear with-project versus without-project framework.

Environmental Considerations in Highway Projects

More generally, this case study has afforded an opportunity to review most of the major environmental considerations that normally arise in the design of highway projects. These include the potential benefits or costs associated with changes in pollution levels (air, water, and noise) as well as forgone benefits from the lands and associated assets, which must be converted from some current use to the new road or its right-of-way. The choice of appropriate spatial boundaries for the analysis of project environmental impacts deserves special mention. To more accurately reflect the true social costs and benefits associated with a development project, it is important that the economic analysis includes not only impacts on the area immediately adjacent to the highway, but also on areas used as sources of building materials and their transport routes, on the area downwind or downstream from the highway, and on the environments around other roads which will see altered traffic patterns as a result of the new highway. It is also important to note that highway projects will often result in some environmental improvements, particularly if slower, congested traffic is replaced by faster, more fuel efficient and cleaner-burning vehicle patterns. Such impacts should be carefully analysed in a with-project and without-project framework, and the with-project scenario should preferably include major design alternatives for evaluation.

Environmental Economic Analysis to Support Evaluation of Development Projects

The feasibility studies on which this case relied did not provide a wide range of with-project design options for analysis. This illustrates the analytical disadvantage of considering too few options and too narrow a range of potential impacts. EIAs and efforts to place economic values on project impacts should be conducted at the earliest possible stage of project design. Too often, EIAs are conducted well after most design decisions have been made, which severely limits the usefulness of either EIAs or extended cost-benefit analyses as a means for improving a project's net benefits (though they can still improve the basis for well informed decision making).

No clear operational relationship has yet emerged between EIAs and extended cost-benefit analysis. Major international donors, such as the World Bank and Asian Development Bank, are moving towards requiring the monetization of environmental impacts whenever feasible, but they are still struggling with how best to integrate the two types of environmental analysis. There is also the issue of available capacity to conduct valuation studies, even if they are required. In practical terms, it seems that the use of the 'benefits transfer' approach to estimating values (in which values obtained through in-depth studies on one project site are adjusted and used in another) will probably expand rapidly in the next few years. Extensive EIA training has been conducted in Asia, but there remains a shortage of environmental economists trained in valuation techniques and the practical skills needed to incorporate the results of such analysis into project design. Although this case study has not presented valuation methods in any detail, the authors hope that the paper illustrates how a systematic framework for the economic analysis of environmental impacts should be constructed and that this study will assist efforts to expand the use of extended cost-benefit analysis for the economic appraisal of road and highway projects, as well as the evaluation of public and private investments in other development sectors.

Acknowledgements

The initial version of this case (Sivagnanasothy, 1993) was prepared with support from the US Agency for International Development under its Natural Resources and Environmental Policy Project in Sri Lanka, and this current expansion of the analysis has been supported by the United Nations Environment Programme. While the authors are thankful to both sponsors and to Sri Lankan Government authorities and others for providing support as well as access to the information needed to prepare this case study, they retain full responsibility for its content and shortcomings.

NOTES

1   Ateneo de Manila University.
2   Resources, Environment and Economics Center for Studies, Inc.
3   See glossary for a brief explanation of dose-response functions.
4   Perch is the local measure of land area; there are 390 perches in a hectare.

References

Asian Development Bank (1996) *Economic Evaluation of Environmental Impacts: A Workbook*. ADB, Manila.

Dixon, J A, Scura, F L, Carpenter, R A and Sherman, P B (1996) *Economic Analysis of Environmental Impacts*. Earthscan, London.

Japan International Cooperation Agency (JICA) (1984) *Feasibility Study for the Colombo-Katunayake Expressway*. JICA, Colombo.

McCauley, D S (1995) Environmental Economics and Environmental Impact Assessment: Seeking Complementarity, in Hay, J (ed) Network for Environmental Training at the Tertiary Level in the Asia-Pacific Region (NETTLAP): Report of the Environmental Economics Thematic Group Meeting. United Nations Environment Programme, Bangkok.

Organization for Economic Cooperation and Development (OECD) (1995) *The Economic Appraisal of Environmental Projects and Policies: A Practical Guide*. OECD, Paris.

Road Development Authority (RDA) (1991) *Review Study of the Previous Feasibility Study: Consultancy Services for the Colombo-Katunayake Expressway Construction Project*. RDA, Colombo.

Road Development Authority (RDA) (1993) *Environmental Impact Analysis of the Colombo-Katunayake Expressway*. RDA, Colombo.

Sivananasothy, V (1993) Extended Benefit-Cost Analysis of a Highways Project: A Case Study of the Colombo-Katunayake Expressway in Sri Lanka. Working Paper, USAID Natural Resources and Environmental Policy Project: Colombo.

Part III

Eastern and Central Europe
Case Studies

8

An Economic Assessment of the Natural Resources of the Baltic Oil Shale Basin: Case Study of Estonia

Maye Kjabbi[1]

Oil Shale in Estonia

Estonia is a small Baltic state, one of the former republics of the USSR, now bordering Russia, Latvia and (by sea) Finland. Estonia is relatively rich in mineral and other natural resources, and indeed mineral resources have provided the basis for its economic development. The most important mineral resource deposits – oil shale, phosphorite, dictyonema shale and carbonate rocks – are found in the north and north-east of the country. The oil shale stocks in Estonia are the largest exploited deposits in the world. Eighty per cent of Estonia's mined oil shale supports the country's energy production and the other 20 per cent supports its chemical industries. It is important to mention that the Baltic Oil Shale Basin extends through Estonia and into the Leningradskaya oblast of Russia, as one continuous natural complex, so the issues of its development should be considered jointly by Russia and Estonia.

While Estonia's oil shale mines cover only 1.5 per cent of the country, a much larger area is affected by the extraction. For example, an area of 300 km² has been scarred by the mining and this area is constantly increasing.

Environmental Problems of Oil Shale Extraction

There are a number of environmental problems associated with oil shale extraction, including loss of land (especially forest land), loss of soil, reduction of animal populations, and depletion of groundwater and surface water reserves. There are also serious problems linked to the loss of non-renewable natural resources, such as limestone, sand, and peat.

Most of these environmental impacts of oil shale extraction are not taken into account in the existing methodology of oil shale deposit valuation and pricing.

Valuing Estonia's Oil Shale Deposits

The value of the main kinds of natural resources of the oil shale basin are presented in Table 8.1. The current size of oil shale stocks in Estonia is approximately 100 million tonnes, the traditional economic value of which is about US$6 per tonne. Other natural resources are consumed or lost during oil shale extraction, and the total cost of depleting these other resources is approximately US$11.2 per tonne of oil shale extracted. So, in order to internalize these external costs, it would be necessary to almost triple the current price of one tonne of oil shale. This would then make the opportunity costs of oil shale extraction higher than the benefits. Obviously the current methods used to assess the efficiency of oil shale mining, which do not take into account the environmental externalities, need substantial revision to enable them to reflect these costs.

Table 8.1 *Quantity and Value of the Natural Resources of Estonia's Baltic Oil Shale Basin*

Natural resource	Quantity	Value (US$/ha)	Total resource value (thousand US$)
Land			
Agricultural	1005 ha	35.2	35,387.3
Forest	2337 ha	16.9	39,498.6
Bioresources	2337 ha	100.0	233,700.0
Mineral resource losses			
Limestone and sand	110 million t	4.2	462,000.0
Peat (for fertilizer)	16 million t	22.0	352,000.0
Total			1,122,585.0

DESCRIPTION OF THIS STUDY

Objective

The aim of this case study is to propose a new methodology for the valuation of natural resource complexes such as oil shale, which can support the internalization of environmental externalities and the search for solutions to the environmental problems concerned with the use of these natural resource complexes.

The proposed methodology would contribute to economically and environmentally rational decision-making on the development of complex natural resources that combine non-renewable resources (such as minerals) and renewable resources. Specifically, the valuation methodology would assist efforts to:

- conserve forests and wildlife, by introducing more efficient extraction technologies or by preventing extraction when it is not justified from an environmental and economic standpoint (once the externalities have been internalized);
- conserve soils and land;
- conserve other mineral resources; and
- increase agricultural production.

Socio-Economic Context

The production and processing of mineral resources constitute a considerable share of Estonia's GDP. Natural resource based sectors contributed about half of the country's GDP at the beginning of the 1990s (though the output of these sectors has since fallen in both relative and absolute terms). The current socio-economic situation in Estonia can be described as a process of transition to a market economy and democratization. However, this transition has not been accompanied by appropriate changes in the regulation of natural resource use. Estonia's natural resources are not being managed in a sustainable manner, in part because of an inadequate institutional and legal framework for regulation. Thus, the successful implementation of the proposed valuation methodology will depend to some degree on positive changes in the institutional and legal framework in Estonia. In its favour, Estonia possesses the required scientific and information base and the technical know-how to be able to make use of these new methodological approaches.

The Need for a New Approach to Natural Resource Valuation

A brief analysis of oil shale exploitation and the existing system of natural resource taxation reveals a lack of economic incentives for the rational use of natural resources or for increasing the efficiency of production.

To improve natural resource taxation it is necessary to provide an integrated account of all the qualitative and quantitative characteristics of natural resources on the basis of inventories, statistical accounting, and annual balances of changes in the level of stocks.

As for mineral resources, it is necessary to revalue stocks, since the accounting methods that were used in the former Soviet Union were based on wholesale prices of mineral production and the costs of geological prospecting, extraction and processing of mineral resources. Other affected natural resources were not taken into account, and were therefore not valued. This approach resulted in the overvaluation of mineral resources, including the Baltic oil shale basin.

Methodology

The theoretical approach used to determine the value of land used for oil shale prospecting and extraction includes the following set of physical and economic parameters:

Physical parameters
- area of land used for geological prospecting and mining (ha);
- area of land which will need to be restored (ha);
- area of land where the topsoil has been removed (ha);
- amount of soil used for land reclamation (m³);
- area of land used per unit of oil shale production (ha/1000 tonnes of oil shale).

Economic parameters (expressed in the national currency)
Cd = the costs of damage compensation (ie for damage caused by withdrawing land from agricultural production), calculated on the basis of regional market prices for agricultural products which could have been grown on the lost land;

Cr = the current expenditures and capital costs of reclamation (ie the costs of reclamation project preparation, and the technical and biological reclamation);

Cc = state compensation payments to owners of land which has been withdrawn for mining works, on account of land nationalization.

So, when valuing oil shale stocks, the total value of withdrawn lands, Ct is determined by:

$$Ct = Cd + Cr + Cc$$

This valuation can also be expressed in per unit parameters by dividing by the quantity of oil shale extracted:

$$Cu = Ct : Q$$

where Q = the total quantity of shale extracted in the withdrawn land.

The extraction of shale requires the pumping out of groundwater, and results in the pollution of both groundwater and surface water resources. Some of this polluted water is later purified in special ponds, but there is still a considerable pollution problem. Approximately 30 per cent of the water used in surface mining operations is left in a polluted state and more than 5 per cent of the water used for underground extraction is polluted in the mining process. Therefore, it is necessary to value this damage done to both surface water and groundwater reserves, by using the following formula:

$$Cw = Cwr + Cl + Cer - Pw$$

where:
Cwr = the reproduction costs of the water resources;
Cl = the value of direct losses of water resources;
Cer = the costs of ecosystem restoration (because of the depletion of flora and fauna populations, due to marsh formation); and
Pw = the benefit from the sale of purified water.

Quarry mining of oil shale and the burning of oil shale at power stations lead to considerable air pollution in the area of the oil shale basin and adjoining territories. The costs of air pollution control measures need to be internalized in the overall costs of both mining and energy production.

Forecasts show that even by the year 2005, air pollution will exceed air quality standards, despite a relative decrease in oil shale production. As a first step, it is necessary to stabilize these emissions, and in the longer term, new methods of processing mineral resources and the associated by-products will need to be developed.

The proposed methodology for valuing the by-products used or the wastes produced during oil shale extraction and processing is based on the direct and indirect costs of these by-products and wastes, including limestone (used during the extraction process) and shale ash (produced from the burning of oil shales). The relevant prices can be determined on the basis of substitutes or the estimated efficiency in their use by different consumers.

It seems reasonable to recommend the introduction of a parameter of 'environmental expenditure rate' for mining production, when planning new mining enterprises and when evaluating existing mining operations. In general, the parameter 'environmental expenditure' (N) can be calculated using the following formula:

$$N = \frac{Pm + Ct + Cw + Cp + Ca + Cg - Pb}{Q}$$

where:
Pm = payments for mineral resources (on the basis of rental valuation);
Ct = the total costs associated with land use and damage;
Cw = the total costs associated with water use and the impact on water resources;
Cp = the valuation of lost peat;
Ca = the costs of air pollution control;

Cg = the costs of geological prospecting works;
Pb = valuation of by-products;
Q = the output (extraction) of oil shale (in units of national currency).

CRITIQUE OF THE STUDY

Comprehensiveness of Proposed Methodology

From the theoretical point of view, the proposed methodology provides a high degree of comprehensiveness, as it can account for an unlimited number of factors. However, only the main factors were taken into account in this study: damage to soils and agricultural land through the loss of agricultural production; the reduction of animal populations; and the loss of non-renewable resources (limestone, sands, and peat).

Treatment of Time Aspects

The treatment of time factors, especially where environmental and natural resource issues are concerned, is disputable, at least in the economics of former Soviet Union countries. Discounting has been avoided in this study because it is impossible to substantiate the implementation of any discount rate. Aside from problems associated with the inflation process and the economic stagnation common in these countries, one particular factor makes discounting of questionable use. This is the increasing scarcity of natural resources, which means that the future values of these disappearing resources will increase.

Methodology

The proposed methodology is an attempt to take into account all possible environmental and economic externalities of oil shale extraction. On the one hand, this is not a new approach from the theoretical point of view. On the other hand, it creates the possibility of making economically and environmentally justified decisions on the development of oil shale deposits, since this method has been designed as a means of weighing all the factors associated with oil shale extraction.

The appropriate implementation of the methodology will depend on the methods used for valuing the various external factors. Some of these factors can be directly or indirectly valued through market prices of certain goods. However, for non-market goods, different valuation methodologies can be applied. In some cases the so-called contingent valuation method (CVM) can be used, but the author prefers the method based on accounting for reproduction costs. The latter is more in line with the principles of sustainable development, because it creates the necessary conditions for reproducing renewable natural resources, while the CVM (especially in countries in transition) is not able to identify the costs of restoring these natural resources. However, as the replacement cost method still needs to be improved, and some key data were not available for this valuation, the assessment made is rather a rough one. The application of more advanced methodological approaches, while technically feasible, given Estonia's scientific expertise, is currently unaffordable.

NOTE

1   State Committee for Environment Protection, Russia.

REFERENCES

Kjabbi, M (1990) *Planning of Natural Resource Use in the Mining Industry.* Nedra ('Subsurface Resources') Publishers, Moscow (in Russian).

IUCN (1993) *Environmental Status Reports. Volume Five: Estonia, Latvia, Lithuania.* IUCN East European Programme, United Kingdom.

Environmental Information Centre of Ministry of the Environment of Estonia (1994) *Estonian Mineral Resources.* Tallinn.

Environmental Information Centre (1994) *Estonian Environment 1993.* Tallinn.

The Pandivere State Water Protection Area (1993) Jyvaskyla, Finland.

The Planning Inspectorate (Department of the Environment) (1994) *Planning Appeals: A Guide.* Great Britain.

United Nations Economic Commission for Europe (1992) *Regional Cooperation to Promote Environmental Protection and Sustainable Development.* United Nations, New York.

9

Valuation of Natural Resources of the Moscow Region of Russia

Olga Medvedeva[1]

Natural Resources of the Moscow Region

This study focuses on the valuation of natural resources in the Moscow Region – an administrative unit of the Russian Federation, and one of the most heavily depleted and contaminated areas of Russia. The Moscow Region, including the city of Moscow, covers 47,000 km² and has a population of about 16 million people. Enterprises representing almost all sectors of industry are located in this region. The main natural resources present are forests, game, wild mushrooms and berries, herbs, wetlands and meadows. The region is also home to some rare and endangered species of plants and animals.

The distinctive feature of the Moscow Region is the combination of Russia's largest metropolis with a heavily forested territory rich in flora and fauna. In fact, forest areas in the Region amount to 2,220,800 hectares, or 42 per cent of the land area. However, in recent years the natural resource potential has been under threat as a result of irrational land use and environmental policies and the virtually uncontrolled privatization of land, which has already led to significant losses in valuable habitats, including forests. The forested land near Moscow performs recreational and ecological functions as well as providing raw materials.

The recreational use of these woods is very important for the economy of the city of Moscow, with its 15 million population. On a fine summer weekend about 5 million people leave the city to spend time enjoying this environmental amenity. The most popular recreational activities include walking, hiking, boating, fishing and hunting. There are more than 130 controlled hunting areas, and the Moscow region ranks as one of the most intensively hunted areas in the Eastern part of Russia, as measured by game output per unit of hunting area. Another use of the forest is the collection of wild flora. The amount of mushrooms, berries, herbs and hay harvested by the local population varies between tens of thousands of tons to hundreds of thousands of tons in a summer season. Up to 70 per cent of the holiday makers visit recreational areas within 1 to 2 hours' travel from Moscow, where much of the recreational infrastructure exists.

The woods in the Moscow area are also important for regulating and preserving the ecological balance in this highly industrialized region. They perform water-preserving and sanitation functions, as well as air-cleaning for the entire Moscow urban area.

Despite their significant ecological and recreational roles, the forests are heavily exploited. Forest felling averages 2.0–2.2 million m³ per annum, including 1.2 million m³ of timber and 1.0 million m³ of firewood. Valuable coniferous trees constitute the major part of the offtake. Until recently, 50 per cent of the province's demand for timber was obtained from the forest resources near Moscow.

CURRENT METHODS USED FOR NATURAL RESOURCE VALUATION

The methods of natural resource valuation currently being used in Russia are far from perfect and are generally confined to timber valuation. Their applications are limited to calculating charges such as stumpage fees and forest land tax rates. Forest use charge rates are calculated on the basis of unit prices for the forest products obtained, and the rates vary according to the forest uses and the geographical conditions. The stumpage value technique is the most widely used. The forest valuation is made by calculating the difference between the prices of timber products and the average costs of their production (including wages, costs of materials, energy, and depreciation). Lately, local authorities have been establishing charge rates according to the results of forest auctions. Thus, the values of forest plots are determined by evaluating their timber stocks, by organizing auctions to sell the standing timber. In these cases, the forest use charge is simply a stumpage fee. The forest land tax is established for commercial forests on the basis of the forest use charge rates and set at 5 per cent of the stumpage fee. So the forest land tax is also based on timber value.

Valuations of some species of animals and plants are carried out, mainly to establish licence fees and fines for their extraction or destruction. The methodology used in these calculations usually involves fixing an indicator (such as the minimum wage rate, to measure the economic significance of these species as multiples of the minimal wage rate). These values obviously do not reflect the real value of the species and so can not be used in the economic analysis of projects involving the use of natural resources.

Likewise, the value of forests in the Moscow region is traditionally referred to only in terms of the amount of timber harvested. Other forest functions are rarely taken into account. This leads to the allocation of forest lands for activities that are not compatible with the conservation of its biological and recreational potential.

Recognizing the need to base land management and taxation policies on the true value of the natural resources involved, the authorities have requested economists to undertake valuations of the biological and recreational functions performed by the forests in the Moscow Region. These valuations can then help the authorities to:

- make rational decisions on the use of recreational land in the Moscow Region;
- determine the size of compensatory payments to be made when municipal lands are transferred to federal ownership;
- differentiate land tax rates and land rents in the Moscow Region;
- determine the amount of effort required to restore the forest parks' ecosystems;
- establish fines for the illegal appropriation of land and violations of land legislation in park territories.

Considerable experience has been accumulated to date, particularly in the USA and Western Europe, in the valuation of recreational functions of forests. However, many of the methods developed are expensive and labour intensive, making them impractical in the context of Russia's economic recession. Another serious impediment to using these valuation methods is the lack of 'markets' for recreational and environmental services in the Moscow Region, and, as a consequence, a lack of information to make the necessary calculations.

DESCRIPTION OF THIS STUDY

Objective

The purpose of the case study is to present and discuss integrated methods of natural resource valuation, by illustrating how these methods can be used to take into account the recreational and ecological functions of the forest resources in the Moscow Region.

The main aims of this case study are therefore to:

- present objective valuations of the recreational and ecological potential of heavily populated urban areas;
- discuss the potential applications of valuations which take into account the non-marketed uses of natural resources; and

- calculate normative parameters that can simplify the process of valuing the ecological and recreational functions of forest areas.

Methodology

The kinds of forest parks and park territories near Moscow can not be valued in the same way as other less-visited forest areas, due to the diverse uses they perform. The following general principles have been applied in this study to value the Region's forests:

- valuation of the biological resources is carried out using the main theoretical principles and techniques of real estate valuation, to consider both the direct and indirect uses of these resources;
- valuation of the recreational resources is carried out by calculating their aggregated biological potential value, including soils, flora and fauna;
- in the case of commercial exploitation of a given forest area, the value of its aggregate biological potential is added to the market price of neighbouring unforested land;
- the most acceptable methods for valuing the forest areas in the Moscow Regions are those which deal with reproduction costs, rent discounting, and transport costs;
- valuations are carried out using several methods simultaneously, to check the validity of the results and to calculate the parameters of different kinds of biological resource value.

Reproduction Cost Method

Valuation of natural resources by the replacement (or reproduction) cost method is done by determining the necessary hypothetical expenditures to create artificial analogues of the same volume and with the same set of consumer properties as the natural resource. In other words, the method involves measuring the costs which society would need to spend yearly on some hypothetical replacement, to completely compensate for the extinction of the resource in question. For example, the valuation of *rare and endangered animal species* by this method consists of firstly determining the minimum population size for each species to enable it to be removed from the endangered category. Let us call this the threshold number of a given species. Then the discounted costs of artificially breeding or keeping in captivity one individual of the species is multiplied by the threshold number to arrive at the total costs of restoring and preserving this species in the wild.

Applying this approach to game species and other economically useful species consists of determining the discounted costs of breeding all the game species living in a given area. The valuation is based on the costs of creating artificial analogues for every species on, for example, fur farms or nurseries. These costs for every species are then added up to calculate the total costs needed for the hypothetical restoration of the hunting resources:

$$C = \sum_{i=1}^{n} Ni * Ki$$

where:
C = reproduction cost of hunting animals;
Ki = capitalized (discounted) costs of artificially breeding the ith species;
Ni = population size of the ith species.

In the case of species for which no artificially bred analogues exist, it is possible to apply some coefficients, calculated on the basis of the weight, size, fodder consumption and other characteristics of the animals in question.

The reproduction cost method can also be used to value *wood and other vegetative resources*, in several ways:

• a valuation based on the cost of installing and growing forest stands of the given tree species' structure and age;
• a valuation based on the cost of growing each separate species in nurseries;
• a valuation based on the cost of reproducing the cumulative biomass of an existing forest.

Applying the reproduction cost method to *entire ecosystems* involves determining the total value of the biological resources of a given ecosystem on the basis of the hypothetical costs of artificially producing all the organic matter naturally produced by that ecosystem. The aggregate biomass of an ecosystem is determined by dry organic matter stocks, contained in separate components of the ecosystem, using the following formula:

$$B = Ba + Bg + Bw + i$$

where:
Ba = biomass of animals, micro-organisms and algae;
Bg = biomass of herbaceous vegetation;
Bw = biomass of wood plants;
i = humus reserve.

Knowing the biomass parameters and the reproduction costs of each component of the ecosystem, it is then possible to value the aggregate potential of biological resources of any area. Since the key characteristic of an ecosystem is the ratio between aggregate biomass and humus stocks (Kovda, 1974), it is possible to use data on reproduction costs of only one component, such as soil humus, if data on the reproduction costs of some other components are not available. Then the reproduction cost of an ecosystem is calculated using the formula:

$$Cr = Cs / Hs$$

where:
Cr = reproduction costs of the ecosystem;
Cs = reproduction costs of soil;
Hs = the proportion of soil humus in the total biomass of the ecosystem.

This calculation relies on the availability of information on the costs of artificial humus production. This method was tested to obtain an aggregate resource potential for Russia and other CIS countries, as well as a value for health resorts in Russia, at the initial stage of developing a land market (Misko, 1991).

Discounted Income Method

In its application to biological resources, the discounted income method consists of determining the profits that could be obtained from the use of a natural resource over the duration of a project, and then discounting future costs and incomes to a certain year. It is essentially a form of cost-benefit analysis. A simplified version of this method is the discounting (or capitalizing) of the expected rent over the time period.

The method of future income discounting is usually applied when making decisions on buying real estate that is expected to bring in some income. Therefore, when valuing biological resources by this method it is expedient to consider the income that could be expected from the exploitation of biological resources, including for example, income from timber, hunting, and recreational uses.

Valuations obtained from these techniques can be presented in either relative or absolute terms. In the latter case, the estimated value of a biological resource corresponds to the price of a piece of land occupied by the given resource, determined by capitalizing (discounting) a profit or rent from the exploitation of the land. The discounting rate should be determined each time, to correspond to the purposes of the valuation and the territory's development pattern. In the case of the commercial use of a territory the discounting rate (or the 'coefficient of capitalization') can be determined by the payback period of capital investment in the given area, selected at the existing bank discount rate. For non-commercial uses of a territory, the discount rate should be related to the length of time required to restore the exploited ecosystems.

Indirect Valuation Methods

Indirect valuation methods, including contingent valuation, usually involve questionnaire surveys, administered to representative groups of the population, on the values of certain biological resources and on the time and money spent on getting to a recreational site. The travel cost technique is considered the most appropriate type of indirect valuation for the conditions in the Moscow region.

This method facilitates fairly objective valuations of the most valuable recreational territories, not only on the basis of interviews on the assumed costs of a natural resource, but also on the basis of observations and records of actual visitation rates for the sites. Data on transport availability and reports on the recreational load of specific areas, prepared in the course of research work on recreational travel patterns in the Moscow Region, can serve as the main sources of information.

Travel Cost Method

On the basis of data available on visits to recreational forests, the average time spent on the trip and transport charges incurred in reaching the sites, it is possible to offer the following method to value forest areas in the Moscow Region.

The value of forest areas in the Region as a whole is calculated as the sum of the value of the closest, most heavily visited forest park belt within a radius of one hour access by transport, and the value of the outlying districts of the forested zone, located within a radius of 2 to 3 hours' accessibility.

The valuation is based on assessing the vacationers' costs in purchasing gasoline for the round trip by car to a recreational area, as well as the time spent on the trip (expressed in terms of an average daily wage).

Calculating the total recreational value of forest areas, using the transport cost technique, consists of the following stages:

1   Determining the most heavily visited area of the forest park zone (ie the area within a radius of 1 hour access by transport). For the Moscow Region, this comprises 75,600 hectares.
2   Calculating the total number of holiday makers, on the basis of data on the average visitation density in forest parks (on a summer weekend, this amounts to 30 persons per ha), as well as the total number of holiday makers in the area during an entire summer season (counting only days off, ie about 12 to 24 days, this figure is between 2.7 to 5.4 million people). This figures corresponds well with data provided by local authorities.
3   Calculating the total costs of travel to recreational sites in the Region. These costs are determined on the basis of market prices of a litre of gasoline, multiplied by the average mileage and by the the fuel consumption per mile. This amounts to an average of US$4 per person, or US$10.8 to US$21.6 million for all vacationers.

An average daily income multiplied by the number of summer vacationers should be added to these figures. The daily income under the current conditions in Russia can be derived by taking an average daily income from selling goods at a market place, as this activity can be regarded as an alternative to taking a day off, for many people in the Moscow Region. The average daily income from trade at a market place is US$44 per person.

Therefore, the alternative value of recreation is between US$118.8 million and US$237.6 million. However, it is not possible to conclude that all holiday makers can earn money this way. Taking into account the fact that only half of the four people in an average family are adults, with a constant source of income, the previous figures should be halved. Therefore, the value of recreational resources amounts to between US$59.1 million and US$118.8 million. Thus, the total value of zones of intensive recreation, calculated by the transport cost method, is US$69.9 to US$140.4 million (ie 10.8 + 59.1; or 21.6 + 118.8 million). The valuation of the second, more remote forest recreation zone, conducted in the same way, gives a figure of US$2051.0 million, of which US$547.2 million cover the actual travel costs and US$1504.8 million are the alternative value of time spent vacationing in the countryside. The calculations were based on the following data:

- area of outlying forest zones   574,000 ha;
- travel time   2 hours;
- cost of gasoline   US$8;
- average vacationer density on a summer weekend   10 persons/ha;
- average number of vacation days (counting
  only Sundays)   12

The total value of recreational forest functions of the first and the second 'belts' is therefore between US$2120.9 million to US$2191.4 million, or about US$3,300 per hectare of forest. Apparently, the real recreational value of the forests may be considerably higher than this, since the number of vacation days may be as high as ninety, rather than the 12–24 range used in the calculations. However, at the same time, the average visitation rate should be decreased. Then, the total recreational value of forests, based on an average density of 5 persons per hectare daily, would be between US$12,000 to US$14,000 per hectare. These figures are quite close to the land market prices, which are fluctuating between US$10,000 and US$50,000 per ha (in the nearby and more remote areas of the Moscow region, respectively).

Opinion Survey Method
Various forms of questionnaire surveys and interviews can be used to value the recreational potential of the forest areas in the Moscow Region, by modelling the hypothetical benefits of recreational activities to

society. One of the few studies which have used a Willingness to Pay (WTP) approach to valuing the forest resources in the Moscow Region is the work by Kamennova and Martynov (1994), who used questionnaire surveys to establish average visitation rates for different uses of the forests in the Moscow Region. The researchers considered the following direct uses: hunting, fishing, mushroom gathering, and berry and nut gathering. They added the values of these uses together to estimate the total biological resource potential of the forests, and they then added the hypothetically calculated existence value. Indirect values were determined on the basis of the social consequences of recreation, including the reduction of paid sick leave and the treatment costs involved.

The existence value of the bioresources and the forest ecosystems as a whole were determined as the hypothetical income that could be earned by the population by forgoing recreational activities. For this purpose the researchers used the average wage in Moscow and the Moscow Region for the appropriate period of time. The total existence value came to between US$227 million and US$272 million, or US$103 to US$124 per hectare. The total value of bioresources, including direct, indirect, and existence values, amounted to US$621 million, or US$311 per hectare.

One shortcoming of this work by Kamennova and Martynov is their failure to account for the high level of inflation which was operating in the time period between their collection of the data and their subsequent analysis. The real inflation rate was actually ten times the official rate used by the researchers, with the result that they considerably undervalued the biological resources.

ILLUSTRATIONS OF HOW THE VALUATION METHODS CAN BE APPLIED

Valuation of Game Species

Valuing the game species present in the Moscow Region can support the following tasks:

- decision making with respect to land use in the Moscow region;
- valuing hunting territories;
- valuing land that is valuable habitat for game species;
- determining fees for the use of hunting territories;
- determining the compensatory payments for damage caused by destruction of the hunting environment.

Two alternative valuation methods are possible: the reproduction cost method, and the discounted income method.

Valuation of Game Species Using the Reproduction Cost Method

Applying the reproduction cost method to the valuation of game species in the Moscow Region involves determining the conventional capitalized costs of breeding the populations of game that exist at the beginning of a hunting season. Firstly, the average costs of breeding (at farms or nurseries) several standard species (for example, mink, fox and sable at fur farms; deer in nurseries; and ducks at game breeding farms) are determined. These costs include all current expenditures on feeding and keeping the animals, and the capital costs of the farm buildings. All costs should be discounted.

The values obtained for these standard species are then extrapolated to other species, using coefficients such as the ratio between the prices obtainable for the shot animals, or the ratio between the average weights of the animals. Then, the revealed costs of breeding one animal are multiplied by the number of wild animals present in the hunting territories, to calculate the total value of the territories. The results of valuing game species in the Moscow Region are shown in Table 9.1. The following species were used as standard ones, for the calculation of the coefficients:

Table 9.1 *Reproduction Costs of Game Species in the Moscow Region*

Species	Number (thousand head)	Coefficient of value	Reproduction cost (US$ thousand)
Otter	0.4	2.9	135.0
Squirrel	270	0.07	8578.0
Marten	4.5	1.42	998.4
Beaver	1.9	2.0	675.0
Ermine	12.5	0.25	488.3
Lynx	0.04	3.35	13.5
White hare	295.5	0.12	5540.6
Hare	47.9	0.16	1197.9
Fox	12.6	1.08	1695.2
Mink	2.9	1.0	453.1
Wolf	0.2	0.7	14.5
Racoon dog	2.9	1.78	978.8
Polecat	3.1	0.5	242.2
Muskrat	14.4	0.11	247.5
Mole	2,246	0.007	2358.0
Elk	13.5	1.0	7031.3
Wild boar	23	0.27	3234.4
Roe deer	3.7	0.07	134.9
Capercaillie	6.5	1.05	71.0
Black cock	41.9	0.48	209.5
Hazel grouse	81.3	0.24	203.9
Waterfowl and marsh game	60.9	0.2	144.0
Goose	2.0	1.0	20.8
Duck	339.5	0.6	2121.9
Woodcock	21.4	0.12	26.8
Pigeon	42.1	0.2	87.7
Total			34,351.7

mink, fox, elk and goose. The capitalized costs of mink breeding were taken to be US$156 per animal; for goose US$10.4 per bird; and for elk US$500 per animal.

Valuation of Game Species Using the Discounted Rent Method
The method of rent capitalization, as applied to game, consists of determining the potential profits obtainable from the use of hunting territories, and then discounting these profits for a particular period of time. Profits are estimated as the price of shot animals minus the costs of using and managing the hunting reserve, including costs of biotechnology and other protective and reproduction measures. The potential economic productivity of a hunting reserve, which is the key value in this method, is usually calculated as the sum of sold production (in selling prices), which it is possible to obtain by the total withdrawal of all animals permitted to be extracted:

$$V = \sum_{i=1}^{n} Ni * Ki * Pi$$

where:
V = the potential economic productivity of hunting territories;
Ni = population size of the ith species;
Ki = the rate of allowable withdrawal of animals of the ith species;
Pi = the commercial price of a shot animal of the ith species.

Estimating the potential economic productivity is made on the basis of data on the size of the game populations in the season before hunting begins (ie in the autumn), averaged over the last three to five years. Hunting rates are established as percentages of the population sizes in the autumn, and should not exceed the annual population increase rates. For migratory species, hunting rates are determined on the basis of established rates of shooting.

The selling price of shot animals is established on the basis of prices obtained at a local or regional market, by aggregating the appropriate prices for those species where different kinds of production are possible (including, for example, fur, meat, and horns). The costs of managing the hunting reserve are taken from data provided by the local government. The individual expenditures of hunters (including both amateurs and professionals) are added to the management costs.

The average bank rate is used as the coefficient of capitalization (ie the discount rate), and this was set at 13 per cent at the time at which this study was undertaken. Table 9.2 provides an example how the hunting resources in the Moscow Region can be valued by the rent capitalization method.

Table 9.2 *Rent Capitalization of Hunting Reserves in the Moscow Region*

Parameters	Value (US$)
Total price of game animals shot in the Moscow Region (per year)	6,072,000
Total annual costs of protection and management of game	2,049,000
Discount rate	0.13%
Total value of hunting reserves in the Moscow Region	30,946,000
Per hectare value of hunting reserves	7.39

Comparison of Valuation Results for Game Species
The valuation of game species in the Moscow Region using the reproduction cost method came to US$34.4 million, while the rent capitalization method gave a value of US$30.9 million. The similarity between these two results helps to confirm the validity of these two methods.

The lower value obtained by the rent capitalization method can be explained by its not taking into account the recreational value of hunting territories, or the costs of passes, licences and other incomes connected with catering to hunters. Including these kinds of incomes would allow the recreational aspects of the hunting reserves to be taken into account.

Valuation of Elk Island Using the Reproduction Cost Method
The national park 'Elk Island' is a large tract of forest on the northeast of Moscow. The park covers 11,000 hectares, including 3000 hectares within the territory of the city of Moscow. The ecosystem is in good condition, and includes typical southern taiga flora and fauna, with coniferous species and birch dominating the forest. The park is home to some bird species which are rare in the Moscow Region. Elk Island performs recreational and nature protection functions, as it acts as a natural filter for the Moscow air.

The following parameters were used for the valuation of Elk Island: the reproduction costs of mixed coniferous ecosystems; the reproduction costs of broad-leaved forests; the market price of vacant sites, based on sales of long-term leases of land in neighbouring districts of Moscow. So, the economic valuation of the park territory was calculated by summarizing the reproduction costs of its natural components and the market price of land in the northeast section of Moscow. The total economic value was estimated as US$430,200 per hectare.

The reproduction costs were calculated by extrapolating the costs of artificially reproducing humus to the costs of reproducing the whole biomass volume (measured in terms of total carbon stocks) accumulated by a given ecosystem. The data on the costs of artificial humus production were taken from Gorbunov et al (1976), modified for inflation. The data on the valuation of carbon reserves of coniferous and broad-leaved forest zones were taken from Kovda (1971). The valuation of market land price was obtained from analyses of auction data on sales of long-term leases.

The calculation of the economic valuation of 'Elk Island' is presented in Table 9.3.

Table 9.3 *Reproduction Cost of 'Elk Island'*

Components	Biomass (tons/ha)	Reproduction cost (US$/ton)	(US$/ha)
Vegetation	455.5	187.5	85,406.3
Soils	157.0	187.5	29,437.5
Micro-organisms and water plants	1.3	187.5	243.8
Animals	0.7	187.5	131.2
Total ecosystem			115,218.8
Market price of a vacant lot northeast of Moscow			315,000.0
Total value of Elk Island (US$/ha)			430,218.8

Valuation of Aurochs Using the Reproduction Cost Method
The value of rare animal species should be added to the valuation of the total biological potential of the territory, since it is impossible to obtain their real value through the parameters of biomass reserves. This is because of the need for special efforts to protect, reintroduce and increase the population sizes of these rare species. Applying the reproduction cost method to the valuation of rare animal species is illustrated here by a simplified calculation of the value of aurochs, which was carried out to assess the efficiency of a programme to restore the number of aurochs in the wild.

Data on the keeping and breeding of aurochs are based on information from the aurochs nursery, located near Moscow. The threshold number of aurochs in their natural territory (which extends through Russia, Ukraine, Byelorussia and Transcaucasian republics) was determined by specialists. The calculation of the reproduction cost of aurochs is shown in Table 9.4. This calculation does not include the costs of settling and reintroducing the aurochs, although these costs would need to be taken into account for a more detailed valuation. When valuing the biological resources of nature reserves or other areas where there are wild aurochs, the economic value of an individual auroch (ie US$50,320), multiplied by the total number of aurochs in the area, should be added to the total economic value of the territory, obtained by the reproduction cost method.

Table 9.4 *Reproduction Cost of Aurochs*

Parameters	Quantity or value
Total capitalized cost of breeding and keeping one auroch in a nursery until it is 3 years old	US$7,346.9
Total number of aurochs to be involved in the programme	10,000
Total costs of achieving the threshold number	US$73,469,000
Actual numbers of aurochs in the wild (1991)	1,460
Economic value of the species	US$50,320 per animal

NOTE

1   Ministry of the Environment, Moscow.

REFERENCES

Englin, J and Mendelsohn, R (1991) A Hedonic Travel Cost Analysis for Valuation of Multiple Components of Site Quality: The Recreation Value of Forest Management. *Journal of Environmental Economics and Management* 21: 275–290.

Gorbunov, N I, Zarubina, T G, Zapevalova, I S and Tunik, B M (1976) Land Reclamation as Part of the Problem of Rational Use of Natural Resources and Protection of Environments. *Pochvovedenie* (Soil Science) vol 1, USSR Academy of Sciences.

Kamennova, I E and Martynov A S (1994) Integrated Valuation of Willingness-to-Pay and Other Elements of Economic Valuation of the Moscow Region's Biological Resources. Report presented at the IUCN/GEF Conference on methods of economic valuation of biodiversity, Moscow.

Kovda, V A, Yanushevskaya, I V (1971) *Biomass and Humus Environment of Soil: Biosphere and its Resources.* Nauka (Science) Publishers, Moscow.

Kovda, V A (1974) Biosphere, Soils and Their Uses: Report of the President of the International Society of Soil Scientists to the International Congress of Soil Scientists, Moscow.

Lampietti, J A and Dixon, J A (1994) *A Guide to Non-Timber Forest Benefits.* Environment Department, The World Bank Washington, DC.

Medvedeva, O E (1992) Economic Valuation of a Region's Biological Resource Potential. Ph.D dissertation, Moscow State University, Moscow.

Medvedeva, O E (1994) Application of the Reproduction Cost Methods to Valuation of Biological Resources of the Moscow Region. Report presented at the IUCN/GEF conference on methods of economic valuation of biodiversity, Moscow.

Misko, K M (1991) *Resource Potential of a Region.* Nauka (Science) Publishers, Moscow.

Ministry of Forestry of the Russian Federation (1989) *The Main Rules of Organization and Development of Forestry of the Moscow Region.* Moscow.

Rodin L E, Basilevich N I (1965) *Dynamics of Organic Substance and Biological Cycle Rotation of Ash Elements and Nitrogen in the Main Types of World Flora.* Nauka (Science) Publishers, Moscow.

PART IV

LATIN AMERICA CASE STUDIES

10

Valuing the Net Benefits of Air Pollution Control in Santiago, Chile[1]

Edgar Fürst, David N Barton and Gerardo Jiménez[2]

Air Pollution Control in Santiago

Particulate concentrations in Santiago during the winter months are among the highest for any urban area in the world, due to heat inversion and lack of wind in the valley basin where the city is located. A closed valley with little wind, little rain and thermal inversions during winter months contribute to worsening the impact of emissions. Climatic conditions differ significantly from those experienced in many capitals of tropical countries in the region where heavy rains in winter months, often windy summer months, and little possibility of severe heat inversions help to reduce relative concentrations, even under equal levels of emissions.

Legal Context

Chile has a legal tradition of strong private property rights, which for policy purposes may aid market prices to move in the direction of social cost. At least, this is mostly true for *local* externalities where emissions sources and victims are clearly identifiable. However, in the case of a *pervasive* externality such as air pollution, traditional property rights are not sufficient to obtain efficient, let alone optimal, levels of pollution without additional incentives being put in place.

In this context, the Basic (Environmental) Law, which was recently passed in Chile, guarantees its citizens their constitutional right to live in an environment free of contamination. The law charges the government with the enforcement of this 'right' and with the conservation of nature (World Bank, 1994). In effect, this implies that air quality rights are allocated to potential victims of pollution and that Pareto improvements in contamination levels may be achieved through the application of the Polluter-Pays Principle.[3] The strong tradition of property rights makes it more feasible, both politically and practically, to introduce market-based instruments such as tradeable permits, or the 'compensation system' suggested in the report (World Bank, 1994).

Prior to enactment of the Basic Law, environmental policy in Chile had been delegated to sectoral ministries. There was no common monitoring system for key environmental indicators, which could have provided a basis for integrated studies. This fact makes the effort under-taken in this study, to collect the required data for the integrated modelling of pollution impacts, all the more noteworthy. In many policy situations, comparable data in developing countries are not available, and the decision-maker has to make do with transferring dose-response functions estimated for other countries. In a supporting study, Ostro et al (1995) conclude that the transfer of estimates from industrialized countries to developing urban areas such as Santiago is feasible, as long as population exposure patterns are relatively similar.

Socio-Economic Context

The Chilean economy has experienced strong economic growth during the past decade, placing it firmly among the middle income countries. The Pinochet government started an export-led policy open to foreign investment, which has been maintained by its successors. An open trade policy may have contributed to uncorrected growth-related environmental problems, although foreign investment is also expected to bring in cleaner technology. The country is experiencing environmental problems typical of countries with a rapid urban growth coupled with significant increases in private consumption. Air pollution emissions (measured by PM-10 levels) lie above the purchasing power parity weighted average for urban areas (World Bank, 1994). However, private income and living standards do not yet appear to have reached a level where there is a significant demand for environmental expenditures and where greener technology is privately profitable.

DESCRIPTION OF THE STUDY

Objectives and Focus

This chapter reviews a study by Eskeland (1994) which examined the costs and health benefits of an air pollution control strategy for Santiago, Chile. The control strategy considered targets a series of broad categories of mobile, point and group sources,[4] quantifying their costs of compliance with emissions and equipment standards, as well as the avoided costs (benefits) of lost productivity due to pollutants that are known to have acute health effects.[5] Pollutants such as CO and lead were not studied, due to a lack of monitoring data. Also, mortality was correlated to ambient pollutant levels on a daily basis, which precluded the possibility of studying chronic (long-term) health impacts such as cancer and cumulative effects to respiratory mortality. Furthermore, non-health environmental impacts, such as corrosion, and damage to vegetation and ecosystems, were not analysed.

The study offers valuable lessons for the assessment and policy design of air pollution control measures in developing countries. For example, the study shows how to estimate important parameters such as the relative priority of pollutants, the relative location-specific impact of emissions, and the overall benefits to the public from emissions reductions.

Guidelines are provided for concrete policy measures such as a 'compensation system' for emissions permits where a premium is placed on the geographical location of the emissions reductions. Also, a lower benchmark is provided for emissions taxes for individual pollutants through the expected minimum benefits per tonne due to health improvements. Increases in energy prices are also offered as a simple alternative approach.

Methodology

The study was one of the first of its kind in developing countries to use a combination of pollutant dispersion, end-point exposure, and epidemiological dose-response models to quantify health impacts, thereby allowing for a full-fledged cost-benefit analysis.[6]

The *air pollutant dispersion model* took the form of a Eulerian multi-box model to simulate the spatial dispersion of pollutants in the Santiago airshed. The airshed above Santiago is divided into a matrix of grid cells of 2x2 kilometres, and the geographical distribution of point and mobile sources is plotted by specific location or, in the case of traffic, based on flow models. The model was calibrated using meteorological data to fit actual ambient pollution levels.

Calculation of *end-point exposure* was done using weights to represent the distribution (density) of the residential population in each grid cell, thereby obtaining a measure of exposure.

The *epidemiological dose-response model* involved time-series correlation studies on the daily health effects of the four pollutants in the study. It was conservatively assumed that impacts occur only after air quality has improved beyond the level required by the existing air quality standards. Confounding effects such as temperature, month, season and day of the week were controlled for, and different functional forms were explored.

Results from these combined models indicate the feasibility of transferring dose-response functions from industrialized to developing countries where health statistics may be scarce.[7]

The health impacts were valued using the 'human capital' and 'mitigation cost' approaches. The cost effectiveness analysis was based on the common quantitative denominator of *work-day equivalents*, by which all health impacts are measured. These were then translated into the 'direct costs' of work-days lost to premature mortality and morbidity. Treatment costs (ie mitigation costs) were also reported on the basis of work-day equivalents, all costs being valued at the average daily wage rate in Chile of US$9.55.

Illnesses were differentiated to allow for partial loss of work-days in the 'cost of illness' calculation. Questions such as *how premature are pollution-related deaths* were addressed by assuming the normal distribution of expected lifetimes per affected age group.

Main Sources of Data

An analysis of the transferability of dose-response functions is based on a worldwide meta-analysis of the health effects of air pollution (Ostro, 1994). As a basis for comparison, epidemiological studies from Santiago are used to calculate site specific dose-response functions (Ostro et al, 1994; Aranda et al, 1994). Dispersion simulations (Ulriksen et al, 1994) and calculation of the unit costs of compliance with control measures (Sanchez, 1994) were also based on background studies commissioned by the World Bank, as well as independent studies (O'Ryan, 1993; Turner et al, 1993).

Main Results

The epidemiological time-series studies showed PM-10 to have the most extensive health impacts. For example, the emipirical analysis from Santiago found a 1.1 per cent increase in mortality for a 10 micrograms/m^3 increase in the three-day moving average of respirable particles (PM-10).[8] Similar values were found in a meta-analysis of health impacts of PM-10 in industrialized countries.

Average premature deaths due to air pollution were calculated at 12.9 discounted productive years and costed at an average wage rate of US$9.55/day. The costs of treatment and partially lost work-days due to morbidity were calculated in a similar fashion for a number of different acute ailments.

A cost effectiveness analysis of compliance by source and pollutant was conducted, providing an initial ranking of cost per ton of pollutant. An example for PM-10 is given in Table 10.1. The table shows variable cost effectiveness with gasoline vehicle standards being the most expensive option at US$37,000/ton PM-10. However, if the spatial distribution

of exposure is taken into account, this has a large impact on the effectiveness ranking. When weights for population exposure are included,
the marginal control costs for PM-10 reductions are approximately equal
across each broad group of emitters.

Table 10.1 *Pollution Control Scenario: Costs and PM-10 Reductions*

	Vehicles			Point sources: convert wood burning to		Combined
	1 Gasoline vehicle standards	2 Diesel truck control	3 CNG buses	4 Distillate fuel oil	5 Natural gas	6 Control strategy (1+2+3+4)
Removes (t/yr)	369	271	1.725	1.438	1.170	3.831
Costs (million US$/yr)	14	4	30	11	19	60
Costs (thousand US$/ton)*	37	17	17	8	15	16

Notes: * All strategies also have effects on other pollutants, so the cost per ton of PM–10 is not
necessarily an important indicator
Sources: Turner et al, 1993; and Ulriksen et al, 1994

Combining the cost-effectiveness and benefit calculations, the authors
calculate that PM-10 reductions are more than 10 times as valuable per
emitted tonne, in terms of health benefits, as any other pollutant (see
Table 10.2). Reductions of PM-10 produce about US$18,000 of health
benefits for every tonne reduced. For policy purposes this can be interpreted as a lower benchmark for a possible emissions tax.

Table 10.2 *Benefits by Pollutant*

Ambient Pollutant	Benefit (US$m)	Emitted pollutant	Tons reduced	Benefit/ton (US$)
PM-10	69.71	PM-10	3,831	18,192
Ozone	32.85	VOC	33,167	495*
		NO_x	12,336	1,315*
NO_x	0.726	NO_x	12,336	59
		NO_x total	12,336	1374
SO_x	0.134	SO_x	1,639	82

Note: * Calculated assuming NO_x and VOC (volatile organic compounds) contribute equally to
ozone generation. The prioritization between VOC and NOx is sensitive to this assumption, but
the prioritization between strategies in the Control Strategy is not.
Source: Eskeland, 1994

Conclusions from the cost-benefit analysis are that the health benefits
from reductions in major air pollutants (PM-10, NO_2, SO_2, and ozone)
are in the range of US$100 million annually, comparing favourably to
total control costs in the range of US$60 million. The authors conclude
that these pollution control benefits are justified on the basis of health

benefits alone, even when several other pollutants and environmental impacts were not taken into consideration.

Comprehensiveness of the Estimates

As previously indicated, the full costs of pervasive and local externalities from air pollution are not considered in the study.

The authors rightly state that the 'human capital' approach underestimates the value of improved air quality in relation to the more theoretically correct 'willingness-to-pay' approach (which captures full consumer surplus). However, they point to the important practical advantages of this approach, as well as its easy interpretation by decision-makers.

In policy terms, the comprehensiveness of the study is limited to the package of measures included in the pollution control strategy. Alternative packages are not proposed, and the performance of each of the individual control measures is not assessed. These aspects are proposed for future studies.

Treatment of Time Aspects

The treatment of time aspects does not play an important role in the study as the costs and benefits of air pollution control are calculated on an annual basis. The time-series studies of dose-response functions assume that the relative importance of the different emissions and impacts, which have been observed in the past, will continue in the future.

A 5 per cent real interest rate is used to discount the future value of lost productive years due to premature mortality.

No explicit treatment is made of irreversibilities. Threshold values for pollutants are assumed when calculating the zero level of illness. As an irreversible effect, individual mortality is considered but no single threshold level can be identified as different population groups have different levels of susceptibility. Separate treatment of the residential risk of pollution exposure is incorporated in the dose-exposure model.

Accuracy and Reliability

Confidence intervals and t-statistics are given for all dose-response functions, whether based on Santiago data, or transferred from other study sites. Sensitivity analysis is used to control for the cyclical nature of total mortality and other confounders such as temperature; to test the effectiveness of control measures weighted or unweighted for population density; and for the loss of work-day equivalents based on age group susceptibility. Sensitivity analysis was also conducted to control for outliers and alternative time-lag structures.

Finally, the meta-analysis of dose-response functions and transferred benefit estimates, lifted from secondary literature sources, was controlled to approximate the measurement and calculation criteria of the Santiago study.

Critique of the Study

Methodology

The following critique is admitted by the authors of the study itself:

- Dynamic time aspects are not taken into consideration. However, intergenerational effects are perhaps of less significance in the case of air pollution, as impacts are largely experienced by the present generation (notwithstanding the cumulative effects of pollutants such as lead on IQ levels observed in children).
- Chronic impacts of air pollution such as cancer were not analysed in the study. The question of how many life years are lost (due to premature death) because of different pollutants is an important question for the *human capital approach*, which requires further research in order to reduce confidence intervals. However, priority policy recommendations can be made with the present results.
- The pollution control strategy as a package of measures does not allow for marginal analysis of individual policy impacts. The analysis of discrete jumps (packages of measures) along the air quality axis only allows for the analysis of cost-efficiency at given levels of air quality. However, measures within the package are disaggregated to give an initial indication of what *category* of control is most cost-effective. Refinements would therefore involve a more detailed study of the *marginal* cost of those measures that seem to be most effective.
- Several air pollutants are ignored (eg CO, CO_2, and lead).
- Several benefits from the reduction of emissions are ignored:
  - non-production benefits of improved health;
  - value of improved visibility;
  - reduced materials damage;
  - reduced emissions of gases with pervasive/global externalities (eg ozone, CO_2).[9]
- The human capital approach to valuation underestimates the economic impacts of air pollution in relation to the more theoretically correct Willingness To Pay (WTP) measure.
- The distribution of environmental impacts among different income groups is not analysed.

Expanding on the last of these limitations, the study made no distinction between the effect of air pollution on poor and wealthy residential areas, nor what the WTP of different income groups would be for improvements in air quality. Baumol and Oates (1988) point out that if air quality differentials are capitalized and reflected in property prices, lower income groups will tend to live in neighbourhoods with heavier pollution. They also point out that different types of control measures tend to affect income groups in different ways (eg taxes, minimum standards of air quality, geographical emission bans). This difference in control measures is not discussed in the study, as the package of measures is evaluated with no disaggregation of the impact of the separate measures. Hypothetical WTP or hedonic property price surveys could be used to differentiate the impacts of the different policy measures on different income groups.

Methodological Alternatives and Complementary Approaches

Contingent Valuation Survey of WTP for Air Quality

Another approach to benefit measurement is the direct one. In a contingent valuation survey of WTP in Santiago, Rogat (1995) found that WTP is influenced by income, age, education and the number of children in the family, although only age proved to be statistically significant. The study was conducted during the Chilean summer when pollution conditions are not so severe. The average WTP lump sum payment was approximately US$46.

A survey applied during the more extreme conditions of winter might reveal higher WTP bids. Furthermore, respondents could be identified by location and their WTP bids correlated to locally observed pollution levels to test the hypothesis presented by Baumol and Oates (1988).[10]

Marginal Cost Calculations for Separate Control Measures

Eskeland (1994) illustrates how more detailed cost-effectiveness analyses could estimate a marginal control cost curve for emissions. The effects of a gasoline tax are also examined for possible improvements in the effectiveness of the traditional command-and-control measures to reduce air pollution in the transport sector.

This approach could be applied to emissions reductions goals for Santiago. Minimum emissions reductions could be established as a function of politically-set goals for minimum reductions in pollution-related health impacts. A detailed cost-effectiveness analysis would seem necessary, whether or not reliable benefit estimates are available. Standards will have to be implemented on the basis of imperfect information on the benefits of reducing air pollution, and there will be a need for efficient measures, even if they may not be Pareto optimal.

Travel Mode Substitution and Effects on Emissions

Further refinements to the cost-effectiveness analysis demonstrated in Mexico are offered by Swait and Eskeland (1995) for the city of São

Paolo, Brazil. The analysis of fiscal instruments, such as a gasoline tax, is expanded to consider several different economic incentives and their impact on the demand for different modes of transport. Inducing substitution to less polluting means of transport through such instruments as subsidies and taxes can constitute a more cost-effective approach to achieving ambient pollution objectives. This type of demand-side management constitutes first-best policy in relation to the more cumbersome direct control of emissions, especially in developing countries where monitoring may be expensive and even impossible.

Non-Health Benefits of Reducing Air Pollution
Air pollution has ecological impacts, especially from sulphur emissions that lead to local and regional 'acid rain'. In addition to the corrosive damage to man-made capital (ie buildings, monuments, and machinery), this is likely to be one of the major negative external effects not considered in the Santiago study. In a recent example from Slovenia, Ayres and Dixon (1995) demonstrate the local timber and non-timber production benefits forgone by not reducing SO_2 from a local thermal power plant. Similar studies of local and regional impacts on recreational and productive ecosystems from sustained emissions in the Santiago Valley would have to be undertaken if the comprehensive benefits of air pollution reduction were to be taken into account.

NOTES

1   This chapter reviews, and therefore draws heavily on, Eskeland (1994).

2   International Center in Economic Policy for Sustainable Development (all authors).

3   See glossary for brief descriptions of the terms Pareto improvement and Polluter-Pays Principle.

4   The categories used are: light duty gasoline vehicles, buses and trucks, industrial point sources, and residential wood burning.

5   SO_2, Ozone, NO_2, PM–10 (respirable particles <10 microns diameter).

6   See glossary for brief descriptions of these different models.

7   The authors mention a number of caveats due to diverging population characteristics between industrialized and developing countries such as age and sex distribution, smoking rates, general health status, exercise and diet, access to and use of medical services, competing risks, averting behaviour, and activity patterns.

8   Confidence interval, 0.9–1.35 per cent

9   The first two of these benefits might be captured as part of a Willingness To Pay (WTP) bid in a Contingent Valuation (CV) survey. The third could be estimated from actual expenses incurred in clearly identified mitigation of damage. See glossary for brief descriptions of the terms WTP and contingent valuation.

10   A simplified example from São Paulo is given by Jacobi (1993) of a contingent valuation survey applied to six different social strata regarding WTP for a reduction in air pollution. The strata were geographically defined according to the standard of housing, which was seen to vary with income.

REFERENCES

Aranda, C F, Sanchez, J M, Angulo, J, Ostro, B, Eskeland, G S (1994) *Air Pollution and Health Effects: A study of Lower Respiratory Illness among Children in Santiago de Chile.* The World Bank, Washington, DC.

Eskeland, G S (1994) The Net Benefits of an Air Pollution Control Strategy for Santiago; in: World Bank, *Chile – Managing Environmental Problems: Economic Analysis of Selected Issues*, Environment and Urban Development Division, Country Department I, Latin America and the Caribbean Region Report no 13061-CH, The World Bank, Washington, DC.

Ostro, B, Sanchez, J M, Aranda, C and Eskeland, G S (1994) Air Pollution and Mortality Results from Santiago, Chile. Policy Research Working Paper no 1453, World Bank Policy Research Department, Public Economics Division, Washington, DC.

O'Ryan, R E (1994) Evaluación de Política para Mejorar la Calidad del Aire en Santiago. *Revista Ingenieria de Sistemas*, XI (2): 11–27.

O'Ryan, R E (1993) 'Cost Effective Policies to Improve Urban Air Quality in Developing Countries: Case Study for Santiago, Chile'. PhD Dissertation, Economics, University of California at Berkeley.

Rogat, J (1995) *Willingness to Pay for Air Quality Improvement: a Case Study of Santiago de Chile.* Studies in Environmental Economics and Development no 1995:6, Unit for Environmental Economics, Department of Economics, Gothenburg University.

Sanchez, J M (1994) 'Unit Cost Estimates of Health Outcomes Associated with Atmospheric Pollution in Santiago'.

Turner, S H, Weaver, C and Reale, M J (1993) 'Cost Emissions Benefits of Selected Air Pollution Control Measures for Santiago'.

Ulriksen, P, Fernandez, M ; Muñoz, R and Eskeland, G S (1994) 'Simulación de los Efectos de Estrategias de Control de Emisiones sobre las Concentraciones de Contaminantes Atmosféricos en Santiago, Mediante un Modelo Simple de Dispersión de Contaminantes'.

World Bank (1994) *Chile – Managing Environmental Problems: Economic Analysis of Selected Issues*, Environment and Urban Development Division, Country Department I, Latin America and the Caribbean Region Report no 13061-CH, The World Bank, Washington, DC.

Other studies valuing air pollution in Latin America
Eskeland, G S (1994) A Presumptive Pigouvian Tax: Complementing Regulation to Mimic an Emissions Fee. *The World Bank Economic Review*, 8 (3): 373–394.

Jacobi, P (1993) *Environmental Problems Facing Urban Households in the City of São Paolo, Brazil.* CEDEC and Stockholm Environment Institute.

Ostro, B (1994) Estimating the Health Effects of Air Pollutants. A Method with an Application to Jakarta. Policy Research Working Paper no 1301, The World Bank, Policy Research Department, Public Economics Division, Washington, DC.

Swait, J and Eskeland, G S (1995) Travel Mode Substitution in Saõ Paulo: Estimates and Implications for Air Pollution Control. Policy Research Working Paper no 1437, The World Bank Policy Research Department, Public Economics Division, Washington, DC.

Other background literature
Ayres, W S and Dixon, J A (1995) Economic and Ecological Benefits of Reducing Emissions of Sulphur Oxides in the Sostanj Region of Slovenia. Environment Department paper 009, The World Bank, Washington, DC.

Baumol, W and Oates, W (1988) *The Theory of Environmental Policy.* Second edition, Cambridge University Press, Cambridge, UK.

11

THE COSTS AND BENEFITS OF REEF CONSERVATION IN THE BONAIRE MARINE PARK, IN THE NETHERLANDS ANTILLES[1]

Edgar Fürst, David N Barton and, Gerardo Jiménez[2]

THE ECONOMIC IMPORTANCE OF CORAL REEF

Bonaire Island in the Netherlands Antilles, like many other Caribbean islands, relies on tourism for much of its income and a major part of its tourism-related earning comes from the diving industry. In 1990 Caribbean tourism generated US$8.9 billion and employed over 350,000 people, an increase from US$5 billion and 300,000 employed in 1985 (Dixon et al, 1993). Dive-based tourism has experienced a rapid increase and in many Caribbean states contributes 15 per cent to 30 per cent of GDP. Direct and indirect revenues from dive-related tourism on Bonaire were calculated at US$23.2 million in 1991. Although not directly comparable, the island's GDP in 1985 (the last year of available statistics) was calculated to be about US$44 million.

The domination by foreign tour operators, and the almost total reliance on imports of food and materials to support dive tourism, has meant that much of the rent generated by the sector is not captured by the island's economy. This, together with the island's liberal capital repatriation laws and free currency exchange, means that the multipliers for the local economy are low. Furthermore, much of the employment growth in the industry is covered by an immigrant workforce, implying additional social costs of any expansion. Because of the low multipliers in the local economy, tour operators tend to see increasing visitation volume as the solution to low net revenues.

The Bonaire Marine Park (BMP) was established as a multiple use area to satisfy recreational, fishing and scientific purposes. Diver visitation rates in BMP have been increasing at 9 per cent to 10 per cent in the past few years, reaching a level of 17,000 dives in 1991. The increase is believed to have caused significant reductions in live coral cover and species diversity at the most heavily visited sites. Other environmental impacts on the coral reefs are believed to be due mainly to untreated sewage as well as sedimentation from coastal development activities such as dredging and construction.

Environmental factors, including a dry climate (with an annual rainfall of only 500 mm) and porous limestone with limited water retention, mean that there are few reliable sources of fresh water on Bonaire. This implies that the coral fringing reefs of the island have little or no value for the protection of aquifers, as has been witnessed on other Caribbean islands (Ryan, 1994).

DESCRIPTION OF THE STUDY

Objectives and Focus

This chapter reviews a study by Fallon Scura and van't Hof (1993) which examined the joint ecological and economic objectives of coral reef conservation in the Bonaire Marine Park. Using quantitative and qualitative reef and diver surveys, the authors conclude that reef degradation has taken place as a result of increasing recreational scuba diving. A threshold level is identified at 4000–6000 dives per site per year, after which reef cover and diversity declines with increasing visitation. This must be interpreted as an absolute physical limit to growth in the dive industry on Bonaire.

On the other hand, the economic analysis reveals the importance of dive-based tourism for the island's economy, as measured by gross private and public sector revenues, and share of employment. A motivational and expenditure survey (a simplified contingent valuation survey) of visitors reveals that the average Willingness To Pay (WTP) of US$27.40 is considerably higher than the current US$10 user fee paid for enjoying BMP's resources.[3]

A total visitation rate, which would ensure the long term recreational quality of the resource and future income generation for the island's economy, is inferred from the reef-carrying capacity. Recommendations are made for improving diver education and park management, which can help to distribute the impact over different diving sites, thereby increasing the effective carrying capacity. Another policy suggestion of the study is the introduction of incentives to increase the local economy multipliers in an industry dominated by foreign tour operators, liberal capital repatriation laws and few currency restrictions, and thereby increase the economic benefits to the local economy of Bonaire.

The study is innovative in a Latin American context for providing an explicit ecological economic 'joint products' analysis of the costs and benefits of marine conservation. The valuation approach is one of gross revenue and expenditure, as well as a general estimate of user WTP, and is a pragmatic example of the level of integrated analysis that can be achieved with relatively limited data and time.

The study explicitly combines an analysis of ecological and economic factors to analyse the following theoretical and policy questions:

- Are protection and tourism compatible?
- What are the trade-offs between protection of biodiversity and the use of protected areas to generate income?
- Are there physical limits on multiple uses of protected marine ecosystems?

In addition, the information gleaned from the simple contingent valuation survey is sufficient to discover that some upward adjustment of the current modest park user fee is possible without reducing demand significantly.

Methodology

The study used the valuation approach of gross revenues and expenditure, and also estimated a general user WTP.

The economic benefits to the Bonaire economy are studied by cross-referencing survey information from the private sector on gross revenue generation with national statistics. A 'loss of income' approach is taken, assuming that without the presence of a healthy coral reef, income from the tourism sector would be seriously reduced. Potential benefits accruing from the reefs and waters of BMP were discussed, including direct use of renewable and non-renewable resources, such as small-scale and recreational fishing, and non-consumptive uses such as dive-based recreation, yachting and other water sports, cruise tourism and ocean transport. Of these, only revenues from dive-based tourism were considered, as other uses are less dependent on the protection of the marine park. Indirect uses related to the ecological functions of the reef as well as passive use values are only briefly introduced as part of the justification for establishing marine protected areas.

Diver expenditure is also examined by way of a survey. Finally, a simplified contingent valuation survey is applied (called a 'motivational and expenditure survey' by the authors). Willingness-to-pay for visits to BMP is elicited with two questions, one a 'take-it-or-leave-it' bid in relation to the current park fee, and a further question similar to a 'payment card' approach using a range of values for the respondent to choose from.

The costs of protection are quantified as direct management costs, indirect costs of resource conflicts between on- and off-site users, as well as the opportunity costs of excluding non-recreational users from the BMP area. The study concludes that indirect costs are relatively small due to the lack of other large reef-dependent economic activities that may be in conflict with diving related activities (although local fishing and anchoring are potentially in conflict if regulation is not continued). Opportunity costs are also at a minimum due to the multiple direct use nature of the conservation area.

A quantitative survey is made of the most frequently visited dive sites using a method of randomly spaced photoquadrats for the identification of the following ecological parameters for reef quality: percentage of live coral cover, the Shannon index (H') for species diversity, and species richness. By examining areas progressively further from the dive moorings, the 'intermediate disturbance theory' was confirmed – species diversity increases with an initial increase in diver impact as niche adaptation is encouraged due to increasing levels of coral stress. As dive intensity continues, however, coral diversity and cover decrease.

A significant result of this quantitative analysis combined with visitors' surveys and tourism statistics is the establishment of a threshold level for the diver visitation rate. The study concluded that, if the current rate of increase of diver visitation continued, the overall carrying capacity of the reef would be reached some time in 1995.

Main Sources of Data

The primary data sources were the reef photo-survey, the diver questionnaire (on environmental perceptions), departing visitors' survey (on motivational and expenditure aspects of their visits), and the dive operator and hotelier survey. Results from interviews with operators were cross-checked with existing tourism statistics.

Comprehensiveness of Estimates

The comprehensiveness of the study needs to be analysed in relation to its objectives. Given the limited information available, the study was sufficiently comprehensive to analyse the policy issues related to one use – scuba diving – facing the Bonaire Marine Park management. However, due to a lack of data and possibly the jurisdiction of the BMP, other important management issues were not analysed adequately enough to propose policy measures on, for example, improving water quality around the reef.

Concerning valuation, consumer surplus is defined as the diver willingness-to-pay in excess of the park user fee of US$10. The measure is however a 'ball-park' estimate as only a rough approximation of the demand curve was possible using data from the diver survey. Indirect and non-user values were not quantified in this study, although they might be substantial depending on the diversity of the reefs and associated fauna.

Treatment of Time Aspects

No treatment of time aspects was made, as benefits and costs were expressed on an annual basis.

Accuracy and Reliability

The authors conducted a cross-check of primary and secondary data sources for the gross revenue calculation. They reported no control procedures for biases in the contingent valuation survey. The diver survey did however divide the sample of respondents according to their dive experience to get a representative cross-section of divers.

CRITIQUE OF THE STUDY

Methodology

The study is an example of a rapid ecological economic appraisal in a situation with poor statistics and limited time available for research. The relatively modest resource endowment on the island and the undiversified economy make such an approach possible. Gross revenue figures are compared to management cost estimates to get an order of magnitude estimate of the benefits of the marine park. The analysis gives a clear indication that the BMP is central to the island's economy. Therefore, research resources are instead focused on obtaining rough estimates of the WTP for a park user fee that will allow the BMP to become self-financing, as well as on the essential issue for conservation management – the absolute threshold level of annual diver intensity per site.

Due to the lack of economic statistics available, the study had to use a less exact approach to the valuation of potential benefits from the marine park's resources. For example, there were no statistics available on fisheries catches, which would have enabled relationships to be established with reef productivity. The economic analysis of a multiple use area, such as BMP, would normally entail the use of several different valuation methods adapted to the various direct and indirect uses of the ecosystem. Due to the very homogeneous nature of the island's economy, few other sectors simultaneously depend on the resources of the park and or in conflict with dive-based tourism, the most important user. For policy purposes the analysis could therefore exclude all other direct uses.

If environmental regulation for water pollution had existed, it would also have been of immediate policy relevance to analyse the costs of this pollution. In addition to the damage done to the reef by deteriorating water quality (an external cost), islanders may also be willing to pay to avoid poorer water quality for health, aesthetic or other reasons. Environmental legislation to this effect may be an implicit economic valuation of the environmental quality of the park waters, due to the costs that must be incurred to ensure compliance. Although the study does not indicate legislation to that effect, it does mention the government's plans to build a sewage treatment plant.

The socio-economic context of the study, while not directly affecting the way valuation exercises might have been carried out, is extremely important for the present problems of the park and suggested future management (see the comment on cost-benefit analysis below). As such, other approaches to decision-making other than those strictly involving economic criteria could have been used (see for example multi-criteria analysis in Saba Marine Park, mentioned below). The introduction of higher park fees or other economic incentives for controlling visitation rates would probably meet with resistance from tourism-dependent sectors of the economy. Top-down decision-making as implied by cost-benefit analysis might only serve to make park management more difficult, by losing for example the cooperation of the dive operators – essential actors in limiting diver impact on the reef. The authors recommend that measures to increase the multiplier are therefore an important part of convincing tour operators to accept a limit on the number of visits and/or higher park user fees.

Even considering the limited research resources available for this study, some comments on the methodology used are worthwhile.

Rent Capture and Cost-Benefit Analysis

The traditional accounting stance of cost-benefit analysis may run into some limitations when foreign users' surplus derived from a locally 'owned' natural resource is incorporated into the calculation. Which value – the user fee or the fee plus consumer surplus – is the economically relevant basis for deciding on management measures in BMP? The government's decision to invest in park management would, without foreign support or altruistic motives, depend only on the economic benefits accruing to the island's economy from foreign visits. However, from a global perspective, consumer surplus from visiting the BMP, regardless of the point of origin of the visitor, is the relevant social economic welfare measure. The BMP shows a relatively large consumer surplus accruing to foreign visitors in relation to the funds actually captured by the park from user fees. In conclusion, more discussion might have been devoted to the economic instruments available, their potential for capturing these global values, and their usefulness in limiting diver impact.

Among their recommendations, the authors suggest the use of marginal cost pricing and differentiation of park user fees according to the area visited, in order to reduce pressure on the most critical sites. They suggest that the variables of congestion and potential coral damage might determine the size of the fee. Some kind of user fee differentiation could be found, but in the long run different pricing schemes do not guarantee that visitation rates will be kept below the damage threshold level. As uncovered in the study, diver demand is increasing rapidly in relation to the supply (ie the accessibility) of attractive reef sites. Therefore, if visitation is to be kept at a safe fixed maximum level per site, a park fee would continuously have to be adjusted upwards in order to reflect the increasing WTP of the divers. Such price differentiation is difficult to put into practice, let alone to optimize, due to information and policing problems of a small island government.

A better system might be to fix some safe maximum visitation rate and auction unit 'dive site entrance rights' to different tour operators. The clearance price established for the entrance right would reflect maximum diver WTP, but the information costs would be passed on to the tour operators, who would have to know their customers' preferences better.

Total Economic Value of a Reef and Full Opportunity Costs of Deterioration

The authors mention three principal categories of benefits from marine parks:

1   direct uses including extractive harvesting and non-extractive recreational uses, ensuring employment opportunities and economic development;
2   maintaining the natural balance of the environment through protecting genetic resources and biological diversity;
3   providing opportunities for scientific research, ecological monitoring and education.

The benefits of a healthy coral reef could also be discussed from a total economic value point of view, as expressed in Figure 11.1 in the Appendix. With a greater focus on analysing the ecological functions involved in 'maintaining the natural balance' of the reef, the study might also have been extended to value the indirect uses of the reef as discussed below.

Methodological Alternatives and Complementary Approaches

Valuation Methods

A maintenance cost approach could have been used to analyse the defensive expenditures needed to comply with some safe minimum standard for water quality that would also prevent reef degradation. Currently, terrestrial polluters are reaping free benefits from using the environment of the BMP as a waste sink. The maintenance costs could be interpreted as the minimum value placed by society on the environmental quality of the park and related benefits, of which dive-based tourism is by far the most important. Alternatively, the mitigation cost could be interpreted as the value of an environmental sink function of the park waters and reef.

Another ecological services value that might have been assessed is the value of the reef as a storm buffer and and its shorefront stabilization function. Order of magnitude values could be obtained for the coastline property values at risk from a loss of live coral cover and the breaking up of the reef. One problem with this method would be the shadow pricing of real estate, given that market prices of internationally attractive beach-front probably grossly exceed the value of the land in its most profitable alternative use.

Alternatively, a replacement cost approach could be used to study the cost of artificial reefs, wave breakers etc. The artificial replacements would of course substitute only one of the reef's many ecological functions, and might not even be a good substitute for that one. This method is partial in its approach and assumes weak sustainability when used alone.

As the focus was on quantifying the ecological impacts on coral cover and diversity, little attention was paid to the associated reef fauna. On the basis of casual observation, the authors assume that no damage has yet occurred to the fauna populations of the reef. Considering the often high level of biodiversity of coral reefs and the niche adaptations of associated fauna, the possibility of threatened and/or endemic species might be of direct economic interest to the tourism industry, as well as of non-user and scientific value. Further ecological surveys of the reef could be used to assess this potential.

Decision-Making Methods
Finally, complementary decision-making tools could be applied alongside the economic analysis, as has recently been done on the nearby island of Saba (Fernandes, 1995). In the absence of sufficient economic data and/or in the presence of important community preferences that may not be appraised monetarily, a multi-criteria analysis (MCA) provides important decision-making information. Fernandes states that one advantage of the method is that it does not necessarily assume rational choice behaviour, perfect markets or equity in the monetary unit of measure. The method was applied to five different management scenarios on Saba using qualitative and quantitative data and preferences expressed by stakeholders through several surveys. The use of MCA on Saba meant that the study could analyse a wider range of management policy options and scenarios than was possible on Bonaire, where only quantifiable economic data were used (though admittedly the objectives of the two studies were different). The alternative options considered were:

1   a marine park with greater communication and education components;
2   a marine park that enforces regulation and prevents over-use;
3   the marine park as it currently is;
4   the marine park without the 'no fishing' zone;
5   no marine park at all.

The performance of each option under different future scenarios (status quo, major oil spill, major increase in tourism, and major coastal construction) was evaluated by stakeholders, and their preferences ordered using an Analytic Hierarchy Process. Each criterion describing policy performance was expressed using qualitative or quantitative attributes. The multiple criteria were:

- ecological sustainability
- economic benefits
- social acceptability
- Saba Marine Park as a global model.

As stated by the author, a limitation of the MCA study on Saba is that it cannot provide a mathematically optimal solution to the successful achievement of the community-identified objectives. However, with or without 'hard data', the approach 'provided a forum for extracting and discussing the various concerns of the community and allowed the surprising degree of general agreement (among stakeholders) to become apparent'. The MCA thus provides a 'bottom-up' approach to decision-making while CBA tends to centralize the evaluation in the hands of a few decision-makers.

APPENDIX

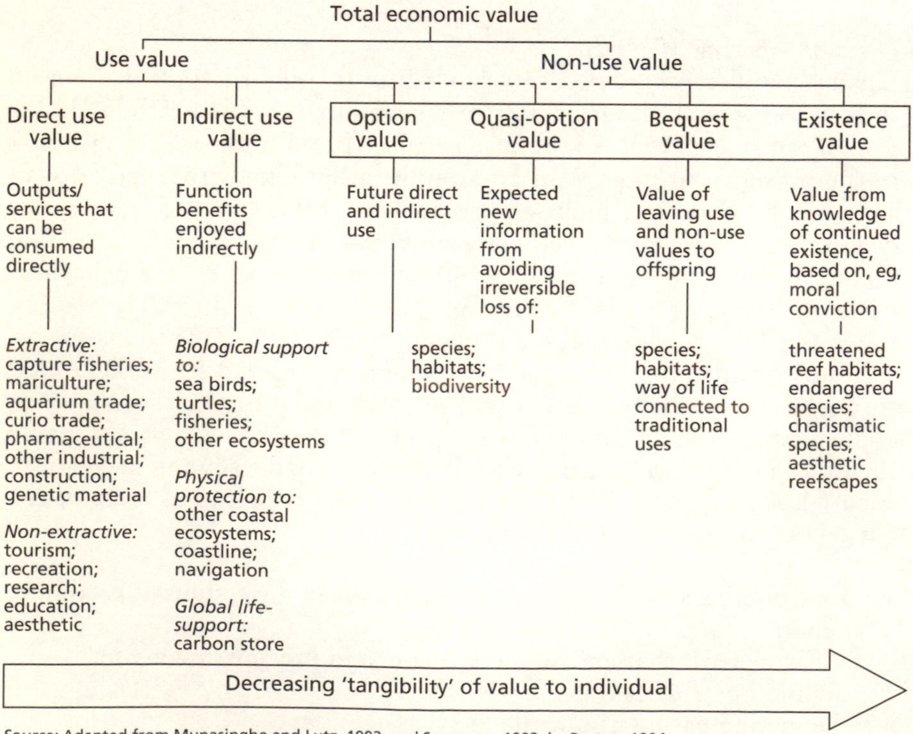

Source: Adapted from Munasinghe and Lutz, 1993, and Spurgeon, 1992, by Barton, 1994

Figure 11.1 *Economic Values Attributed to the Environment: a Coral Reef*

NOTES

1   This chapter reviews, and therefore draws heavily on, Fallon Scura and van't Hoff (1993).

2   International Center in Economic Policy for Sustainable Development (all authors).

3   See glossary for brief descriptions of the terms contingent valuation and WTP.

REFERENCES

Barton, D N (1994) Valoración Económica Parcial de Alternativas de Manejo Para los Manglares de Térraba-Sierpe, Costa Rica. Tesis Magister Scientiae, Maestría en Política Económica, Universidad Nacional, Costa Rica.

Dixon, J A (1993) Economic Benefits of Marine Protected Areas. *Oceanus* (Fall 1993): 35–40.

Dixon, J A, Fallon Scura, L and van't Hof, T (1993) Ecology and Microeconomics as 'Joint Products': the Bonaire Marine Park in the Caribbean; in: C.A. Perrings et al (eds) (1994) Biodiversity Conservation. Kluwer Publishers, Amsterdam.

Dixon, J A, Fallon Scura, L and van't Hof, T (1993) Meeting Ecological and Economic Goals: Marine Parks in the Caribbean. *Ambio* vol 22 (2–3): 117–125.

Fallon Scura, L and van't Hof, T (1993) Economic Feasibility and Ecological Sustainability of the Bonaire Marine Park – The Ecology and Economics of Bonaire Marine Park. Divisional Paper no 44, World Bank Environment Department, Washington, DC.

Fernandes, L (1995) Integrating Economic, Environmental and Social Issues in an Evaluation of Saba Marine Park, Netherlands Antilles, Caribbean Sea. A report to Saba Marine Park and Saba Conservation Foundation, East West Center, Honolulu.

Ryan, J (1994) Corn Island Coral Reef Survey – Summary of Findings and Recommended Action. CEES/AEL-University of Maryland and Tropical Ecology and Ecosystems Management, Universidad Centroamericana (UCA), Final Report to NORAD.

van't Hof, T (1986) The Economic Benefits of Marine Parks and Protected Areas in the Caribbean Region. NOAA, Sanctuary Programs Division, United States Department of Commerce, Washington, DC.

12

Estimating the Willingness to Pay for Water Services in Haiti[1]

Edgar Fürst, David N Barton and Gerardo Jiménez[2]

Socio-Economic Conditions in Haiti

Haiti is among the poorest countries in the world, as measured by GNP per capita. In 1980 more than two-thirds of the population of five million had a per capita annual income of less than US$155 (Whittington et al, 1990). Between 1980 and 1985 GDP fell by 0.9 per cent per annum in real terms, while GNP/capita declined by a full 2.6 per cent per year (World Bank figures, cited in Lundahl, 1993). The socio-economic context for decision-making on public water supply was similar to situations in parts of Africa and Asia.

Given average annual population growth rates, Haiti's population is expected to reach at least 7.8 million by the beginning of the next decade. According to Lundahl (1993), the structural interplay of population growth, composition of output, cultivation techniques and soil erosion has been responsible for falling agricultural production and increasing rural poverty during the 1980s. Increasing population growth has led to increased demand for fuelwood and land for grazing and agriculture. It has also resulted in a move away from perennial crops, towards crops with annual and multi-annual harvests. This problem has been made worse by policies which have affected the allocation of scarce natural resources such as land and forest, and which have therefore had an indirect influence on the hydrological functions involved.

A traditional policy of high export taxes (in operation until 1985) as well as the overvalued national currency (Gourde) have, for example, provided a combination of disincentives for the cultivation of coffee (Foy and Daly, 1989). This led indirectly to a shift from this perennial crop to annual crops, and, with this, increased soil erosion. Furthermore, price controls on various cooking fuels, as possible alternatives to firewood, were not designed to minimize deforestation. Land distribution has also been skewed in favour of the rich, crowding poor people onto marginal lands and thereby worsening soil erosion problems.

Macroeconomic policies introduced at the time of the study have done little to improve the social and environmental situation in the country.[3] IMF-induced fiscal reforms, introduced during the early 1980s, resulted in mainly token changes to the tax system, and whatever fiscal discipline that was imposed was implemented at the cost of cuts in development expenditure. Between 1981 and 1983 total government expenditure was reduced by US$58 million, while over the same period government investment in development projects fell by US$57.4 million (Lundahl, 1993).

Foy and Daly (1989) also mention poor or non-existent credit markets and poor access to institutional credit as factors that have contributed to low investment in agricultural projects. This would also help explain the lack of direct investment in water supply projects for irrigation, and the even greater lack of indirect measures such as watershed management. While water supply has the nature of a public good, there was no mechanism in the country for making private supply projects profitable.

WATER SUPPLY IN HAITI

In 1979 only 7 per cent to 9 per cent of forest cover remained in Haiti. Only 29 per cent of its territory is suitable for planting while 43 per cent is actually cultivated. At the same time, rural access to piped water was only 8 per cent at the beginning of the 1980s. Some 67 per cent of the country is mountainous, and the widespread problem of watershed degradation is a significant factor in the shortage of potable water, as well as the cause of other related environmental problems (Foy and Daly, 1989).

Furthermore, Haiti is the second most densely populated (235 inhabitants per km[2]) country in Latin America after El Salvador, while water use per capita is the lowest in the region. The water shortage problem is illustrated in the study area by the time spent obtaining water fit for drinking, washing and bathing. In 1980 only 8 per cent of the population had access to piped water, while the proportion in urban areas was higher. During the 1980s this figure increased considerably to 35 per cent of the rural population thanks to, amongst other things, public water system projects such as the one considered in this study.

LEGAL CONTEXT

The primary government department responsible for preserving agricultural and forest productivity and (indirectly) watershed management, MARNDR, has inadequate personnel working on soil and water conservation or forestry (Foy and Daly 1989). The legislation in place has not been able to slow the process of land and forest degradation, which ultimately affects water renovation functions. Bureacratic inefficiencies and corruption in the government institutions charged with rural development and conservation are also cited as reasons for non-implementation of the environmental laws that do exist.

Fear of expropriation and government distrust are mentioned as 'political' reasons for the lack of investments in efforts to halt land degradation. Foreign aid projects such as the installation of public water supply and reforestation were being conducted mainly through local NGOs, because these groups were generally more interested in development than the Haitian government of Jean-Claude Duvalier at the time.

DESCRIPTION OF THE STUDY

Objectives and Focus

This chapter reviews a study by Whittington et al (1990) of household willingness-to-pay (WTP) for improved water quality and quantity in a village in rural southern Haiti. In the village (Laurent) where the study was conducted, households had poor access to abundant sources of clean water for domestic use. At nearby sources people had to wait up to several hours to draw supplies. A strong preference for clean water meant that inhabitants would often walk for considerable distances or pay for public transport in order to do their washing in the nearest river. The objective of the study was to test for various survey-related biases that have been reported to reduce the validity of contingent valuation surveys in developing countries as a tool for the planning of rural water supply services. The study considered strategic, starting-point and hypothetical biases. Furthermore, the study provided the NGO that was constructing the water supply system (CARE) with a probable demand curve for the new service. This information could be used in planning a system to ensure recovery of operating costs and possibly investment costs, through an appropriate user fee. A rule-of-thumb assumption in rural water projects in developing countries has been that financial requirements greater than 5 per cent of household income will prevent households from switching to the 'improved' system.

The contingent valuation survey revealed a WTP of approximately 1.7 per cent and 2.1 per cent of income, for public standposts and private connections respectively. This was well below the 5 per cent rule-of-thumb employed by development agencies and the up to 10 per cent of household income spent on water as observed in some developing countries (Whittington and Choe, 1992). This gives an initial indication of the feasibility of the project.

An ordered probit model was used to explain the variations in WTP bids, providing a demand schedule that could be used to predict how changes in prices would affect how households would use the new service. The independent variables which, according to economic theory, have an impact on WTP had the correct sign and the majority were significant to within the 5 per cent level for both public and private connections. These variables were: wealth, income, occupation, sex, education level, distance from source, and quality of source.

Biases were checked using several different survey formats on a sample consisting of 75 per cent of the village population. The non-response rate of 25 per cent and 14 per cent 'don't know' responses provided a good statistical basis for the analysis. The low response rate and significance of economic variables confirmed that hypothetical bias was not a problem in the survey. The expected 'free-rider' problem was detected in the test for strategic bias, but was not statistically significant. Finally, no starting-point bias could be detected although confidence intervals were wide.[4]

The study served the dual purpose of a methodological experiment in contingent valuation, as well as being directly relevant for the decision to invest in and operate a public water system. During the 1980s institutions such as the World Bank had rejected the usefulness of contingent valuation for determining willingness-to-pay. The authors question this conclusion and formulate hypotheses that test whether the method can in fact be used in developing countries to develop useful estimates of willingness to pay for water services. The study concludes that it is possible to do a contingent valuation survey among a poor, illiterate population and obtain reasonable, consistent answers of willingness-to-pay for household access to potable water. These answers are of use in planning the provision of this public service.

Methodology

The benefit considered in the study was domestic water supply. Parameters for quantity (volume) as well as quality (an ordinal index) of the water were specified in the survey. By presenting colour photographs of the public standposts intended to be built, the study attempted to take into account some benefit measure of the perceived practicality of the installation.

As previously explained, the contingent valuation method (CVM) was used to elicit WTP for domestic access to clean and potable water. The survey was designed in several steps to avoid several types of bias. Firstly, focus group discussions were held in the village to get an accurate description of local perceptions of the public good in question which could then be recognized in the survey. Secondly, a pretest questionnaire was administered, to examine different ways of asking the WTP question. Direct (open-ended) questions were formulated to reveal the maximum amount the respondent would be willing-to-pay; and two types of 'bidding-game' procedure were also used. A series of possible biases related to the survey instrument and hypothetical market situation were also analysed (see below).

Bias Testing

Three important biases were tested for in the study:

- starting point bias;
- strategic bias;
- hypothetical bias.

Strategic bias was tested by using two different types of opening statement, one of which offered greater uncertainty as to whether the respondent would actually have to contribute financially to the project. *Starting-point bias* was controlled for by distributing three different types of surveys with different opening bids for WTP, as possible 'anchors' for respondents. Finally, *hypothetical bias* was reduced by giving an accurate description of the good being considered – one of the functions of the focus groups – and by including colour photographs of the installations to be provided. Moreover, the authors contend that this sort of bias is not a major problem for public services such as water supply, as these services are well-known in developing countries.

In reference to the starting-point bias, one may point to a broader category of 'information bias' – which also includes 'design bias' and 'instrument bias'. Design bias was implicitly controlled for in the survey by using focus groups and pretrials, which adapted the formulation of the hypothetical context to local perceptions. Instrument bias was not tested for as only one payment alternative was suggested – a monthly user fee, presumably collected by the local community managing the project.

Diamond and Hausmann (1994) point out that survey respondents identify more easily with 'acts' than with 'states of the world'. This implies that the hypothetical situation described should include how payment will be collected as part of the project package (of acts). They also point to a possible 'embedding effect' sometimes observed for WTP bids for 'non-use values'.[5] Simply put, using a hypothetical example, this is a situation where the WTP for the preservation (existence) of an entire endangered species is different from the sum of WTP bids for each individual of that species. However, this effect does not appear to pose a problem for use values related to a well-known good such as water.

Incidentally, the contingent valuation survey was conducted during the dry season when WTP bids can be expected to be at their highest, due to water shortages. This introduces a seasonal bias which is not discussed by the authors.

Treatment of Time Aspects

Time aspects were not considered, willingness-to-pay bids being solicited as a monthly user fee. However, monthly aggregate village demand could feasibly be discounted at a socially relevant discount rate to derive net present value.

Accuracy and Reliability

The various tests for biases could be interpreted as *sensitivity analyses*, where the sensitivity of WTP was being tested for different hypothetical market situations. *Confidence intervals* were stated in the form of t-ratios for each of the explanatory variables in the statistical probit models (wealth, income, occupation, sex, education level, distance from source, and quality of source). The quality of the responses was controlled as the survey was conducted, based on the experience of the researchers. Accuracy and reliability of the estimates were probably significantly increased by the use of *pretrials* and extensive bias testing, as explained above.

Field survey procedures included two-day training courses for local surveyors/enumerators and on-the-spot modification of surveys, as problems were uncovered in the pretrials.

CRITIQUE OF THE STUDY

Methodology

The type of distortions witnessed in the economy and government of Haiti during the early 1980s, and the lack of applicable environmental legislation, may generally affect the choice of valuation methodology, if not in this specific case study. Direct surveys of resource user willingness-to-pay may be more reliable than using methods that rely on observation of very distorted market prices, or on the costs of complying with often non-existent public environmental standards.

Until recently, most economic evaluations of water projects valued benefits indirectly, based on the costs which households would *not* have to incur, thanks to the water project (Whittington and Choe, 1992). In this sense, the study conducted during the mid-1980s was an innovation. However, some qualifications are made below, based on more recent work by Whittington.

Benefits Not Included in the Study

Whittington and Venkateswarlu (1994) cite large positive externalities as the main justification for water projects. Household willingness to pay for public water supply may not reflect all of these externalities, nor the full savings of reducing opportunity costs associated with the new water system. Firstly, there may be complicated causal relationships between water quality and epidemiological effects, which are hard to quantify; and secondly, certain effects may not be perceived by the respondent. One possible critique of the survey is that it makes no attempt to detail important externalities or possibly unperceived effects to the respondents such as:

• direct and indirect health-related benefits (dysentery, cholera);
• improved property value due to proximity to public water post.

The survey therefore provides a lower bound measure. However, Whittington and Venkateswarlu (1994) caution that just because externalities are hard to measure, they are not necessarily large, nor are benefits unperceived by the users necessarily equivalent to the externalities. On the other hand, the contingent valuation method may capture some of the positive 'altruistic' values derived from knowing that other households or the community as a whole benefit from the water system.

As previously mentioned, the WTP bids were quite low in relation to household income and bids observed in other cases. Whittington and Choe (1992) give possible explanations for low bids, although they are not specifically referred to in the study. Key determinants of household WTP are price, reliability, quality and convenience, and more specifically:

• past government policy and a heavy doubt that government can provide a reliable service, something households place a high value on;
• a sense of entitlement to water services; and
• payment arrangements not in tune with the reality of poor people's income flows.

The first explanation does not seem to be the case in the present study because an NGO is in charge of the project. The other two explanations were not tested for in the survey.

The ordered probit model employed in the study can be used to predict the number of households in a community which will use a new source, depending on the prices charged (Whittington et al, 1990). In addition to this 'demand schedule' which is essentially discontinuous, it would also have been interesting to design a survey that estimated households' willingness to pay *per cubic metre of water*, and a demand function. This would facilitate a marginal analysis of potable water demand that might determine to what extent the population of Laurent was able to pay for a project which supplied water beyond the satisfaction of basic needs. This would in turn be important information for a differentiated tariff structure that could ensure satisfaction of basic needs for the population, possibly with a progressive fee structure for consumption beyond that point, if this was necessary for project financial feasibility.

Methodological Alternatives and Complementary Approaches
Whittington and Venkateswarlu (1994) suggest the following alternative valuation methods that could possibly have been used for comparative purposes in the Haiti study.
Cost-savings approach based on:

- *Water not purchased from vendors.* Households with no direct access to public standposts or piped water may buy their supplies from door-to-door vendors. This method therefore involves a straightforward summation of the household savings on the price charged by vendors minus the water price of the new water utility. The information needed for this calculation is: (i) the average quantity of water a household purchases from vendors; (ii) the price vendors charge for water; (iii) the price of water charged by the water utility; and (iv) the number of households that would choose to connect to the new system. The method does not quantify the possible additional demand due to a lower price, nor the consumer surplus gained from additional consumption of water from the new source.
- *Value of time saved not having to fetch water.* In communities where water vending does not exist, households may spend a considerable amount of time travelling to, and transporting water from, traditional sources. This time has an opportunity cost in the sense of lost wages from forgone employment or other household chores. Data needed for this approach would be: (i) the amount of time the household spends fetching water each day; (ii) the amount of water collected; and (iii) the monetary value of time spent fetching water. While in many cases the minimum wage rate, corrected for seasonal variations in employment, may be used as the monetary value of time, there is some controversy about the correct assumptions to make in this calculation. Another problem with this method is how to accurately measure household water consumption.
- *Value of avoided expenditure in improving water quality.* This approach focuses on the expenses involved in improving the quality of water sources to which the household already has access. Better water quality from a new system may result in avoided defensive expenditures on fuel for boiling drinking water, additives such as alum, and in time savings related to travelling to cleaner sources. Additionally, the time and resources spent on obtaining the current water of poor quality must be known, in order to estimate total savings from the new system.

Consumer surplus calculation based on:
* *An estimated demand function* and the increased quantity of water used, as a result of a fall in the shadow price. As this case study has shown, obtaining detailed micro-economic data on water demand with which to calculate a demand function is not possible, due to a lack of market data and/or the very resource intensive research that would be required for this. Instead of transferring demand functions from better-known sites, the author recommends a second best approach of assuming a functional form based on an assumed ratio between expenditures and the consumer surplus. This would be based on the analyst's experience from similar projects and so is not fundamentally different from the transfer of benefit estimates. However, the author points out the advantages for decision-makers of a clear analytical separation between relatively reliable cost estimates and more uncertain consumer surplus.

Hedonic property value approaches
* The basic assumption of this approach is that in the decision to buy a house, relative access to potable water sources, ie property location, will be one of the attributes reflected in the house price and willingness to pay. The statistical analysis of property markets and household attributes can reveal the correlation between house price and this specific attribute, while controlling for other characteristics of the property. A weakness of this method in developing countries and traditional cultures may be the lack of competitive housing markets or the lack of sufficient data where they do exist.

While the first two approaches attempt to value consumer surplus, they are all indirect, in contrast to the direct method provided by contingent valuation. These methods are complements that, time permitting, could provide a basis for comparison with the CVM. However, it has been pointed out that alternative methods using derived market data do not necessarily provide the basis for a 'validity' test of the contingent valuation results (Mitchell and Carson, 1989).

NOTES

1   This chapter reviews, and therefore draws heavily on, Whittington et al (1990).
2   International Center in Economic Policy for Sustainable Development (all authors).
3   Although the study was published in 1990, the data were collected before 1986.
4   See glossary for brief descriptions of the terms hypothetical bias, starting point bias, strategic bias, and free rider problem.

5   See glossary for brief descriptions of the terms embedding effect and non-use values.

References

Diamond, P A and Hausman, J A (1994) Contingent Valuation: Is Some Number Better Than No Number? *Journal of Economic Perspectives* vol 8 (4 (Fall)): 45–64.

Foy, G and Daly, H (1989) Allocation, Distribution and Scale as Determinants of Environmental Degradation: Case Studies of Haiti, El Salvador and Costa Rica. Environment Department Working Paper no 19, The World Bank, Washington, DC.

Lundahl, M (1993) The Haitian Economy Facing the 1990s. Department of International Economics and Geography, Stockholm School of Economics, Reprint series no 100, Stockholm.

Mitchell, R C and Carson, R T (1989) *Using Surveys to Value Public Goods: the Contingent Valuation Method.* Resources for the Future, Washington DC.

Whittington, D and Venkateswarlu, S (1994) The Economic Benefits of Potable Water Supply Projects to Households in Developing Countries. Economics and Development Resource Center, Asian Development Bank Staff Paper no 53, Manila.

Whittington, D, Briscoe, J, Xinming, M and Barron, W (1990) Estimating the Willingness to Pay for Water Services in Developing Countries: A Case Study of the Use of Contingent Valuation Surveys in Southern Haiti. *Economic Development and Cultural Change* vol 8 (2): 293–311.

Whittington, D and Choe, K (1992) Economic Benefits Available from the Provision of Improved Potable Water Supplies. USAID, WASH Technical Report 77, Washington, DC.

13

TOTAL ECONOMIC VALUE OF FORESTS IN MEXICO[1]

Edgar Fürst, David N Barton and
Gerardo Jiménez[2]

FOREST VALUES

Forest resources have a number of values including intrinsic, ecological, economic, cultural and aesthetic values. However, market transactions provide an incomplete picture of the total economic value, because in most cases they only consider cases of immediate economic benefit, such as the demand for timber, for agricultural land or the need to export forest products to generate foreign exchange. If forests are used only in response to short term economic criteria, society as a whole, including future generations, will lose many other benefits. This is the principal justification for an empirical analysis of total economic value of forest, which gives special attention to values other than those derived from direct use.

DESCRIPTION OF THE STUDY

Objectives and Focus

This chapter reviews a study by Pearce et al (1993), which demonstrates a number of techniques for estimating the total economic value (TEV) of forests in Mexico. This aggregate value is estimated from considering the value of the main components of non-timber values for the Mexican forestry sector, such as non-timber forest products, non-consumptive direct uses including tourism and carbon storage services, as well as the potential future uses of the genetic resources and pure existence values. The largest proportion of economic value is derived from the ecological service values of watershed protection and carbon storage. The study represents the first attempt in Latin America to calculate the total economic value of a particular ecosystem for a national economy. The study also makes a series of general policy recommendations on how to 'capture' or internalize the non-market benefits within the borders of Mexico's economy. The principal instruments suggested are:

- entrance fees for tourist resorts;
- easements and franchise agreements;
- debt-for-nature swaps;
- offsets (carbon); and
- contracts for biodiversity prospecting.

The results show an annual *lower* bound value of the services of Mexico's forest to be in the order of US$4 billion (see Table 13.1).

Table 13.1 *Estimated Value Elements of TEV of Mexican Forests*

	Area (million ha)	Tourism	NTFPs	Carbon	Watershed protection	Option value	Existence value
Tropical evergreen	9.7		$330/r ha/y	$100/ ha/yr		$6.4/ ha/yr	
Tropical deciduous	16.1			$56/ ha/yr			
Temperate coniferous	16.9			$103/ ha/yr			
Temperate deciduous	8.8		$330/ ha/yr	$20/ ha/yr			
Total ($million/yr)	51.5	$32.1	n/a	$3788.3m	$2.3m	$331.7m	$60.2

Source: Pearce et al (1993)

The primary function of the study is to illustrate the concept of 'total economic value' in practice for the forests of Mexico. By demonstrating the total value of current direct, indirect and passive uses of the standing forest, it is hoped to provide arguments for its conservation. The valuation exercises in the study are very rough first approximations and are used more as a means of putting forest conservation issues on the economic policy agenda, rather than as a basis for rigorous analysis of alternative policy options (such as would be the case, for example, in a cost-benefit analysis). The aim of the authors is to show that forests should be conserved on economic as well as ethical grounds.

The demonstration of the considerable 'non-captured' benefits in conserving Mexico's forests prompts a series of national economic policy recommendations, which require further research. Particular attention is given to policies that would capture the global benefits provided by Mexico's forests to other societies, and much less attention is given to how the national-level policies would have to be adapted to fit specific local conditions.

Methodology

Main decision-making method

The derived total economic value is not explicitly used to evaluate alternative policy scenarios. The demonstration of potential conservation value may be interpreted as a basis for a decision to develop and implement policies for rent capture, although no formal decision-making procedure is given in the study. However, the study's focus on total economic value could imply some kind of opportunity cost argument. The problem with such an implicit assumption is discussed in the critique section below.

Benefit Categories

Benefits of preserving the forest in Mexico as a whole ecosystem are evaluated by considering the benefits of the goods, services and attributes outlined in Table 13.2.

Table 13.2 *Forest Benefits Considered in the Study*

Direct use values	Indirect use values	Passive use and information values
Non-timber forest products (food, ornamental, medicinal plants, firewood, derived pharmaceutical products) Tourist recreation	Carbon storage Watershed protection	Option on pharmaceutical uses of biodiversity Continued existence (conservation)

As discussed below, the values quantified in the study are not easily defined as pure option or existence values, and there is some lack of clarity as to whether carbon storage or carbon sequestration is being considered. The categorization in Table 13.2 is therefore an interpretation by the reviewer of the values that were included in the study.

Ecological Modelling

Although the focus of the study was not on modelling, the valuation of carbon storage services and of watershed protection relied on some simple models prior to the valuation stage.

Forest Type and Changing Land Use

The valuation of carbon storage requires as a first step the calculation of the net carbon flux due to changing land use. Different types of forest ecosystem (eg coniferous, evergreen etc.) have different types of carbon storage capacity. Furthermore, the conversion process from forested land to other activities such as permanent pasture and agriculture usually involves a number of intermediate stages. Fluxes are therefore calculated over these intermediate stages to arrive at 'once and for all carbon fluxes' for complete conversion, for each main type of forest ecosystem and alternative land use. This forms the basis of the calculation of carbon dioxide emissions avoided and the associated benefits of avoided global warming damage.

Cobb-Douglas Production Function for Sediment Loading and Water Quality

The watershed protection services offered by forests in the form of avoided erosion and sedimentation are based on a 'black box' modelling relationship with water quality:

$$Q = Q(S,X)$$

where Q is ambient water quality, S is sediment loading, and X is a vector of environmental variables (streamflow and reservoir capacity). In turn, ambient water quality influences the potential costs of water treatment through the relationship:

$$C = C(Q,Z)$$

where C is treatment costs and Z is a vector of economic variables.

The 'black box' and treatment cost relationships were calculated based on US data which were then transferred to the Mexican setting.

Valuation Techniques

A series of valuation methods are used in this study: damage cost, mitigation cost and lost production avoided, contingent valuation and the travel cost methods.

Direct-use values were estimated by considering two sources of revenue: (i) tourism and recreation; and (ii) the use value of non-timber forest products. *Tourism and recreation* is considered in two groups: multipurpose tourism and ecotourism. In the first case, the consumer surplus is estimated using both contingent valuation and travel cost models, based on a local survey in a recreational forest area. In the case of ecotourism, the economic value was estimated by considering simple tourist expenditure (not including consumer surplus). The *use value of non-timber forest products* is discussed for selected non-timber forest species, based on a series of ethnobiological studies at the local level. One study examines the management and utilization of areas of forest groves by indigenous Huastec people in the southeastern part of San

Luis Potosi, known as te'lom, in cloud forest and tropical rainforest ecosystems.[3] However, due to the difficulty of extrapolation from highly localized studies, the final estimate of TEV does not include a value for non-traditional forest products.

Indirect use values were estimated based on the economic losses avoided by conserving the forest. Carbon storage is calculated in the two step procedure outlined above. Once and for all carbon fluxes are valued using conservative estimates from the literature, in this case US$20 per tonne of carbon. This figure is based on average global damage cost estimates due to global emissions of CO_2. The study includes a conceptual discussion of the value of watershed protection, particularly by avoiding deforestation, soil erosion, sedimentation and infrastructural damage. However, the only value actually imputed is the potential defensive mitigative expenditure or treatment costs associated with water purification of suspended sediments, as described above. The option value of forests is calculated by estimating the expected value of successful pharmaceutical development derived from the genetic material in Mexico's forests. A model is used to estimate this option value which takes into account the number of species present in the forests; the probability of a species yielding a useful product; the royalty rate on sales of such a product which would be payable to Mexico; a coefficient of rent capture; the likely value of an internationally traded pharmaceutical product; and the area of forests. Finally, the existence values are estimated by considering the willingness to pay for conservation, measured by the lump sum debt-for-nature swaps realized by international conservation organizations.

Main Sources of Data

The main sources of the results obtained were a combination of empirical research by the authors and the application of existing studies to the case at hand. In many instances the study uses a *meta-analysis approach*, with the transfer of benefit estimates from different areas of Mexico and from the US 'inferred' or extrapolated to the whole country.

Comprehensiveness of Estimates

Economic values of forests are calculated at the national level, including a partial assessment of the global value of carbon storage, biodiversity conservation, and the existence of the forest ecosystem. The study is therefore comprehensive in its scope, but because of the level of analysis, necessarily limited in its detail of local level variations in forest uses and values.

Non-user values have been taken into account as well as partial consideration of consumer surplus, non-user value being considered explicitly as one of the innovations of this study. At the level of the individual valuations, most estimates are cost-based, not including consumer surplus explicitly (the exception being travel cost calculations of consumer willingness-to-pay to visit forested areas).

Treatment of Time Aspects

The treatment of time aspects does not play a major role in the study since the estimation of the total value of forests has been made on an annual basis in most cases. However, time aspects are considered implicitly in the study's examination of the need to preserve the forests and the possibility of using their services in the future. Moreover, the estimation of the option and existence values implies a consideration of the future. In the case of existence values, annual debt-for-nature swaps are amortized using a discounted rate of 6 per cent to obtain the annual value attributable to the forest area conserved.

Accuracy and Reliability

At the aggregated level it is hard to judge the accuracy of the total economic value estimate, even considering the illustrative purposes of the study. Minimum estimates are added to average estimates while cost estimates are used in some cases and other values include consumer surplus. This may be an 'eclectic' approach to valuation conditioned by the availability of data, although greater attention could have been given to pointing out the weaknesses of the estimates.

T-statistics are not given in the study, although confidence intervals are frequently expressed through the sensitivity analysis of high-low assumptions for key variables in the individual valuation exercises.

A simple validation test is performed by comparing the results of the travel cost and contingent valuation models. Average WTP estimates are similar, although the assumptions of both models may mean that this 'convergence' is no more than coincidence.

CRITIQUE OF THE STUDY

Factors Influencing the Study

The study was prompted by a reform of the constitution and changes in the law relating to forestry, which represented radical modifications to forest ownership and exploitation. Changes in property rights regimes are the starting point for many of the study's recommendations for 'capturing' non-timber benefits of the forests. As discussed below, several of the valuation approaches also depend on institutional conditions in the country as well as on recent international agreements such as the Climate and Biodiversity Conventions.

The model used to calculate the expected value of pharmaceutical developments based on forest biodiversity requires the use of a rent appropriation/capture parameter. Evaluation of this parameter depends on national institutional capacity to negotiate royalty agreements, and the existence of patent laws and local R&D facilities that would enhance the information value of the original samples. Mexico's recently established National Biodiversity Commission is intended to have the same role as Costa Rica's INBIO, although no ethnobiological inventory had yet got underway at the time of the study. The authors also point to the country's lack of appropriate patent laws and an 80 per cent market share for transnational corporations in the pharmaceuticals business as other factors influencing rent capture.

Although not mentioned explicitly in the study, the degree of effectiveness of protection may influence the way some value components are quantified. Poor enforcement of protected areas and high uncertainty about forest conservation should increase the 'insurance premium' or option value that society is willing to pay to keep those areas under forest. The possibility of debt-for-nature swaps and the potential 'existence value' of Mexico's forests also depend on the administrative effectiveness of the country's national parks and biosphere reserves. Foreign NGOs will not be willing to invest unless they receive assurances of effective protection.

The same argument applies to the appropriated value of carbon storage – unless a convincing argument can be made that the business-as-usual scenario involves an area being under threat of deforestation, that area should logically not be included in the calculations of avoided carbon emissions. If a country has legislated that certain forested areas are to be protected regardless of the economic value or political importance of alternative uses, the carbon stored in these areas cannot be included as potential emissions of CO_2 in projections of global warming damage, on which the avoided damage valuation is based.

The wide range of values discussed in the study makes it difficult to detail how individual values are affected by environmental conditions. Obviously these conditions vary greatly across the national territory, according to different ecological zones and the associated types of forest ecosystems. This is precisely the weakness of an aggregate, national level approach to total economic value. There is no indication of how policy might be adapted to these widely varying ecological conditions.

Valuation Approach

Although not the intention of the authors, the fact that monetary values have been given to the different use and non-use categories makes it tempting for decision-makers to apply some kind of opportunity cost argument and compare these values to possible forgone benefits of conversion to other land uses. According to this argument, the *opportu-*

nity cost of forgone development due to conservation would need to exceed the lower bound estimate of forest value of US$4 billion for deforestation and conversion to other uses to become economically attractive.

This type of argument would however ignore the partial nature of the TEV quantification, the order-of-magnitude nature of the estimates, the great uncertainty associated with future values of the forest, the irreversible nature of conversion, and large differences between local forest values and the estimated national average. Also, the total economic value concept used in the study does not include, *de facto*, values that may not be quantified using economic valuation methods, but which are highly relevant for determining socially optimal policies (including, for example, ethical and religious values).

These are some of the reasons why the study should be interpreted as an awareness-raising and 'political agenda setting' exercise, rather than as a formal economic valuation study.

Scope of the Study

The principal innovation of the study may be considered to be the proposals made for different national rent-capture mechanisms justified by the presence of potentially large externalities. However, the breadth of the study's focus and its generalization to the national level mean that the study has limited relevance for local level management. Policies on how to 'capture' and internalize the important indirect use values due to ecological services could have been given more emphasis at the local level, through illustrative case studies. How can TEV be applied to decision-making in local areas 'at the crossroads of conservation or conversion', under conditions of limited information, typical in developing countries? Addressing this question might have been more fruitful than attempting to find the total economic value of standing forest and aggregating values with only an order-of-magnitude accuracy. It can be argued that the total economic value approach at the national level provides few applied policy guidelines that may not otherwise be deduced from environmental economics theory.

Finally, timber values were not included in the study as the focus was on valuing non-marketed or service aspects of the ecosystem. Strictly speaking, however, forest management practices can be designed so as to minimize and even avoid use conflicts with the other benefits identified in the study. This is especially true for fuelwood harvesting, although highly selective timber extraction may also preserve most of the ecological and aesthetic characteristics of the forest. For local policy purposes, a TEV estimate that does not include income from these types of ecologically sustainable timber extraction schemes will not reflect the opportunity cost of unsustainable timber extraction and deforestation. Whether this 'full' opportunity cost is a sufficient criterion for society's decisions on forest conversion is a polemical question already touched upon.

Valuation Methodologies

Non-Timber Forest Products

Curiously, this is one of the forest values where most local level studies are cited, as a relatively large body of empirical ethnobiological information was available. Because of the localized nature of these studies, the authors conclude that it is difficult to extrapolate the results to the national level. Paradoxically, access to detailed local level information makes it more obvious that 'inference' and generalization to the national level is less useful for actual policy. In many of the valuations below, where such detailed local information was not available to the same degree, extrapolation may have been considered less of a problem because there were fewer 'reminders' of this lack of local applicability. This is a general problem with economic valuations that are based on very partial baseline data.

A relevant question to consider here is: 'Is an inaccurate monetary value more useful than the alternative of no value at all?' The answer would probably depend on alternative quantitative/qualitative means of expressing policy trade-offs, as well as the heterogeneous preferences and interest groups of stakeholders (including the analyst) involved in the decision-making process.

Tourism and Recreation

The recreational service value consists of an aggregation of different estimates of varying degrees of accuracy. Ecotourism value is calculated by multiplying the average travel expenses per hectare of forest, which is derived from average travel costs and local park visitation rates, by the total number of hectares of protected forest in the country. Although this is the only way to extrapolate the available data to the national level, it is immediately obvious that visitation rates and travel expenses probably do not depend on the number of hectares of forest available, but rather on a number of unique attributes of each individual site. This is the rather intractable problem that must be faced in a national level study such as this one.

In some cases extrapolations, although a necessary 'evil' to obtain some kind of national estimate, may do more to reduce confidence in overall results than provide useful policy advice. This may be the case for example with the average stated WTP of US$3.20 for each multipurpose tourism visit, which was revealed in a 60-sample survey in the Barranca de Cobre area. This result is close to what the authors report as the average weighted consumer surplus found in the travel cost model. However, this may be coincidence as the sensitivity of the results to the assumptions of the travel cost model employed is very large. The contingent valuation result is then chosen as representative and multiplied by (or 'inferred to') the approximately six million annual visits to protected areas all over the country. A more appropriate approach for policy development purposes might have been to provide conclusions based only on relationships between the specific attributes of the area surveyed and the observed WTP.

Watershed Protection

As recognized by the authors, only minimum estimates are provided because other avoided costs of watershed protection have not been included in the valuation (including damage to infrastructure, reduced recreation possibilities, flood hazard, wetland loss, and benefits from groundwater recharge). However, the order of magnitude accuracy of the estimate is of little policy relevance even as a minimum estimate for dedicating resources to mitigation. Firstly, the consideration of only one hydrological function makes the value reported of limited use for illustrating the concept of total economic value. Secondly, the cost estimates for purification of sedimentation are transferred from studies in the United States to the quite different conditions in Mexico. Furthermore, calculations of value are based on national erosion and sedimentation averages, while local conditions vary widely (a fact also admitted by the authors).

It should also be noted that the Cobb-Douglas functional form used to quantify mitigation costs implies the use of a weak sustainability criterion, namely that the service that assures water quality (Q) can be substituted by artificial treatment measures (Z). It also assumes constant water quality returns to scale of treatment inputs (Z). Both these assumptions may be satisfactorily covered by Cobb-Douglas in the particular case of sediment loading, but the consequences of transferring the benefit estimate and functional form to a different setting should be discussed. This is a typical problem encountered in meta-studies of this sort.

Carbon Storage or Sequestration?

The study uses these two terms interchangeably, although as ecological functions they have very different implications for the future increase in global carbon dioxide levels and consequently their imputed social economic value.

The present study calculates 'once-and-for-all' carbon fluxes due to possible future conversion from forest to other land uses. The value imputed therefore is for 'storage' rather than 'sequestration' and represents an average global avoided damage cost. The critical assumption is that the forest would otherwise have been partially or completely converted to other uses. Only under this assumption does the storage function have economic value, which obviously depends on a more detailed analysis of how effectively protected forest areas are managed in Mexico and how large an area is under real threat. The authors correctly point out the necessity of demonstrating some kind of threat of deforestation for international financing to be available, but do not incorporate this conclusion into their calculations.

Policies aimed at 'internalizing global CO_2 reduction benefits' based on this valuation approach do not actually promote reduction, but rather the maintenance of the global emissions status quo (ie they only prevent future increases in the rate of emissions, *ceteris paribus*). Economic incentives based on imputed values for carbon storage do not even promote the principle of returning emissions levels to their 1990 levels as specified in the Climate Convention. This is especially true when tradeable certificates – such as the internationally tradeable carbon offsets – are sold by forested countries, thereby 'justifying' continued CO_2 emissions from industrialized countries.

Land use changes involving permanent reforestation which provides net increases in biomass are the only ones providing true 'sequestration', thereby reducing the 'distance' between the level of CO_2 in the atmosphere and possible threshold levels where different climate change damages start to occur. In other words, storage and sequestration of each tonne of carbon have equal benefits at the margin only if scale issues are ignored. Basing policy on the damage costs avoided approach, assumes that one tonne of *avoided future increase* in CO_2 emissions is equal in social value to one tonne of *actually sequestered* CO_2. However, society should be willing to pay an 'insurance premium' for reducing actual ambient CO_2 levels (ie sequestration), as opposed to avoiding future increases (ie storage). The premium would reflect the WTP of a risk-averse society for increasing the distance to damage thresholds which are not known with certainty.

In conclusion, the valuation approach chosen has important policy implications that might have been analysed at greater length, to differentiate between the societal value of storage and sequestration.

Option Value of Genetic Resources

Is the expected commercial value of pharmaceutical developments an adequate expression of forest option value? The authors point out that the 'option value can be conceptualized as being similar to an insurance premium, paid to ensure the supply of an asset, the availability of which may otherwise be uncertain'. However, according to this review, two different types of uncertainty may have to be distinguished when discussing the option value of conservation.

One is the uncertainty of whether the area will be deforested and whether the full range of ecosystem goods and services will be available in the future. The second uncertainty is whether, once the area is conserved, there will be species of potential pharmaceutical value present.

The first case is referred to by the authors when they state that the 'insurance premium society is willing to pay to conserve species for future uses and values may in practice be represented by the costs of establishing a reserve and the opportunity costs of any forgone development in the reserve area'. This is the broad concept of option value. Under the uncertainty of deforestation, society should be willing to pay insurance premiums for maintaining options open to *all* the potential uses and values of the system – not just pharmaceutical material. Under this argument the option value of only pharmaceutical uses is an undervaluation.

Another conceptual problem may be present in the valuation in this study. Mitchell and Carson(1989) and Pearce and Turner (1990) give similar definitions:

option value = option price (ex ante) minus expected
consumer surplus (ex post)

Option price is the *ex ante* willingness to pay for an uncertain future state of the world, or in this case the sum of the *ex post* price of a successful development of the pharmaceutical product, the expected consumer surplus above product price and the 'insurance premium'. According to this definition, the probability-weighted expected sales value of pharmaceuticals expressed by the model in the study quantifies only part of the option price (the expected market price), not including expected consumer surplus, nor the 'insurance premium' that must be paid to ensure biodiversity conservation.

In conclusion, expected pharmaceutical value is not a sufficient valuation of the forest species in danger of extinction that may provide future pharmaceutical products, nor is it a complete expression of option value related to conserving future supply of all non-timber forest benefits. On a case-by-case basis it would have to be determined whether conservation expenses and forgone conversion benefits related to specific areas were justified totally or only partially on the basis of the threatened biodiversity/species argument. For specific areas, surveys could be used to ascertain stakeholders' conservation interests as well as their potential risk-aversiveness to losing economic forest uses, as distinct from the expected market price of these uses.

These unresolved doubts illustrate the difficulty of empirically measuring option value as a basis for policy decisions, although the concept is definitely useful as a justification for a risk averse or 'safe-minimum standards' approach to conservation policy.

Existence Values as the Willingness To Pay of International NGOs
Debate continues as to whether or not debt-for-nature swaps by international NGOs constitute an acceptable and useful estimate of existence value. As an example, membership of such organizations usually involves material or social benefits other than the pure satisfaction of knowing that natural resources are being preserved. Willingness to pay for swaps may also have other conditionalities than simply conservation (including, for example, the achievement of social goals among communities living in the protected area).

One general problem faced by the study is that the existence value and the value of carbon storage are expressed as lump sum figures, while other values are expressed as annual income streams. It is therefore not clear how values are to be aggregated or amortized, as the case may be, in order to obtain a unique measure of total economic value. The value/year figures implicitly admit large uncertainties about the future, while net present value figures assume some certainty about future income streams. Even if aggregation and comparison were not intended by the authors, the discounting of future values, necessary to arrive at a total economic value of forest conservation benefits, begs some discussion.

Methodological Alternatives and Complementary Approaches

A large number of alternative valuation methods are available for the different aspects analysed in this study. Their choice would depend on the data available, which were scant in most cases in the study.

The policy usefulness of the total economic value concept would seem to be greater at the local level for small areas of diverse and unique ecosystems, even though there are several important caveats. In many cases conversion is only partial, there are several intermediate levels of development and important 'quality' aspects of the ecosystem under threat must be evaluated. In this case 'total' economic value is an inappropriate concept for decision-making.

For policy purposes at a local level, partial valuation approaches such as cost-benefit analyses might be more successful because of their reduced data needs, especially in developing countries. An important limitation exists in cases where irreversible loss of unique ecosystems or endangered species may result from policy alternatives being considered. If trade-offs are to be permitted, they at least require a well informed participative decision by all stakeholders (excluding future generations).

Decision-making processes capable of considering differing value concepts and stakeholders' interests would be necessary. Analysing total economic monetary value provides only one criterion for analysing policy options. Alternative decision-making approaches to cost-benefit analysis, such as Multi-Criteria Analysis, Positional Analysis and Integrated Assessment, have been proposed during recent years.[4] The trade-offs between conservation and development that must be considered by these approaches require opportunity cost reasoning, but the opportunities 'lost' have dimensions that seldom if ever will be adequately expressed by total economic value.

NOTES

1   This chapter reviews, and therefore draws heavily on, Pearce et al (1993).

2   International Center in Economic Policy for Sustainable Development (all authors).

3   It is estimated that over 2000 plant species are utilized from Mexican forests. These range from products such as resins, turpentine and pitch from pine forest, and chicle from the chicle forest in the Yucatan, all of which are internationally traded, to a multiplicity of medicinal plants and wildfoods utilized at subsistence level.

4   See glossary for brief descriptions of these approaches.

REFERENCES

Adger, W N, Brown, K, Cervigni, R and Moran, D (1995) Total Economic Value of Forest in Mexico. *Ambio* vol 24 (5).

Mitchell, R C and Carson, R T (1989) *Using Surveys to Value Public Goods: The Contingent Valuation Method.* Resources for the Future, Washington, DC.

Pearce, D W, Adger, W N, Brown, K, Cervigni, R and Moran, D (1993) Mexico Forestry and Conservation Sector Review Substudy of Economic Valuation of Forests, Report prepared for the World Bank Latin America and the Caribbean Country Department II, by CSERGE, University of East Anglia and University of London.

Pearce, D W and Puroshothurum, S (1992) Protecting Biological Diversity: The Economic Value of Pharmaceutical Plants. CSERGE, University of East Anglia and University College London, Global Environmental Change Working Paper no 92–27.

Pearce, D W and Turner, K R (1990) *Economics of Natural Resources and the Environment.* First edition, Harvester Wheatsheaf, London.

14

PARTIAL ECONOMIC VALUATION OF MANGROVES IN NICARAGUA[1]

Edgar Fürst, David N Barton and Gerardo Jiménez[2]

MANGROVE ECOSYSTEMS

Mangrove ecosystems are home to a diverse series of natural resources and ecological functions with possible economic value. They are known for their multiple-use characteristics and consequently also the multiplicity of the possible resource use and administrative conflicts that may arise there. Because they are located in the land-ocean interaction zone, typically many different agencies have jurisdiction over them. The complexity of the development and user interests will condition the approach to economic analysis of management alternatives.

LEGAL CONTEXT

The administrative situation in Nicaragua's mangroves is similar to that found in other Central American countries (Suman, 1994), with different ministries in charge of their management – the Ministry of Natural Resources and the Environment (MARENA) and the Ministry of Economics and Development (MEDE). In neighbouring Costa Rica, unclear jurisdictional boundaries currently exist between departments charged with wildlife management (flora and fauna) and forestry, as well as between ministries charged with terrestrial resource management (agriculture, environment) and the fisheries authorities. In Nicaragua some potential administrative conflict has been avoided by placing the responsibility for both fisheries and aquaculture within MARENA.

Very few laws governing the use of mangrove systems exist in Nicaragua, and those that do cannot be enforced due to a lack of administrative personnel and resources. A law of 1976 and a decree in 1991 by the then IRENA prohibit the cutting of mangroves for commercial purposes, and state that any use of natural resources in the mangrove must be given by government concession. The deforestation rate evident in this case study is an example of the lack of effectiveness of these regulatory incentives when faced with the subsistence needs of the population.

SOCIO-ECONOMIC CONTEXT

At the time of the case study (1990/1991), Nicaragua had just entered a period of relative peace, and large amounts of foreign aid (47.6 per cent of GNP in 1991), coupled with monetary and fiscal stabilization programmes, had brought hyperinflation rates of up to 22,000 per cent at the beginning of 1990 down to single digit figures. However, high unemployment and underemployment levels prevailed, and in the case study area (Región II) unemployment was well above the national average. No data on income distribution are available, but it is believed the average recovery in real wage rates observed at the time may have mostly benefited the urban population.

In addition, national energy shortages; low rates of electrification especially in rural areas; and falling household food production during most of the previous decade demonstrate possible links between subsistence fuelwood needs of the local population and the high levels of deforestation prevailing in the mangroves of Héroes y Mártirez in Región II in 1990/91.

MANGROVE DEGRADATION IN NICARAGUA

The generation of net income streams from the mangrove ecosystem relies on its main structural component – the mangrove forest. At the time of the study the local population was extracting mangrove wood well above the Maximum Sustainable Yield (MSY), subsistence extraction of firewood alone contributing to an annual deforestation of nearly 400 hectares.[3] Taking into account deforestation due to other uses as well, the mangrove was predicted to sustain only another seven years of exploitation before total depletion. At that time, not only would all direct forest benefits be lost under a business-as-usual scenario, but so would the majority of ecological services supporting non-consumptive and indirect uses of the system.

DESCRIPTION OF THE STUDY

Objectives and Focus

This chapter reviews a study by Windevoxhel (1992) which evaluated the net benefits of management alternatives for an 8,700 hectare mangrove area on Nicaragua's north Pacific coast. The study is the first of its kind in Central America and the Caribbean to evaluate sustainable and unsustainable mangrove forestry management options, taking into consideration both the goods and services provided by the ecosystem. The study uses a variety of valuation methodologies, including a simple *net income approach*, *change in productivity*, *contingent valuation (CV)*, and *travel expenditure* (as distinct from travel cost). Beside net benefit estimates, the combined use of valuation techniques within a cost-benefit analysis (CBA) framework provides several methodological insights into their use on mixed subsistence and commercial resource-based economies.

The economic valuation was complemented by ecological analyses of carrying capacity, to determine possible limits to future income flows within the ten-year horizon of the analysis. The MSY level was determined for the forestry activity using net primary productivity estimates transferred from similar mangrove stands elsewhere in the tropical world. Another approach to production functions was adopted, using time series regression analysis, where a progressive decline in mangrove area was shown to be significantly correlated to a sustained fall in shrimp catch.

Two management scenarios were evaluated using a CBA: *scenario 1* in which present levels of unsustainably high forest extraction lead to deforestation of the mangrove within seven years, thereby cutting off the provision of goods and services; and *scenario 2* in which the forest is managed at MSY, guaranteeing a constant flow of goods and services over the 10 year horizon of the analysis. At a 10 per cent discount rate, net benefits from the 8,700 hectares of mangrove are valued at US$5,740,000 in the unsustainable alternative, and at US$10,968,000 under the sustainable alternative. Direct extractive value was dominated by the benefits from the subsistence collection of firewood.

Significantly, despite the limited consideration of services, they still accounted for about half of the total net present value derived from the ecosystem, as estimated in the study. The author concludes that a more comprehensive consideration of services would provide much higher aggregate values than for direct extractive goods, despite the importance of subsistence uses in the local economy. Finally, sensitivity analyses were conducted for higher labour costs, as well as changes in market prices for extractive marine goods.

The approach is one of both methodological testing and policy analysis. The main objectives of the study were to apply methods of economic valuation to mangroves in Central America, and to test the following hypotheses: that a sustainable mangrove management policy is economically more beneficial than the *damages caused by existing conditions* of overexploitation; and that the aggregate of ecosystem services represents greater economic benefits than do extractive goods.

Methodology

Policy analysis is conducted for two scenarios using a *cost-benefit analysis*: scenario 1 representing a business-as-usual rate of forest extraction that eventually leads to the depletion of the resource; and scenario 2 assuming a rate of extraction equal to MSY, and implying sustainable income flows from direct and indirect uses of the mangrove. Although many components of the mangrove are valued in a total economic value framework, the use of CBA and the limited access to data both require a partial economic valuation approach.

Benefit Categories

The study considers direct uses of *renewable* stocks including both subsistence and commercial artisanal activities: the extraction of timber for firewood, charcoal and tannins production; small-scale estuarine fishing, and the collection of molluscs. The only indirect use value considered is also related to a renewable stock, described as the external support provided by the ecosystem to the adjacent commercial shrimp fishery.

Also considered is the value of the *ecosystem and its landscape* – the beaches and estuaries around the mangrove forests – to local and national recreational visitors.

Ecological Modelling

No direct empirical estimates are made of net primary productivity of wood biomass in the study, due to a lack of on-site data. However, using a meta-study of literature on mangrove productivity from other tropical areas, a probable value for productivity is determined for the semi-arid mangroves of Nicaragua's Pacific coast. A simple stock flow approach is then used to determine the years remaining before depletion, under current patterns of overexploitation.

A more sophisticated approach was possible in determining a production function for the coastal shrimp fishery. It is hypothesized that the catch depends on the importance of the mangrove as a spawning ground and source of nutrients, represented by total mangrove area. Using available *time-series data* (23 years) for fishing catch of the Penaeus genus of shrimp, the corresponding fishing effort, and changes in mangrove cover, a *regression analysis* revealed a significant correlation between mangrove deforestation and a decline in fisheries productivity, while holding fishing effort constant.

Valuation Techniques

For direct extractive uses, the commonly applied approach was the *loss of income or production* due to the multiple impacts of deforestation. In the valuation, the uncorrected market prices of goods were used directly as economic prices. On the inputs side, one significant exception was made for labour costs, where market wage rates were corrected for significant long-term and seasonal unemployment. Where goods were extracted for subsistence purposes they were valued at the market price of the best substitute, usually the same product sold in the local market.

The recreational benefits from the mangroves were considered using both the travel cost and the contingent valuation survey (direct willingness-to-pay (WTP)). However, the travel cost method (TCM) 'failed' to estimate a demand curve for visitors, as it was limited to the estimation of average travel expenses multiplied by the number of visits. This approach fails to capture the consumer surplus that visitors derive from the experience, above and beyond the expenses they incur in reaching their recreational destination.

In the contingent valuation survey a simple open-ended question was used to estimate willingness-to-pay for the experience of the mangrove beaches and estuaries. There was only limited control for biases, with questions on whether other sites had been visited on the journey (a specification-related bias). No standard specification was made of the hypothetical environmental service for which the respondents were offering their WTP bids, nor was the payment vehicle specified. Furthermore, there is no discussion in the study of the representativity of the sample (n=680) of the population of visitors of foreign, national and local visitors, nor of the percentage of non-response rates to the questionnaire.

A type of 'validity test' or comparison is then made between the travel cost and contingent valuation approaches. However, considering the limited control for biases in the CVM and travel expenses calculation, the comparison is of limited value. In fact, the travel expenditure approach, which does not take into account consumer surplus, revealed an average annual expenditure many times higher (US$176) than the WTP estimate obtained from the contingent valuation question (US$53), when theory suggests that the reverse should be true (since the WTP as expressed in a CV study includes the whole area under the estimated demand curve).

Main Sources of Data

Empirical research consisted of current sources of income of the population being surveyed using a questionnaire sample covering about 17 per cent of the population. The travel cost and contingent valuation surveys were administered to 680 respondents. In addition primary data were gathered on the cost structure of commercial operations such as tannin production. *Existing secondary sources* were used for time-series data on the shrimp fishery and changes in mangrove area, as well as for net primary productivity estimates.

Comprehensiveness of Estimates

There are important questions on the results obtained in this study. It is not clear, for example, if an effort was made to correct market prices for distortions, such as value-added taxes, or for imperfect competition. Although the principal input, labour, was valued at an estimated shadow price, preferences revealed by uncorrected market prices cannot be expected to give a complete picture of consumer surplus in the study, without important caveats. This methodological critique is qualified by the field study situation of poor access to other market data in rural Nicaragua, and the limited research resources available to study market distortions.

Treatment of Time Aspects

No social discount rate had been calculated for Nicaragua. Therefore, a *discount rate* of 10 per cent was adopted following a literature review of valuation studies from other developing countries. This rate is also recommended by Lutz and Munasinghe (1994), and represents the lower range of World Bank interest rates in development related projects.

A *time horizon* of 10 years was selected after studies of carrying capacity revealed that the business-as-usual scenario would lead to resource depletion within seven years. The otherwise short time horizon can be considered to capture the major impacts on the system, although it will inevitably underestimate the benefits from the sustainable management scenario.

A case can be made that the explicit calculation of the carrying capacity of the forest constitutes a *separate treatment of irreversibilities*. In this case, the mangrove is considered irreversibly damaged once deforestation is complete, as the analysis makes no allowances for reforestation.

Accuracy and Reliability

Sensitivity analyses are performed for critical economic variables such as the wage rate for labour inputs and the price of marine products. As previously indicated, a limited validation comparison was performed on the CVM and TCM results, although the 'validity' of the test itself must be called into question, as estimates of consumer surplus and expenditure are not directly comparable.

Confidence intervals and significance levels are reported for the multiple regressions conducted on mangrove deforestation and loss of fisheries productivity. Where available, confidence intervals are also reported from the meta-study of net primary productivity. However, a single figure is used instead of a probable range when estimating forest carrying capacity for timber products.

CRITIQUE OF THE STUDY

Factors Influencing the Study

The difficult economic context of the study conditioned the methodology in several ways. The unsustainable management scenario was based on rates of deforestation (1000 ha/year) more than twice as high as those actually observed in the area, presumably due to predictions of a deteriorating unemployment situation and increased subsistence pressures on the mangrove resources. *Ex post* deforestation rates would have to be reviewed to corroborate this prediction under present economic conditions.

In situations of very high inflation, barter trade becomes an important exchange mechanism for avoiding the transaction costs associated with holding currency. Although not reported in the study, problems may have existed in the observation of market prices for locally produced and traded products. The availability of reliable indices with which to calculate real prices may also be a problem under conditions of hyperinflation, as prices for locally-traded products and inputs may not adjust at the same rate, as calculated by general indices based on a nationally representative basket of goods and services. Despite drastic reductions in the nominal inflation rate by the time the study was completed, the author assumes constant prices and calculates all values in real 1990 US dollars. This improves the usefulness of the results for cross-country comparisons.

The shadow wage rate was calculated as the minimum wage corrected downwards by the percentage of local unemployment. Considering the extremely high rates of equivalent *under*employment affecting more than half the workforce, it is possible that the shadow wage rate was even lower. The use of very low shadow wage rates improves the relative economic profitability of management alternatives that are labour intensive. This should favour subsistence-related activities, given their high ratio of labour to capital inputs, but it tells us nothing about whether the minimum wage used for accounting purposes actually covers the basic needs of the population. This distributional issue is particularly relevant in Nicaragua, which has one of the lowest GNP/capita in the world.

The multiple use characteristics of mangroves require the use of complementary decision-making tools to cost-benefit analysis. The provision of a variety of goods and ecological services, as well as possible non-use values, requires the use of multiple valuation methods. Due to this user diversity, the data on resource extraction are at best partial in developing countries, while 'hard' data on indirect uses may be almost entirely absent. This problem is as much a reflection of the neglect of ecological services in national accounting practices as an ecological characteristic of mangroves. The diversity of components, functions and attributes does however mean that serious aggregation problems must be confronted when using cost-benefit analysis, due to the highly varying quality of individual valuation results.

The location of the ecosystem in the land–ocean interaction zone, often at the mouth of rivers, requires the definition of sustainable management alternatives that also take into account benefits to and impacts from land use activities in the watershed upstream and outside the bounds of the mangrove forest itself. The study attempts to value one ecological service downstream through the analysis of the impact of deforestation on shrimp fisheries, while possible upstream effects, such as protection of the freshwater aquifer and coastline, are omitted due to a lack of data and resources. Ultimately though, the integral management of mangroves cannot be based only on traditional zoning within the forest area, but must also include for example upland erosion and water contamination issues (Barton, 1995).[4] Economic analysis of these highly open systems will increasingly need to focus on evaluating indirect impacts, as these impacts become recognized by decision-makers and in the legislation of the countries involved.

The great importance of ecological services requires any comprehensive valuation exercise to be firmly based on hydrological, ecotoxicological, biological, ecological and other relevant natural science quantitative studies. Although monitoring information is largely absent for ecological indicators in the mangroves of the region, any valuation assumptions must at least be based on informed opinions from other disciplines. In this respect the study is a success, with its detailed treatment of the sustainable yield characteristics of various resources in the study. However, the multiple direct and indirect uses of mangrove systems 'condemn' most (if not all) studies to being partial approaches (as announced by the study's title). The problem with determining the 'total' economic value – admittedly not the objective of the study – is so evident in the case of mangroves due to their multiple direct uses, but is in fact a common trait of any analysis that goes beyond the direct uses of an ecosystem.

Methodology

The operational feasibility of economic analysis in developing countries hinges on the trade-offs between accuracy and transparency of the results to decision-makers. Crude market prices will often give the clear first approximations needed to take rapid decisions, which seems to be the eclectic approach adopted in this study. However, valuation exercises under conditions of hyperinflation considerably increase the difficulty of calculating real market prices. It may be conceivable that some other intermediate unit of accounting for recognized barter value in the local economy might be used in extreme cases. Multiple criteria analysis may then be employed to study stakeholders' trade-offs between non-monetary attributes of goods and services.

An important socio-economic characteristic of the recreational demand for mangroves in Nicaragua should be mentioned as it may limit the use of the travel cost method. The author notes the difficulty in applying a standard survey to the diverse modes of travel encountered in a country such as Nicaragua (including bicycle, bus, lorry, and private car). Distances and modes of travel represent very different levels of travel expenditure and opportunity cost, which may not depend as much on willingness-to-pay for the recreational experience as on restricted access to transportation, low income and employment opportunities (ie the opportunity cost of time). These factors can in theory be controlled for in statistical analysis using ordered probit models, but the multiple modes of travel significantly complicate data collection.

An examination of how household budget restrictions in subsistence income areas may affect willingness-to-pay bids in the contingent valuation question also needs to be addressed. Furthermore, property rights issues were not discussed, which makes it difficult to establish whether the WTP or willingness to accept (WTA) format would have been most appropriate in the question put to visitors. A clear distinction would have to be made between the part of the sample composed of local or national recreationers and questions included in the survey concerning their perceived user rights to the mangrove recreational areas.

The exclusive use of CBA in evaluating management alternatives which affect the subsistence livelihoods of very poor populations is another questionable aspect of the study. The cost-benefit analysis illustrates the economic opportunity costs of the current destructive forestry practice, and external costs imposed on fisheries and recreation. However, the net present value criteria do not consider the distribution of impacts of alternative forestry policies, for example, on groups subsisting on mangrove extraction. Nor does CBA provide a tool for revealing and resolving the complex conflicts of interest among users and government bodies associated with the ecosystem.

The partial utility of CBA is a common methodological limitation for project evaluations in many developing country contexts. The use of net present value as a unique policy indicator would be a mistake in a multiple use system such as the mangroves, as the study points out by its detailed analysis of the ecological sustainability of different resource uses. The study's analysis of extraction rates in relation to maximum sustainable yields, as well as the economic valuation, may be taken as warning indicators that should bring stakeholders to the table. However, additional methodological approaches, such as multiple criteria analysis, are needed to integrate the possibly different preferences of stakeholders, if efforts are to be made to gain consensus on the design of the most favourable management option.

Methodological Alternatives and Complementary Approaches

The following are some alternative approaches to those used in the study:

- *Examination of local property rights, regimes and perceptions* in order to apply an appropriate measure of the change in consumer surplus. Willingness-to-accept (WTA) measures will usually be associated with perceptions of resource ownership, for example by the local population. A loss of access to recreational uses of the mangrove may be accepted, but only with some form of hypothetical compensation as expressed by the WTA concept. For non-local and foreign recreationers who do not perceive usufruct or ownership rights to the resource, a willingness-to-pay (WTP) measure is suggested as most relevant by the literature (Mitchell and Carson, 1989).
- *Multiple-criteria approaches* may be applied as a response to the information and aggregation difficulties of 'social environmental economic cost-benefit analysis' and in order to take into account the non-monetary preferences of multiple stakeholders and trade-offs.
- *Definition of relevant decision-making criteria of stakeholders* before undertaking the economic study, in order to examine the political relevancy of the valuation results and how these results will be interpreted by them. In addition to multiple criteria analyses (examples of which can be found in van Pelt, 1993, and Fernandes, 1995), a negotiated approach to a socially optimal management strategy may be based on a positional analysis of stakeholders and interest groups (Søderbaum, 1990).
- *Data quality ranking method* applied to information sources and results. The assumptions on which the evaluation are based may need to be systematically and summarily presented in the main report to improve the quality of decision-making. The multiple criteria approach provides a possible format for this analysis.

NOTES

1   This chapter reviews, and therefore draws heavily on, Windevoxhel (1992).
2   International Center in Economic Policy for Sustainable Development (all authors).
3   See glossary for description of the term MSY.
4   Despite their negative effects on upland agriculture, erosion and the resulting nutrient loss and silting of estuaries may have beneficial effects for mangrove colonization and extension.

REFERENCES

Ammour, T, Sención, G and Solís, H (1992) Proyecto Evaluación Económica de Humedales – Peten Guatemal – Caso de Petexbatun Proyecto OLAFO CATIE, Costa Rica.

Barbier, E B (1992) Valuing Environmental Functions: Tropical Wetlands. Discussion Paper no DP92–04 London Environmental Economics Centre (LEEC), London.

Barbier, E B, Costanza, R and Twilley, R R (1991) Guidelines for Tropical Wetland Evaluation. Report from 'Taller Internacional de Trabajo para la Elaboración de un Manual de Evaluacion Económica de los Bienes y Servicios de los Humedales Tropicales', Centro Agronómico Tropical de Enseñanza y Investigación (CATIE), Costa Rica.

Barton, D N (1995) Valoración Económica Parcial de Alternativos de Manejo para los Manglares de Térraba-Sierpe, Costa Rica Tesis Magister Scientae, Maestría en Política Económica, Universidad Nacional de Costa Rica.

Fernandes, L (1995) Integrating Economic, Environmental and Social Issues in an Evaluation of Saba Marine Park, Netherlands Antilles, Caribbean Sea. A report to Saba Marine Park and Conservation Foundation, East West Center, Honolulu.

Lutz, E and Munasinghe, M (1994) Integration of Environmental Concerns into Economic Analyses of Projects and Policies in an Operational Context. *Ecological Economics* 10: 37–46.

Mitchell, R C and Carson, R T (1989) *Using Surveys to Value Public Goods: the Contingent Valuation Method.* Resources for the Future, Washington, DC.

Suman, D (1994) Legislación y Administración de los Manglares en América Central. *Revista Forestal Centroamericana* (September-November): 6–12

Søderbaum, P (1990) Economics in Relation to Environment, Agriculture and Rural Development. A Non-Traditional Approach to Project Evaluation. Department of Economics, Working Paper no 31, Sveriges Lantbruksuniversitet.

van Pelt, M J F (1993) Sustainability-Oriented Project Appraisal for Developing Countries. PhD thesis, Wageningen Agricultural University.

Windevoxhel, N J (1994) Valoración Económica de los Manglares: Demostrando la Rentabilidad de su Aprovechamiento Sostenible. *Revista Forestal Centroamericana* (September-November): 18–26.

Windevoxhel, N J (1992) Valoración Económica Parcial de los Manglares de la Región II de Nicaragua, M Sc Thesis, Turrialba, CATIE, Costa Rica.

Further Reading: Valuation Studies in Developing Countries

The following is a selection of other literature on valuation studies in Africa, Asia, and Latin America and the Caribbean. The regional listings were prepared by the coordinators, namely Hugo van Zyl, Thomas Store and Anthony Leiman (Africa Region); Marian delos Angeles (Asia Region); and Edgar Fürst, David Barton, and Gerardo Jiménez (Latin America and Caribbean Region). No such bibliography was prepared for Eastern and Central Europe.

Africa Region

Most of the following references of valuation studies conducted in Africa are taken from two studies: one conducted by Anders Ekbom (1993) of the Department of Economics at Gothenburg University, Sweden entitled, '75 Case Studies on Environmental Economic Evaluation in Developing Countries'; the other being the study by Pearce et al (1994) on 'Economic Values and the Environment in the Developing World', published by Edward Elgar for UNEP.

Change in productivity studies:

Anderson, D (1987) The Economics of Afforestation: A Case Study in Africa. World Bank Occasional Paper, Johns Hopkins University Press, Baltimore, Maryland.

Aongola, L B (1993) Soil Conservation and Agroforestry Extension Programme. Chipata North and South Agricultural Districts: A Cost-Benefit Approach. Unpublished Msc thesis from The Agricultural University of Norway.

Arntzen, J (1990) A Framework for Economic Valuation of Collective Fencing in Botswana. In: Dixon, J and Sherman, P B (eds) *Drylands Management: Economic Case Studies*, Earthscan Publications, London.

Bishop, J and Allen, J (1989) The On-site Costs of Soil Erosion in Malawi. *Environment.*

Bojö, J (1991) *The Economics of Land Degradation: Theory and Applications in Lesotho.* Stockholm School of Economics, Stockholm.

Bojö, J (1993) Economic Valuation of Indigenous Woodlands; in: Bradley, P N and McNamara, K (eds) Living With Trees: Policies for Forestry Management in Zimbabwe, Technical Paper no 210, World Bank, Washington, DC.

Convery, F and Tutu, K (1993) *Estimating Gross Costs of Environmental Degradation – Sectoral Analysis: a Ghana Case Study.* Department of Economics, University College of Dublin.

Marenga, P K N (1992) An Economic Evaluation of the Mgeta Community Based Wildlife Management Project: Selous Game Reserve – Tanzania. Unpublished MSc thesis, Agricultural University of Norway.

Ruitenbeek, J (1992) The Rainforest Supply Price: a Tool for Evaluating Rainforest Conservation Expenditures. *Ecological Economics*, vol 6 (1): 57–78.

Loss of Earnings Studies:

Nur, E M (1984) The Socio-Economic Impact of Water Associated Diseases in Sudan; in: Osman, A F and Baily, C R (eds) *Water Distribution in Sudanese Irrigated Agriculture: Productivity and Equity.*

Nur, E M (1986) Impact of Schistosomiasis and Malaria on Agricultural Productivity in Sudanese Irrigated Agriculture. Final Report, TDR/TL6/181/SER/1, WHO, Geneva.

Replacement Cost Studies:

Newcombe, K J (1989) An Economic Justification for Rural Afforestation: The Case of Ethiopia. In: Schramm, G and Warford, J (eds) *Environmental Management and Economic Development.* Johns Hopkins University Press for the World Bank, Baltimore, Maryland.

Stocking, M (1986) The Cost of Soil Erosion in Zimbabwe in Terms of the Loss of Three Major Nutrients. Consultant's working paper no 3, Soil Conservation Programme, Land and Water Development Division, FAO, Rome.

Hedonic Pricing/Property Value Approach Studies:

Grootaert, C and Dubois, J L (1986) The Demand for Urban Housing in the Ivory Coast. Working Paper no 25, World Bank, Washington DC.

Travel Cost Studies:

Brown, G J (1989) The Economic Value of Elephants. LEEC paper 1989-12, IIED, London.

Durojaiye, B and Ikpi, A E (1988) The Monetary Value of Recreational Facilities in a Developing Economy: a Case Study of Three Centres in Nigeria. *Natural Resources Journal*, vol 28 (2): 315–328.

Liken, R (1987) Economic Analysis: Canal Cities Water and Wastewater Phase 2. Unpublished report for USAID, Cairo.

Maille, P and Mendelson, R (1993) Valuing Ecotourism in Madagascar. *Journal of Environmental Management* vol 38 (3): 213–218.

Contingent Valuation Studies:

Abala, D (1987) A Theoretical and Empirical Investigation of Willingness to Pay for Recreational Services: a Case Study of Nairobi National Park. *Eastern Africa Economic Review* 3 (2): 111–119.

Boadu, F (1992) Contingent Valuation for Household Water in Rural Ghana, *Journal of Agricultural Economics*, vol 43

Brown, G, Swanson, T, Ward, M and Moran, D (1994) Optimally Pricing Game Parks in Kenya, CSERGE, University College London, mimeo.

Edwards, S F (1987) Willingness to Pay for Potable Groundwater: A Case Study. In: *An Introduction to Coastal Zone Economics*, Taylor and Francis, New York.

Kramer, R A, Sharma, N, Shyamsundar, P and Munasinghe M (1994) Cost and Compensation Issues in Protecting Tropical Rainforests: Case Study of Madagascar Environment. Department Working Paper, World Bank, Washington, DC.

Lyman, T J P, Vermeulen, S J and Campbell, B M C (1991) *Contingent Valuation of Multi-purpose Tree Resources in the Smallholding Farming Sector in Zimbabwe*, IDRC, Canada.

Moran, D (1994) Contingent Valuation and Biodiversity: Measuring the User Surplus of Kenyan Protected Areas. *Biodiversity and Conservation* 3.

Vermeulen, S J, Campbell, B M C and Lyman, T J P (1991) *Value of Trees in the Small-scale Farming Sector in Zimbabwe*, IDRC, Canada.

Whittington, D et al (1988) Willingness to Pay for Water in Newale District, Tanzania: Strategies for Cost Recovery. Water Sanitation for Health Project Field Report No 26, USAID, Washington DC.

Whittington, D et al (1989) Paying for Urban Services: A Study of Water Vending and Willingness to Pay for Water in Onitsha, Nigeria, Report INU 40, Infrastructure and Urban Development Department, The World Bank, Washington DC.

Whittington, D et al (1989) Strategies for Cost Recovery in the Rural Water Sector: a Case Study of Nsukka District, Anambra, Nigeria. Infrastructure and Urban Development Department, The World Bank, Washington, DC.

Asia

Arifin, B (1997) *Searching Alternatives to Shifting Cultivation in Forest Land.* University of Lampung Jakarta, Indonesia.

Bann, C (1998) An Economic Analysis of Tropical Forest Land Use Options, Ratanakiri Province, Cambodia. Economy and Environment Programme for South East Asia (EEPSEA) Research Report Series. International Development Research Centre (IDRC), Singapore.

Delos Angeles, M S and Pabuayon, I M (1994) Economic Valuation of Impacts of Environmental Degradation in Laguna Lake. Integrative Report submitted by REECS-PDFI to the MetroManila Environmental Improvement Project.

Delos Angeles, M S and Pelayo, R (1997) Philippine Mangrove Resource Valuation Project. Integrated Final Report (revised). Philippine Institute for Development Studies (PIDS), Makati City.

Economy and Environment Programme for South East Asia (EEPSEA) and World Wide Fund For Nature-Indonesia (WWF) (1998) *Economics Value of the 1997 Haze Damages to Indonesia*, International Development Research Centre (IDRC) Singapore.

Francisco, H (1986) Economics of Soil Erosion and Conservation: The Case of Magat Watershed. Unpublished Dissertation, University of the Philippines Los Banos (UPLB).

Israngkura, A (1997) *Entrance Fee System for National Parks.* National Institute for Development Administration (NIDA) and Thailand Development Research Institute (TDRI), Bangkok.

Jansen, R and Padilla, J (1997) Valuation and Evaluation of Management Alternatives for the Pagbilao Mangrove Forest. Collaborative Research in the Economics of Environment and Development (CREED) Working Paper Series No 9, International Institute for Environment and Development (IIED), London.

Jesdapipat, S and Kiratikarnkul, S (1997) Surrogate Pricing for Water:The Case of Mini Hydro-Electricity Cooperatives in Northern Thailand. Draft Final Report, Thailand.

Shahwahid H O et al (1997) Economics Benefits of Watershed Protection and Trade-off with Timber Production: A Case Study in Malaysia. Economy and Environment Programme for South East Asia(EEPSEA) Research Report Series, Singapore.

Shaw, D et al (1997) *An Alternative Approach to Combining Revealed and Stated Preference Data: Valuing Water Quality of the River System in Taipei.* Academia Sinica, Taiwan.

Yaping, D (1998) The Value of Improved Water Quality for Recreation in East Lake, Wuhan, China: Application of Contingent Valuation and Travel Cost Methods, Economy and Environment Programme for South East Asia (EEPSEA) Research Report Series, International Development Research Centre (IDRC) Singapore.

Latin America and the Caribbean

Acosta, J (1995) Elements for Calculating the Value of Biological Diversity Losses: The Case of Oil Exploitation at Cuaybeno Reserve in the Ecuadorean Amazonian Region. In: Munasinghe, M (ed) *Protected Area Economics and Policy*, World Bank, Washington, DC.

Ammour, T, Sención, G and Solís, H (1992) Proyecto Evaluación Económica de Humedales – Peten Guatemal – Caso de Petexbatun. Estudio proyecto OLAFO, CATIE.

Aylward, B A, Echeverría, J, Fendt, L and Barbier, E B (1993) The Economic Value of Species Information and its Role in Biodiversity Conservation: Costa Rica's National Biodiversity Institute. London Environmental Economics Centre, LEEC Paper DP 93–06, IIED, London.

Barton, D N (1995) Valoración Económica Parcial de Alternativas de Manejo para los Humedales de Térraba-Sierpe, Costa Rica. Tesis Magister Scientae en Política Económica con enfasis en Economía Ecológica, Universidad Nacional de Costa Rica.

CAURA (1994) Evaluación de Impacto Ambiental del Sistema Hidroelectrico Guayabo y Siquirres. Informe final, volumen v, Instituto Costarricence de Electricidad (ICE).

Cuesta, M, Carlson, G and Lutz, E (1994) An Empirical Assessment of Farmers' Discount Rates in Costa Rica and its Implications for Soil Conservation. World Bank Environment Department, Washington DC (mimeo).

Current, D, Lutz, E and Scherr, S (1993) Economic and Institutional Analysis of Agroforestry Projects in Central America and the Caribbean. World Bank, Washington, DC (mimeo).

Darling, A, Gomez, C and Niklitschek, M (1993) The Question of a Public Sewarage System in a Caribbean Country: A Case Study. In: Munasinghe, M (ed) Environmental Economics and Natural Resource Management in Developing Countries. Committee of International Development Institutions on the Environment (CIDIE), World Bank, Washington, DC.

Echeverría, J, Hanrahan, M and Solórzano, R (1995) Valuation of Non-Priced Amenities Provided by the Biological Resources within the Monteverde Cloud Forest Preserve, Costa Rica. *Ecological Economics* 13 (1): 43–52.

Fallon Scura, L and van't Hof, T (1993) Economic Feasibility and Ecological Sustainability of the Bonaire Marine Park – The Ecology and Economics of Bonaire Marine Park. World Bank, Environment Department, Divisional paper No 1993–44, Washington, DC.

deGroot, R S (1986) *Functions and Socio-Economic Importance of the Natural Environment in the Galapagos Islands, Ecuador.* Nature Conservation Department, Agricultural University of Wageningen.

Gutman, P (1992) Venezuela Natural Resources Management Project, National Parks: Costs and Benefits of the Project. World Bank, Washington DC.

Jacobi, P (1993) *Environmental Problems Facing Urban Households in the City of São Paolo, Brazil.* CEDEC and Stockholm Environment Institute.

Kishor, N and Constantino, L (1993) *Forest Management and Competing Land Uses: An Economic Analysis for Costa Rica.* Latin America Environment Division, World Bank, Washington DC.

Lutz, E, Pagiola, S and Reiche, C (1994a) Cost-Benefit Analysis of Soil Conservation in Central America and the Caribbean. World Bank, Environment Department Paper No 8, Washington DC.

Lutz, E, Pagiola, S and Reiche, C (eds) (1994b) Economic and Institutional Analysis of Soil Conservation Projects in Central America and the Caribbean. World Bank Environment Department Working Paper No 8, Washington DC.

Marcondes, M A P (1981) Adaptación de una Metodología de Evaluación Económica, Aplicada al Parque Nacional Cahuita, Costa Rica Centro Agronómico Tropical de Investigación y Enseñanza, Serie Técnica 9.

Margulius, S (1992) Back-of-the-Envelope Estimates of Environmental Damage Costs in Mexico. World Bank working paper.

Pearce, D W, Adger, N, Brown, K, Cervigni, R and Moran, D (1993) Mexico Forestry and Conservation Sector Review Substudy of Economic Valuation of Forests. Latin America and the Caribbean – Country Department II (LA2), World Bank, report prepared by CSERGE, University of East Anglia and University College London.

Posner, B E et al (1981) *Economic Impact Analysis for the Virgin Island National Park St Thomas, US Virgin Islands.* Island Resources Foundation.

Rogat, J (1995) *Willingness to Pay for Air Quality Improvement: A Case Study of Santiago de Chile.* Unit for Environmental Economics, Department of Economics, Gothenburg University, Studies in Environmental Economics and Development No 6.

Solorzano, R, de Camino, R, Jimenez, J, Repetto, R, Tosi, J, Vásquez, A, Villalobos, C, Watson, V and Woodward, R (1991) La Depreciación de los Recursos Naturales en Costa Rica y su Relación con el Sistema de Cuantas Nacionales. Centro Científicio, Tropical,World Resources Institute.

Swait, J and Eskeland, G S (1995) Travel Mode Substitution in Saõ Paulo: Estimates and Implications for Air Pollution Control. World Bank, Policy Research Working Paper 1437, Washington, DC.

Whittington, D, Briscoe, J, Xinming, M and Barron, W (1990) Estimating the Willingness to Pay for Water Services in Developing Countries: A Case Study of the Use of Contingent Valuation Surveys in Southern Haiti. *Economic Development and Cultural Change* 38(2): 293–311.

Windevoxhel, N J (1992) Valoración Económica Parcial de los Manglares de la Región II de Nicaragua. Tesis de Magister Scientiae, CATIE.

World Bank (1994) Chile – Managing Environmental Problems: Economic Analysis of Selected Issues. Environment and Urban Development Division, Country Department I, Latin America and the Caribbean Region Report No 13061-CH, World Bank, Washington, DC.

GLOSSARY

adjusted likelihood ratio: a measure of the 'goodness of fit', the equivalent of R^2, but for a *logit* or *probit* model.

analytic hierarchy process: a method of multi-criteria analysis which combines judgement and personal value in a logical way. The process involves the organization of objectives within a hierarchy and a pairwise comparison of objectives on a nine-point scale (Fürst et al, 1996).

benefit transfer: the transfer and application of estimates of economic benefits of particular resources from previous studies to a site for which no such benefit values are available. This transfer of benefits obviously assumes that the value of the resource in question is the same (or similar) across the different sites (Pearce and Moran, 1994). See *off-the-shelf values*.

bequest value: the amount of payment an individual is willing to pay to preserve the environment for the benefit of their children and grandchildren (Pearce and Turner, 1990).

biases: referred to in the context of the contingent valuation method, biases arise from limitations of the survey design, sampling procedure, interview situation or the hypothetical nature of the environmental amenities studied, which move the *willingness-to-pay* result away from a theoretical correct value. Biases have been divided into *hypothetical bias*, *strategic bias*, and *information bias*, the former including *instrument bias* and *starting-point bias*. Biases are also found in travel cost surveys (Fürst et al, 1996).

bidding games: in a bidding game, each individual is asked to evaluate a hypothetical situation and to express his or her *willingness-to-pay (WTP)* for, or *willingness-to-accept (WTA)* compensation for, a certain change in the level of provision of a good. There are two major types of bidding games: single bid games and iterative bid games. In the former, an interviewer, after describing a good (for example, preservation of an endangered species or a certain improvement in air quality) to a respondent, asks him or her to name their maximum WTP for the good or their minimum WTA compensation for losing the option to purchase the good. The responses are then averaged and extrapolated to arrive at an aggregate WTP or WTA for the population as a whole. In iterative bidding games the respondent, rather than being asked to name a sum, is asked whether he would pay $X for the situation or the good described. This amount is then varied iteratively until a maximum WTP or minimum WTA is reached (Dixon et al, 1988). See *payment card*.

bid-rent curve/function: a relationship which indicates the amount a household or firm will be able to pay for the use of a given quantity of land (the bid-rent) at varying distances from the centre of an urban area, while maintaining a constant level of utility or profit (Pearce, 1992).

black box modelling approach: an approach to the modelling of dose-response relationships that does not actually describe the intermediate mechanisms or linkages between the changes of a dependent and related independent variable. It usually refers to the correlation of some anthropogenic action with an alteration in a characteristic of a natural system or human end-point, for example the negative impacts of pollution. Statistical regression analysis based on historical data is a quantitative example of this modelling approach (Fürst et al, 1996).

border price: the border price for internationally-traded goods is the price received (f.o.b.) for exports, or the price paid (c.i.f.) for imports. See *parity prices.*

ceteris paribus: a common assumption in economics, meaning 'all other things remaining constant'.

Change of Productivity Method: a valuation method that can be used if it is possible to measure the effect of one activity on the production function (ie the relationship between inputs and outputs) of another activity.

COBB-Douglas function: a nonlinear production function.

confidence level: in statistical analysis, the desired probability, selected by the investigator, that the universe mean will be included in the calculated limits. For most ecological work, 95 per cent (0.05) or 99 per cent (0.01) confidence limits are considered satisfactory.

construct validity: in assessing the results of a *Contingent Valuation Method (CVM)* study, construct validity includes *theoretical validity*, which looks at whether the CVM measure conforms to theoretical expectations; and *convergent validity*, which looks at whether the CVM measure is closely correlated with measures of the good found using other valuation techniques (Pearce and Moran, 1994).

consumer surplus (CS): the difference between the amount paid for a good or service, and the total utility enjoyed. Since many environmental goods and services have low or zero prices, the CS component in total utility of those goods and services may be very large. In turn, if these 'free' environmental goods and services are lost, the loss of welfare (CS) is large (Dixon et al, 1988).

content validity: as used in assessing the results of a *Contingent Valuation Method (CVM)* study, content validity looks at whether the WTP measure estimated in the study accurately corresponds to the good in question.

Contingent Valuation Method (CVM): a *direct valuation* method, which involves asking people what they are willing to pay for a benefit, and/or what they are willing to receive by way of compensation to tolerate a cost. This is usually done through a questionnaire survey, but can also be done through experimental techniques. In either case, the objective is to elicit the personal valuations of the respondent for increases or decreases in the quantity of some environmental good, contingent upon a hypothetical market. Structured questions and various forms of 'bidding game' can be devised, involving 'yes/no' answers to questions regarding maximum *willingness to pay*. Econometric techniques are then used on the survey results to find the mean bid values of willingness to pay. One advantage of using CVM, rather than *indirect valuation* techniques, is the fact that it can be used to elicit *non-use values*. See also *bias*, *payment card*, *reliability* and *validity* (Pearce and Turner, 1990).

convergent validity: see *construct validity.*

cost-benefit analysis (CBA): a conceptual framework for the evaluation of investment projects (or conservation projects), which considers gains (benefits) and losses (costs), regardless of to whom they accrue. In practice, some benefits of conservation or preservation projects will be difficult to monetize, in which case an *opportunity cost approach* is useful as an extension of the traditional cost-benefit analysis.

criterion validity: in assessing the results of a *Contingent Valuation Method (CVM)* study, criterion validity compares the estimates obtained with the 'true' value (the criterion) of the good in question. This is not feasible for many environmental goods (and is why CVM is carried out in the first place). However, some experiments have compared hypothetical *willingness-to-pay (WTP)* values from CVM with 'true' WTP, as determined by simulated markets using real money payments (Pearce and Moran, 1994).

damage cost (avoided) technique: a valuation method which places a monetary value on the cost of damage (from, for example, flooding) which would occur if the natural resource in question was lost or degraded (for example, upstream deforestation).

dB: decibel, a numerical scale that expresses the relative loudness of sound (Raven et al, 1993).

debt-for-nature (DFN) swaps: involve the purchase, usually by an international conservation organization, but also by governments and even individuals, of developing countries' secondary debt in the secondary debt market. Such secondary debt is sold by existing holders at a discount, reflecting the market's judgement on the probability of repayment. In a DFN, the new holder then offers to give up the debt holding in exchange for an undertaking by the country government or acting conservation organization to protect a given area, train conservationists, etc. The idea of valuing the biodiversity so conserved through DFNs is that the payment made reflects some kind of *willingness-to-pay (WTP)* on the part of the conservation body purchasing the debt (Pearce and Moran, 1994).

demand function: a curve showing the relationship between willingness-to-pay and the quantity/quality of the good or service in question. Estimation of the demand curve permits the quantification of the change in *consumer surplus* derived from a change in the quantity or prices of the good or service in question. See also *Marshallian demand function.*

direct valuation methods: valuation methods which elicit preferences by either conducting experiments or by using questionnaire surveys. *Contingent valuation* is an example of a direct valuation method. See also *indirect valuation methods.*

discount rate: a measure of the rate at which individuals or governments prefer the present over the future (ie the implicit reduction of costs and benefits which occur in the future). Discount rates are applied to determine the present values of future benefits (of, for example, a country's forests) or future costs (of, for example, the loss of these resources through deforestation). Discounting is a highly controversial issue, particularly when dealing with environmental valuation, as the approach has a built-in bias against future generations and makes unsustainable exploitation seem preferable, in economic terms, to sustainable use (Pearce and Turner, 1990).

discounted income method: a valuation method that consists of determining the profits that could be obtained from the use of a natural resource over the duration of a project, and then discounting future costs and incomes to a certain year.

discrete choice model: those statistical models which specify the probability of discrete dependent variables as a function of independent variables and unknown parameters. They are relevant in economics because the decision of an economic unit frequently involves discrete choice: for example, the decision as to the number of cars to own, the choice of the mode of transport, or the choice of which source of water to use (Eatwell et al, 1987).

dose-response technique: an indirect valuation technique which aims to establish a relationship between environmental damage (response) and some cause of the damage, such as pollution (dose), such that a given level of pollution is associated with a change in output that is then valued at market, revealed/inferred, or shadow prices. Dose-response techniques have been used for example to look at the effects of pollution on health, aquatic ecosystems, and vegetation. The damage done is found using a *dose-response function*, which relates physical/biological changes in the ambient environment to the level of the pollution. The dose-response function is then multiplied by the unit 'price' or value per unit of physical damage (Pearce and Moran, 1994).

economic internal rate of return: see internal rate of return.

environmental impact assessment (EIA): the identification, prediction and evaluation, mitigation and management of impacts from a proposed development and its reasonable alternatives (UNEP, 1996).

embedding effect: a problem sometimes observed in *Contingent Valuation Method (CVM)* studies, where respondents may interpret the hypothetical offers of a specific good or service to be indicative of an offer for a broader set of similar goods or services. This is known as the embedding problem since the value of the good being sought is embedded in the value of the more encompassing set of goods and services reported by the respondent. This kind of problem is particularly apparent in environmental issues, because they evoke deeply held moral, philosophical and religious beliefs, which respondents may find difficult to separate out from their preferences for the specific environmental good or service being valued (Pearce and Moran, 1994).

end-point exposure model: referred to in the context of *impact* and *dose-response analysis*, where a chain of impacts are followed to their points of last observable impact. In the context of economic valuation, end-point exposure is a measure of the susceptibility of human livelihood or well-being to changes in environmental conditions (for example, exposure to pollution).

epidemiological survey: a survey of particular factors influencing the occurrence, distribution, prevention, and control of disease, injury, or other health-related events in a defined human population.

Eulerian multi-box dispersion model: a type of air dispersion model which is used to describe the dispersion of pollutants in an airshed, by dividing the area into a number of two-dimensional boxes. Each cell of the matrix represents a specific concentration of pollutants for that geographical area and, using Euler's matrix mathematics, changes in concentrations can be modelled (Fürst et al, 1996).

existence value: a value placed on an environmental good, which is unrelated to any actual or potential use of the good. For example, endangered species have an existence value to many supporters of wildlife conservation campaigns, even though these people are very unlikely to make use of these wildlife resources (Pearce and Turner, 1990).

forest economy: that part of a local, regional or national economy concerned wholly or largely with forest production.

free-rider problem: a general problem in the management of public goods, whereby some individuals avoid paying for their use of the good in question.

functional form: the shape of the curve that describes the mathematical formalization of the relationship whereby the values of a set of independent variables determine the value of the dependent variable.

Gross Domestic Product (GDP): a measure of the total production and consumption of goods and services in a country.

Gumbel distribution: a type of distribution of random variables that is assumed when using a logit-type function.

Hausman test: Hausman tests are based on testing whether or not the estimates from two different estimating procedures differ significantly from one another.

hedonic pricing method: an indirect valuation method, which attempts to estimate an implicit price for environmental attributes by looking at real markets in which those characteristics are effectively traded. Thus, for example, 'clean air' and 'peace and quiet' are effectively traded in the property market, since purchasers of houses and land do consider these environmental dimensions as characteristics of property. The *hedonic property value method* is thus one application of hedonic pricing (Pearce and Moran, 1994).

hedonic property value method: a form of hedonic pricing, which looks for any systematic differences in property values between locations and tries to separate out the effect of environmental quality on these values (Pearce and Moran, 1994).

human capital technique: also referred to as the *loss of earnings/income technique*, this technique assumes that environmental impacts leading to human morbidity and mortality can be valued by quantifying the resulting lost wage earnings and increased medical expenses. Although social policies frequently implicitly value human life, this is one of the most controversial valuation approaches, due to the moral implications of valuing human suffering and life (Fürst et al, 1996).

hypothetical bias: a potential *bias*, in *contingent valuation* surveys, that arises because such surveys seek to elicit hypothetical bids for goods, for which in many cases no actual market exists. Respondents' stated *willingness-to-pay (WTP)* for goods in hypothetical markets may be different to what they would be willing to pay in actual markets, where they can suffer real costs if, for example, they pay too much.

impact analysis: in an economic valuation context, impact analysis involves the quantification of changes in welfare resulting from the (negative) impacts of a specific development policy or project in relation to a 'without project' alternative. This is distinct from a more comprehensive analysis of alternatives such as in *cost-benefit analysis*.

indirect valuation methods: indirect valuation techniques seek to elicit preferences from actual, observed market-based information. Preferences for the environmental good are revealed indirectly, when an individual purchases a marketed good that in some way relates to the environmental good. Indirect valuation methods include *hedonic price* and wage techniques, the *travel cost method*, and *replacement/reproduction cost technique*.

information bias: a potential *bias*, in *contingent valuation surveys*, which arises from the type and amount of information provided to respondents. *Starting point bias* can be considered one type of information bias.

instrument bias: in some forms of *contingent valuation* surveys, an instrument bias can arise if the respondent is hostile to the means by which payment would be collected. The vehicle chosen for payment – entrance fee or user fee – may result in different *Willingness-to-Pay* responses. Moreover, some people accustomed to certain public goods being provided free of charge may protest at any kind of payment and be unwilling to pay anything. Adding an additional question to make sure that any zero bid from the respondent actually reflects zero value to them, rather than a 'protest' against payment, can often eliminate this kind of bias (Dixon et al, 1988).

integrated assessment: also known as 'integrated adaptive ecological economic modelling and assessment', the principles behind this consensus-building approach are openness, transparency, acknowledgement of uncertainty, creativity, flexibility and adaptivity, long-term focus, acknowledgement of value judgements, and simplification to principle relationships.

internal rate of return (IRR): the internal rate of return is defined as the rate of return on an investment which will equate the present value of benefits and costs. The IRR is the discount rate that would result in a zero *net present value* for a project. Once calculated, the IRR is compared to some other financial interest rate or discount rate to determine whether the project is financially or economically attractive (Dixon et al, 1988).

logit model: a linear probability model, created using the logistic function. Similar to the *probit model*, but more popular as it requires less computational cost.

loss of earnings/income method: see *human capital technique*.

loss of productivity method: see *change of productivity method*.

lower bound: conservative estimate. See *upper bound*.

maintenance cost technique: involves the quantification of the costs associated with maintaining resource stocks or environmental quality at or above some predefined standard. The method can be used to value society's minimum *willingness-to-pay* for the benefits derived from maintaining a particular environmental standard (Fürst et al, 1996).

Mann-Whitney U test: an ordering method test for two independent samples, which uses the actual ranks of the various observations to test hypotheses about the identity of the two populations (van Zyl et al, 1996).

marginal utility of income: the rate at which an individual's utility (or welfare) increases as his/her personal budget (income) is expanded by one unit (£1, $1, etc.) (Pearce, 1992).

marginal value: the extra value (benefit) obtained from an extra unit of any good.

Marshallian demand function: a demand curve for environmental goods in which income is held constant. In contrast, a Hicksian demand curve takes into account the effect of income, and is more appropriate when the elasticity of demand and the ratio of *consumer surplus* to income are very high. In practice, there is usually only sufficient data available to define the uncompensated Marshallian demand function (Pearce and Turner, 1990).

maximum likelihood estimation technique: in econometrics, the maximum likelihood principle of estimation is based on the idea that the sample of data at hand is more likely to have come from a 'real world' characterized by any other set of parameter values. The maximum likelihood estimate of a vector of parameter values is simply the particular vector which gives the greatest probability of obtaining the observed data (Kennedy, 1985).

maximum sustainable yield (MSY): the maximum we can take from a natural resource stock (for example, fish stocks in a river, or timber stocks in a forest) on a sustainable basis, ie without reducing its long-term stock. MSY is used to describe the maximum biological productivity or regeneration of renewable living resources and/or their habitat. In extractive activities where there are declining marginal returns to extractive effort, the MSY does not coincide with the optimal economic level of extraction (Fürst et al, 1996).

meta-analysis: a 'study-of-studies' where valuation estimates for a particular resource or amenity are based on a number of *off-the-shelf values* from other geographical areas or similar environmental goods and services. Often used as first approximation where local data are not available, it is an increasingly common approach to estimating option and existence values (Fürst et al, 1996).

mitigation cost technique: involves the quantification of the costs associated with mitigative actions *ex ante*, aimed at diverting degradation, as well as *ex post*, aimed at compensating for loss or degradation that has already occurred (*replacement cost* or *reproduction cost*). For preventive expenditure, optimal mitigative behaviour is based on expected damage costs, with the associated uncertainties related to predicting environmental impacts. Replacement or reproduction costs may be substantially simpler to use as they are usually an accounting exercise after the fact (Fürst et al, 1996).

multicollinearity: a problem with *hedonic price* studies, as many of the explanatory variables will be related to one another – ie will be collinear. This makes it difficult to identify which factor is determining movements in house prices (Pearce and Moran, 1994).

multi-criteria analysis (MCA): a decision-making support tool designed to incorporate multiple categories of information in the analysis of alternative policies or projects. A number of approaches exist to logically structure information of varying quality and multiple units of measurements relating to environmental impacts and stakeholders' preferences for impacts or environmental attributes (see *analytical hierarchy process*). Algorithms may then be used to develop an ordered list of policy preferences of the decision-maker(s) or the logically structured information may be used as a basis for further negotiations between stakeholders (Fürst et al, 1996).

net income method: valuation method based on the calculation of the difference between costs and benefits. If the costs and benefits are discounted, the method can also be called the *discounted income method*.

net present value (NPV): the difference between the streams of benefits and costs of a good or service, discounted to the present.

NGOs: non-governmental organizations.

non-timber forest products (NTFP): all biological materials other than timber which are extracted from forests for human use. These include foods, medicines, spices, essential oils, resins, gums, latexes, tannins, dyes, ornamental plants, wildlife (products and live animals), fuelwood and raw materials, notably rattan, bamboo, smallwood and fibres (De Beer and McDermott, 1996).

non-use values: also referred to as *passive use values*, they include *existence values* and *option values* (including *bequest values*). Non-use values are the most intangible among the categories of total economic value posited by economists. Non-use values are per se not observable from revealed preferences and are only quantifiable through direct polling of consumers, using *contingent valuation surveys*. Some authors argue that *debt-for-nature swaps* and contributions to conservation and animal rights groups are the expression of non-users of their appreciation for the intrinsic natural rights of existence of individuals, species and natural systems.

NO_x: nitrous oxides, ie NO (nitrogen monoxide) and NO_2 (nitrogen dioxide).

O_3: ozone, a blue gas which is a human-made pollutant in one part of the atmosphere (the troposhere) but a natural and essential component in another (the stratosphere).

OECD: the Organization for Economic Co-operation and Development, OECD's fundamental task is to enable its members to consult and cooperate with each other to achieve the highest sustainable economic growth in their countries and improve the economic and social wellbeing of their populations. The OECD offers advice and makes recommendations to its members to help them define their policies. On occasion it also arbitrates negotiations of multilateral agreements and establishes legal codes in certain areas of activity. OECD currently has 29 member countries, including western European countries, North America, Japan, Australia, New Zealand, Finland, Mexico, the Czech Republic, Hungary, Poland and Korea (OECD, 1998).

off-the-shelf values: in cases where research resources or local data are scarce, some studies transfer benefit estimates (or biological productivity estimates or damage functions) from previous studies of similar resources to the local problem being studied. In the case of valuation studies in developing countries, these *benefit transfers* (which are commonly taken from western countries where the required data are more available) need to be carefully assessed for their applicability to the local situation. See *meta-analysis*.

one way ANOVA test: in econometrics, an analysis of variance test to determine whether or not a particular classification of the data is meaningful.

opportunity cost approach: not an actual valuation technique, but an approach which involves estimating the benefits of an activity causing environmental deterioration – say, a housing development – in order to set a benchmark for what the environmental benefits would have to be for the development *not* to be worthwhile. This approach can be used to indicate the kinds of economic returns that must be secured by biodiversity use if such land uses are to be economically preferred to the alternative land use (Pearce and Moran, 1994).

option value: the extra payment an individual is willing to pay to ensure that he or she can make use of the environment in the future. Option value therefore represents the potential benefit, as opposed to the actual present use value. Option value is essentially an expression of preference, a willingness to pay, for the preservation of an environment against some probability that the individual will make use of it at a later date. Option value can also include the willingness to pay to preserve the environment for use by future generations (ie can include *bequest value*) and for use by other individuals (Pearce and Turner, 1990).

ordinary least squares estimation technique: in econometrics, the ordinary least squares estimator is the estimator that generates the set of values of the parameters that minimizes the sum of squared residuals. This is probably the most popular estimator among researchers doing empirical work.

parameter values: the values of the constants, as opposed to the variables, in an economic equation, which are used as summary values for a population.

pareto optimum/optimality: a pareto optimum situation is one in which it is impossible to make any individual better off without making someone else worse off (Pearce and Turner, 1990).

pareto improvement: a net gain in social benefits.

parity prices: using parity prices for exported or imported goods involves adjusting the *border prices* for these goods, to take account of transport and distribution charges.

partial economic valuation: in contrast to the *opportunity cost approach*, partial economic valuation refers to the quantification of the net impacts of various policy alternatives. This approach forms the basis of *cost-benefit analysis*.

passive use values: see non-use values.

payment card: sometimes used in contingent valuation studies, a payment card shows a range of *willingness-to-pay (WTP)* (or *willingness-to-accept (WTA)*) values, and is presented to the respondent, who is asked to state their maximum WTP (or minimum WTA) by indicating the acceptable figure on the card. Payment cards can be used as an alternative to more open-ended *bidding games*.

PM-10: particulate matter (ie dust or mist particles) less than 10 microns in diameter, known to cause respiratory diseases. The term 'total PM' refers to dust and mist particles, of unspecified diameter, suspended in the atmosphere; this can include soil, soot, lead, asbestos, and sulphuric acid droplets.

polychotomous model: a probability model with more than two probability categories; as opposed to *dichotomous models* which have only two different probabilities.

positional analysis: similar in approach to multi-criteria analysis but with a focus on stakeholder and decision-makers' preferences and the resulting interest groups that arise in connection with conflicts of interest over policy alternatives (Fürst et al, 1996).

pre-testing: used here to refer to the testing of a survey instrument for *biases*, often involving focus groups to identify relevant issues and problems relating to the design of the survey. A pilot questionnaire can also be used to test for problems in the actual interview process. Pre-testing is recommended in the preparation of *contingent valuation surveys* or *travel cost method* studies.

price elasticity: the extent to which price falls (rises), as supply increases (decreases).

probit model: a linear probability model, created using the cumulative normal function. Similar to the *logit model*.

production function: models of how inputs relate to outputs in a productive process at the level of the household, economy or for natural resources and systems. When sufficient data are not available to describe natural or man-made productive processes, production functions are often assumed by economists to have a prescribed functional form, such as the Cobb-Douglas function (Fürst et al, 1996).

random bidding models: utility models based on discrete choice theory, based on the probability that an individual will be the highest bidder for a specified bundle of housing attributes. Random bidding models can be used to derive the marginal bid function for individual attributes from an estimate of the *bid-rent function*, and so can be used for valuation purposes.

random utility models (RUMs): utility models based on *discrete choice theory* in which the utility of a given choice is based on the utility derived from different attributes of that choice plus an unobservable component of utility that is assumed to be random. RUMs can be used when analysing the probability that people will choose to visit one particular recreation site, rather than other, potential substitute sites (van Zyl et al, 1996).

regression model: a regression equation (or mathematical relationship) which is fitted to a set of data points, usually by the method of *ordinary least squares*, for the purposes of establishing quantitative economic relationships (estimating the values of parameters), or testing economic hypotheses. Simple linear regression refers to the fitting of a linear function between two variables. Multiple linear regression involves the fitting of a linear function containing two or more independent variables (Pearce, 1992).

reliability: as used in assessing the results of a *Contingent Valuation Method* study, reliability is the degree to which the variance of *WTP* responses are attributable to random error. The greater the degree of non-randomness, the less reliable the study, such that mean WTP answers are of little value. In order to assess reliability, a number of practitioners have advocated the use of replicability tests, ie by repeating an experiment using different samples to see if there is a correlation between the variables collected.

replacement cost technique: an indirect valuation technique which looks at the cost of replacing or restoring a damaged asset to its original state, and uses this cost as a measure of the benefit of restoration. Information on replacement costs can be obtained from direct observation of actual spending on restoring damaged assets, or from professional estimates of what it costs to restore the asset.

reproduction cost method: see *replacement cost technique*.

revealed preference technique: a valuation technique that relies on the observation of people's behaviour, to reveal their preference for, for example, a particular kind of water source. This is in contrast to a contingent valuation technique, which elicits people's preferences through questionnaire surveys.

safe minimum standard (SMS): applying the SMS criterion involves calculating a margin of safety to prevent irreversible damage to a resource. If such a standard can be maintained without 'excessive' costs, the resource should be protected. This criterion is appropriate when dealing with resources which are renewable up to a point but are subject to irreversible damage once exploitation exceeds a certain level. These include soil resources and biodiversity resources as a whole (Dixon et al, 1988).

sensitivity analysis: sensitivity analysis involves changing the parameters of a decision problem and studying how this affects the outcome. It is particularly associated with *Cost-Benefit Analysis* where the most common form is the use of alternative discount rates. The purpose of the analysis is to identify the important assumptions upon which the analysis is based – those to which the outcome is sensitive (Pearce, 1992).

shadow prices: an imputed valuation of a commodity or service which has no market price, or whose market price does not reflect the opportunity costs involved. Shadow prices are used, for example, for health, environmental quality, or labour (if market distortions are operating in the labour market).

shadow project method: In cases where an economic development project would cause irreversible environmental losses, a shadow project approach would increase the development project by an amount sufficient to fund a 'shadow project' designed to substitute for the lost environmental asset. For example, if the development project would result in the destruction of a particularly valuable wetland, a shadow project could be designed to restore a partly degraded wetland elsewhere in the region (Pearce and Turner, 1990).

Shannon H' index: a relative measure of species diversity.

significance level: sometimes used as a synonym for *confidence level*.

SO_x: sulphur oxides, ie SO_2 (sulphur dioxide) and SO_3 (sulphur trioxide), produced primarily through the combustion of fossil fuels. These gases can lead to respiratory tract irritations in humans, as well as acid rain. SO_2 will dissolve in moisture in the atmosphere to form sulphuric acid.

social benefit: the sum of the gains or benefits deriving from an activity or project to whomsoever they accrue. Occasionally used to describe 'external benefits', ie benefits to others, rather than to the individual who predominantly enjoys the private benefit (Pearce, 1992).

social cost: the social cost of a given output is defined as the sum of money which is just adequate when paid as compensation to restore to their original utility levels all who lose as a result of the production of the output. The social cost is the *opportunity cost* to society, rather than to just one firm or individual. One of the major reasons why social costs differ from the observed private costs is due to the existence of *externalities* (Pearce, 1992).

social optimum: that allocation of a society's resources, pattern of production and distribution of output which is the 'best' attainable, according to some stated set of objectives. The concept is most usually applied in welfare economics where there may be several alternative situations, all of which are *pareto optimal*. By introducing a social welfare function, which represents the welfare of society at large as some function of the welfare of the individuals forming that society, it is then possible to chose the best of all the Pareto optimal solutions – the social optimum (Pearce, 1992).

starting point bias: a potential *bias*, in *contingent valuation* surveys, that arises when the first bid suggested by the interviewer (for the amount of *willingness-to-pay (WTP)* or *willingness-to-accept (WTA)* influences the respondent is some way, perhaps by suggesting the range over which the 'bidding game' is to be played.

strategic bias: a potential *bias*, in *contingent valuation* surveys, that arises from a respondent's perceived payment obligation and his/her expectation about the provision of a good. Where individuals actually have to pay their reported *willingness-to-pay (WTP)* values, then there is the temptation to understate their true preferences in the hope of a free ride (see *free rider problem*). Or, if the price to be charged for the good is not tied to an individual's WTP responses, but the provision of the good is, then over-reporting of WTP may occur in order to ensure provision (Pearce and Moran, 1994).

theoretical validity: see *construct validity*.

time series analysis: the analysis of data observed for variables over time (time-series data), as opposed to cross-sectional analysis, where observations are made over, for example, individuals, objects, or geographical areas.

Total Economic Value (TEV): actual *use values* plus *non-use values* (the latter including *option value* and *existence value*). TEV expresses the range of social economic values that economists associate with society's use and enjoyment of the natural world.

travel cost method (TCM): an indirect valuation method which uses observed expenditures on the travel to recreational sites to estimate the benefit arising from the recreational experience. The travel cost method typically uses information on money and time spent by people in getting to a site, to estimate their *willingness-to-pay* for the site's facilities or characteristics.

truncation bias: a bias in travel cost studies, which arises from the fact that the studies generally elicit information on people who have actually visited the site, but not on non-users.

t-test: a statistical test to compare the values of two samples, involving the null hypothesis that the difference between the values is no greater than expected for two samples coming from the universe. The t-test is used to determine if the null hypothesis is rejected (no significant difference exists between the samples) or accepted (a significant difference does exist).

upper bound: an estimate likely to be at the top end of the range of probable values; in contrast to a more conservative *lower bound* estimate.

use value: benefits (expressed as economic values) derived from the actual use of the environment. Use values include direct use values (from exploitative or recreational activities) and indirect use values (from the ecological services provided by the environment). When calculating the *Total Economic Value* of a natural resource or ecosystem, its *use values* and *non-use values* are added together.

utility function: a function stating that an individual's utility is dependent on the goods s/he consumes and their amounts (Pearce, 1992).

validity test: valuation methods may be assessed for their *construct* and *content validity*. Validity tests therefore examine whether the estimates obtained are similar to those produced using different valuation methods; whether the estimates are consistent with real market behaviour; and whether the estimates conform to theoretical expectations.

volatile organic compounds (VOCs): any organic compounds that participate in atmospheric photochemical reactions.

Wilcoxon signed ranks test: an ordering method test for two matched samples (pairs of scores), that uses differences in both direction and size, that can be ranked (van Zyl et al, 1996).

Willingness to Accept (WTA): the amount of money an individual feels he or she would need to be paid before they are willing to forgo an environmental benefit or tolerate an environmental loss.

Willingness to Pay (WTP): the amount of money an individual is prepared to pay to secure an environmental benefit or to prevent an environmental loss. WTP for a natural resource or an ecosystem is elicited through *contingent valuation surveys*.

with-and-without project analysis: an analysis which compares the impacts (costs and benefits) associated with a (conservation or development) project, with the likely impacts if the project is not undertaken.

zonal travel cost method: a variation on the travel cost method, which defines zones of distance from the environmental facility being valued. The total number of sampled users from each zone is divided by the population of each zone, to obtain a per capita visitation rate from each zone.

REFERENCES

De Beer, J H and McDermott, M J (1996) *The Economic Value of Non-Timber Forest Products in Southeast Asia*. Netherlands Committee for IUCN, Amsterdam.

Dixon, J A, Carpenter, R A, Fallon, L A, Sherman, P B and Manipomoke, S (1988) *Economic Analysis of the Environmental Impacts of Development Projects*. Earthscan Publications, London.

Eatwell, J, Milgate, M and Newman, P (1987) *The New Palgrave: A Dictionary of Economics*. The Macmillan Press, London.

Fürst, E, Barton, D N and Jiménez, G (1996) Case Study Analyses on the Application of Environmental and Natural Resource Valuation Methods in Developing Countries and Countries in Transition to Market Economies: Latin America and Caribbean Substudy. Report for the United Nations Environment Programme by the International Center on Economic Policy for Sustainable Development and Universidad Nacional, Costa Rica, mimeo.

Kennedy, P (1985) *A Guide to Econometrics*. Second edition, The MIT Press, Cambridge, Massachusetts.

OECD (1998) Webpage 'About OECD', edited 31 July 1998.

Pearce, D W (ed) (1992) *Macmillan Dictionary of Modern Economics*. Fourth edition, Macmillan Press, London.

Pearce, D and Moran, D (1994) *The Economic Value of Biodiversity*. Earthscan Publications, London.

Pearce, D and Turner, R K (1990) *Economics of Natural Resources and the Environment*. Johns Hopkins Press, Maryland.

Raven, P H, Berg, L R and Johnson, G B (1993) *Environment*. Saunders College Publishing, Harcourt Brace Jovanovich College Publishers, Orlando.

UNEP (1996) Environmental Impact Assessment: Issues, Trends and Practice. Prepared for the Environment and Economics Unit of UNEP, by Scott Wilson Resource Consultants. UNEP, Nairobi.

van Zyl, H, Store, T and Leiman, A (1996) A Case Study Analysis on Valuations of Environmental and Natural Resources in Africa. A Report to the United Nations Environment Programme. University of Cape Town, School of Economics, mimeo.

INDEX

wildlife viewing (Kenya) 36–8,
44–5, 48–9, 50
travel costs 37–8, 44
travel time savings, expressway (Sri
Lanka) 105–6

Ukunda, Kenya 24, 27
urban land market, Accra 56–60

validity
Contingent Valuation Method 46–7
land values study 61
Travel Cost Method 49
variables, land values (Ghana) 54–5
Vehicle Operating Costs (VOCs),
expressway (Sri Lanka) 104–5
visitation rates, national park 36–7
VOCs *see* Vehicle Operating Costs

water collection, Kenya 23–34
critique 29–32
discrete choice theory 24–7, 30
evaluation 32
policy relevance 31–2
water sources 24
water pollution
expressway (Sri Lanka) 117–18
oil shale extraction 130–1
water services, Haiti 172–81
bias testing 176–7
contingent valuation method 175–6
critique 177–80

demand 173, 180
Willingness to Pay 174–7
water sources, Kenya
kiosks and vendors 24, 25–6, 27–8
pipeline 24
wells and pumps 24, 26, 27, 28
watershed protection, forests
(Mexico) 185, 191
wildlife viewing, Kenya 35–52
Contingent Valuation Method
38–9, 42, 43–4
critique 42–9
evaluation 49–50
pollution threat 35, 39
Travel Cost Method 41, 44–5
validity 46–8
Willingness to Accept (WTA)
mangroves (Nicaragua) 204, 205
wildlife viewing (Kenya) 38, 40, 43,
47–8
Willingness to Pay (WTP) 11, 14–15
air pollution control 94, 96, 158
coral reef park 163, 164–5
forests (Mexico) 193–4
format types 47–8
recreational forests 142
water services (Haiti) 172–81
wildlife viewing (Kenya) 36, 38, 40
With/Without Analysis, expressway
(Sri Lanka) 110–12
WTA *see* Willingness to Accept
WTP *see* Willingness to Pay